LEGENDARY LOCALS

OF

DENTON

TEXAS

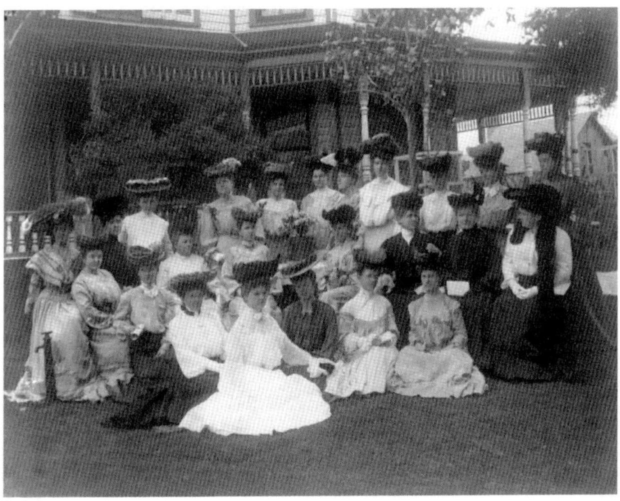

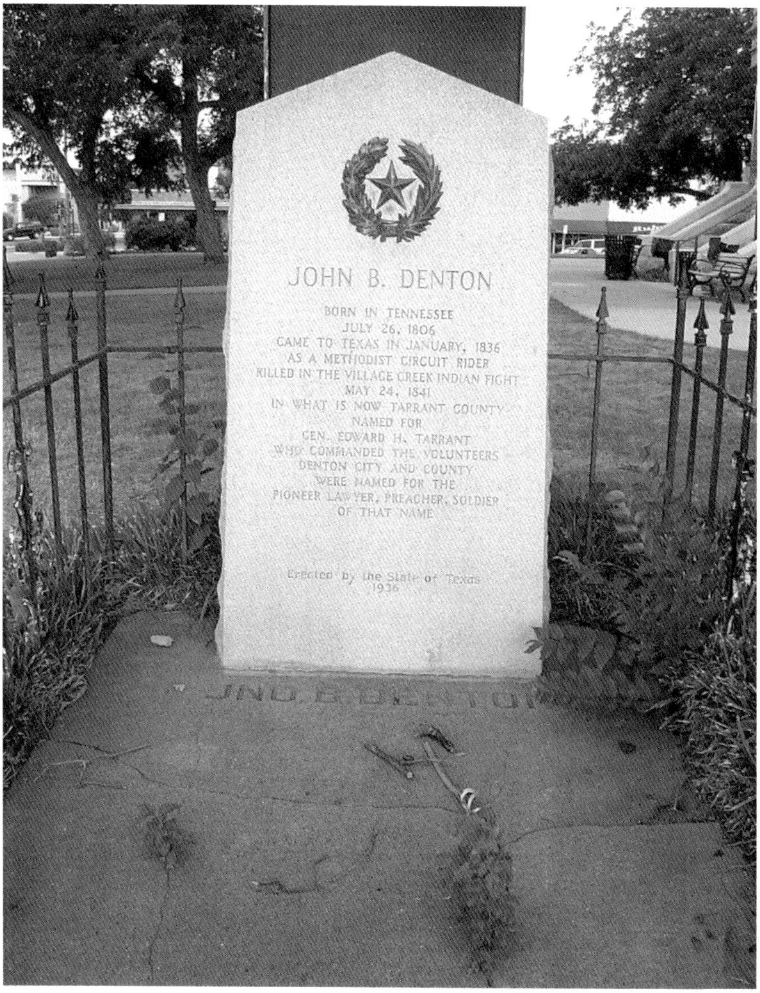

Final Resting Place?
John B. Denton, a pioneer itinerant Methodist preacher and lawyer for whom the county and city of Denton are named, died in a Keechi Indian ambush in May 1841 at the battle of Village Creek. His militiamen buried him in an unmarked, stone-lined grave near Oliver and Denton Creeks. John Chisum, whose father, Claiborne Chisum, was on the raid, disinterred what survivors of the raid believed to be Denton's remains. Chisum buried them on his ranch in northwestern Denton County. He left directions for the location of this second unmarked grave when he moved to New Mexico. In 1901, the Denton County Old Settlers Association exhumed Denton's bones once again and interred them for the third time, in the southeastern section of the courthouse lawn. Many question Chisum's belief that he had found Denton's bones. In their opinion, he buried them rather cavalierly on his ranch. Lately, there has been renewed interest in ghostly appearances on the downtown Denton Square. These apparitions may stem from the restless bones in Denton's grave. (Courtesy of Denton County Office of History and Culture.)

Page 1: **Ladies of the Club**
The Ariel Club, established in 1891, is Denton's oldest club for women. The organization's purposes are exclusively charitable, educational, and literary (see page 10). (Courtesy of *Denton Record-Chronicle*.)

LEGENDARY LOCALS

OF

DENTON

TEXAS

DR. GEORGIA CARAWAY

LEGENDARY LOCALS

ISBN 978-1-4671-0165-3

Legendary Locals is an imprint of Arcadia Publishing
Charleston, South Carolina

Printed in the United States of America

Library of Congress Control Number: 2014933319

For all general information, please contact Arcadia Publishing:
Telephone 843-853-2070
Fax 843-853-0044
E-mail sales@arcadiapublishing.com
For customer service and orders:
Toll-Free 1-888-313-2665

Visit us on the Internet at www.arcadiapublishing.com

Dedication
To past, present, and future residents, who are the very soul of this captivating city; and to the legendary man in my life.

On the Front Cover: Clockwise from top left:
Hal Jackson, World War II hero (Courtesy of Denton County Office of History and Culture; see page 41), Bob Rogers, piano man (Courtesy of the *Denton Record-Chronicle*; see pages 53, 117), Homer B. Bly, city manager/banker (Courtesy of Denton County Office of History and Culture; see page 8), Brenda Marshall, actress (Courtesy of the author; see page 79), 1904 Ariel Club members (Courtesy of *Denton Record-Chronicle*; see page 10), Leon Breeden, director of One O'Clock Lab Band (Courtesy of *Denton Record-Chronicle*; see pages 54, 55), Phyllis George, 1971 Miss America (Courtesy of Denton County Office of History and Culture; see page 110), Mary Evelyn Blagg Huey, first female president of Texas Woman's University (Courtesy of *Denton Record-Chronicle*; see page 90), "Mean" Joe Greene, professional football player (Courtesy of Denton County Office of History and Culture; see page 98).

On the Back Cover: From left to right:
Curtis H. Collins, winning high school coach (Courtesy of Denton County Office of History and Culture; see page 96), Daugherty family, influential pioneers (Courtesy of Denton Public Library; see page 13).

CONTENTS

ACKNOWLEDGMENTS

Several longtime residents who have been involved in community activities were consulted to help select these "legendary locals." Consideration was also given to those already appearing in the three other Denton histories published by Arcadia Publishing. I tried to avoid repetitions; however, some of our superstars make up the very fabric of the city and had to be included here. If there is someone missing among these legendary locals, please consult the other Arcadia publications. It is likely that their stories will be told there.

The author extends her gratitude to the *Denton Record-Chronicle* (DRC), Denton Public Library (DPL), University of North Texas Archives and Portal to Texas History (UNT), University Relations, Communications & Marketing (UNT URCM), Texas Woman's University Archives (TWU), *Dallas Morning News* (DMN), Greater Denton Arts Council (GDAC), Independent Order of Odd Fellows (IOOF), Denton Chamber of Commerce (DCofC), Denton Convention and Visitors Bureau (DCVB), the staff of the Denton County Office of History and Culture (DCOHC), and the city of Denton for assistance in my gathering research material for the stories here and the images that accompany those stories. Our Superstars also provided photographs from their personal collections. Great appreciation goes to Monte B Photography and Eagleton Photography. A photographer extraordinaire cannot go unmentioned: Al Key (AK), *Denton Record-Chronicle*.

Indispensable access to research materials, books, and articles by those whose footsteps have been followed cannot go without mention. The following persons and institutions deserve thanks: E. Dale Odom, Ed F. Bates, James L. Rogers, C.A. Bridges, Richard Himmel, Bob LaForte, Phyllis Bridges, Joyce Thompson, Mary Carolyn Hollers George, Holly Hervey, Gayle Strange, Mike Cochran, *The North Texan*, Texas State Historical Association *Handbook*, Michael Burgess's *Capitol Words*, *Pioneers in Modernism*, and websites about the featured individuals. Phyllis Bridges allowed me to paraphrase her tribute to Gertrude Gibson. Thanks to UNT Press for the Martin Shockley excerpt from *Last Roundup*, and to Karla K. Morton for her poem, "Clearing the Woods." The Otis G. Welch poem was found in an April 18, 1897, article printed in the *Dallas Morning News*. A special thank-you and love goes to Martha Len Nelson and her "understudy," Peggy Capps, dear friends who shared encyclopedic knowledge of Denton history. Thanks also goes to Robyn Lorraine Lee, whose way with words and friendship have nourished and sustained me.

INTRODUCTION

Denton is located 39 miles north of Dallas and Fort Worth. Together, the three cities form what is often referred to as the "Golden Triangle." Denton, the peak of that triangle, is the North Star. Imagination drives people to refer to past and present residents of Denton as supernovas, or superstars. Indeed, they are, in the hearts and minds of fellow Dentonites. Their accomplishments burst forth from the chapters of this book to outshine their counterparts in those other two cities of the Golden Triangle for their generosity, talents, skills, activism, adventurous spirits, energy, civic pride, business acumen, courage, and creativity.

Denton has used various marketing slogans throughout the years to promote itself, such as "Dynamic Denton," "North of Ordinary," "Denton . . . and all that jazz," "Denton, a good place to live, work, and play," "Denton, Texas, gives you room to breathe . . . and reason to want to," "Denton: a model city," and "Denton: It's a Whole Other Country." The city even has an unofficial slogan, created by Bill Ford, director of the University of North Texas student-managed advertising and public relations agency: "Denton: always a few degrees cooler than Dallas."

No matter what brand is used to describe this vibrant city, it is the people who make the community. Our history defines our community. And our people define our history.

That history began when Denton was founded in 1857, when county residents needed a location near the geographic center of Denton County to house a county seat. William Loving, Hiram Cisco, and William Woodruff donated 100 acres for the site of the town, which, like the county, was named in honor of John B. Denton. Families named Wright, Welch, Daugherty, Carroll, Williams, Bell, Egan, and Schmitz were among the early men and women who settled the city.

Rail connections in 1881 caused a shift from subsistence farming to cash crops, such as corn, wheat, and cotton. Milling industries were organized to process the increased production. Offshoot industries, such as blacksmith shops, grocery stores, and implement and hardware stores opened around the square, the market center for the city. From the 1920s to 1940s, residents grew their businesses into thriving operations. In the 1950s, the Federal Emergency Management Agency built an underground shelter on the edge of town, and in the 1960s, Denton State School was established. These two major employers added to the city's growth in population and employment.

Proximity to Dallas and Fort Worth, good interstate highway connections, and increased enrollments at the two universities were also foundational to the city's population growth. With the opening of Dallas–Fort Worth International Airport in the 1970s, many airline employees and company executives who traveled frequently moved to Denton.

The opening of the Golden Triangle Mall in 1980 and the attraction of large companies to Denton, such as Peterbilt, Tetra-Pak, Andrews Corporation, Aldi's, and Flowers Foods, enhanced the opportunities for growth. By 2013, the population of Denton had grown to more than 100,000. The success of these businesses, and the town's economic and population growth, enabled citizens to share their wealth with others in need.

Denton men and women proudly served their country in all branches of the armed services during all of the wars in which the United States was involved. Bravery was demonstrated not only during conflicts overseas, but in the United States as well when the nation was threatened. Whether here or abroad, Denton residents respond with compassion and determination to retain their freedoms. Civic-minded citizens are not heralded enough for their service to the community on the local, state, and national levels. This book is an effort to encourage such lasting recognition.

The two universities and the performance venues scattered about town provide nurturing environments for students. Writers, actors, artists, and musicians hone their talents in Denton. In many cases, these residents take their place on the world stage.

With the opening of North Texas Normal College in 1890 and the establishment of Girls' Industrial College in 1903, Denton became a "town and gown" community. The two universities enhance the city's economic, intellectual, and cultural life.

The high schools and universities produced many athletes who moved on to professional careers, some with international recognition. Integration of the University of North Texas in the 1950s led to opportunities for several students to become professional football players, a championship golf team produced PGA champions, an award-winning gymnastics program claimed an Olympic gold-medal winner, and a family of brothers created a wrestling dynasty.

Science and engineering programs produced space scientists, doctors, inventors, engineers, and innovators in world-class digital technology. The "can-do" spirit enabled five amateur car jocks to create a vehicle that would break the land speed record.

That same environment allows cheerleaders and civic heroes to thrive as they perform community service to make their hometown a better place for everyone.

One of Denton's prominent historians, C.A. Bridges, described it as "a city of homes, churches, schools, and law abiding, peace-loving people." He went on to express what all Dentonites would applaud: "Our wish for Denton," he said, "is that she have a share in the best of all things—all ways, and always."

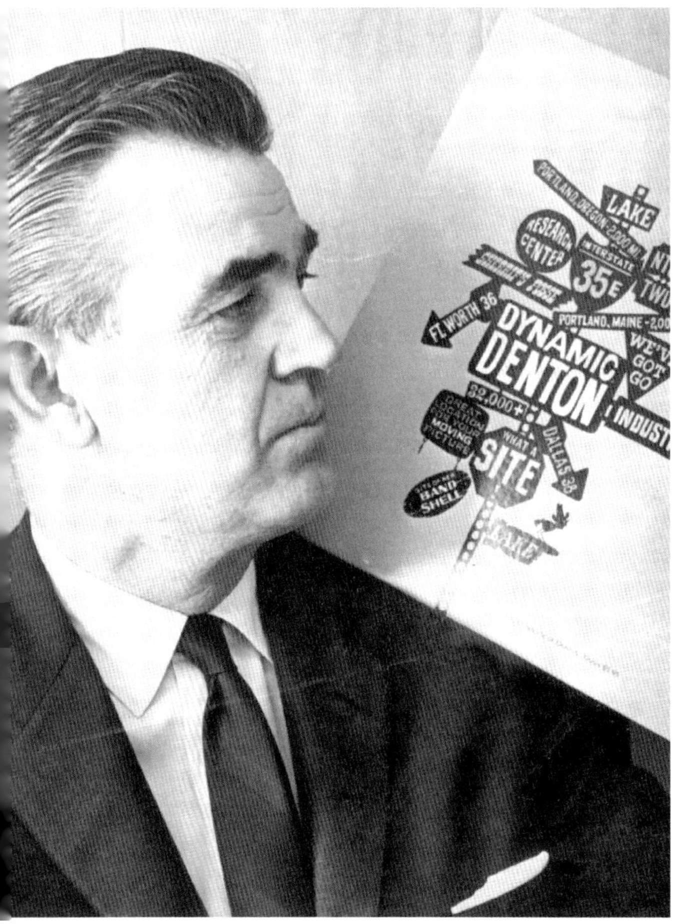

Dynamic Denton
Homer B. Bly began his career in Denton as city manager and served the chamber of commerce during the time that the city's slogan was "Dynamic Denton." A 1968 movie by the same name promoted the city and featured a young Dentonite who would later become Miss America and have a career in television and movies, Phyllis George. Bly made a career change when he joined First State Bank in 1963. He became president of the bank in 1972 and chairman of the board in 1988. Bly was instrumental in bringing the Federal Emergency Management Agency to Denton, was campaign manager of the United Way, and served on the UNT Foundation. Homer Bly won the Otis Fowler Award and was presented with honorary alumnus status from UNT. (Courtesy of DCOHC.)

CHAPTER ONE

Superstars of Early Denton

Pioneers lay the roads for those who follow to walk on.

—Unknown

The threads that bind the individuals selected for this chapter weave the fabric of the rest of the book. Courageous, hearty souls, these men and women were merchants, lawyers, judges, farmers, ranchers, bankers, sheriffs, soldiers, and even outlaws who laid the groundwork for the dynamic Denton of today. Mothers, daughters, and wives fashioned the city's diverse cultural and domestic tapestry.

The four streets that rim the immediate Downtown Square are named for indigenous trees: Oak, Elm, Locust, and Hickory. Encircling those main arteries are Pecan, Walnut, Ash (now Austin), and Cedar Streets. Chestnut, Mulberry, and Sycamore are feeder streets into and out of the residential areas to downtown. Oak Street is also known as "Silk Stocking Row" for the large homes of prominent families. The Oak/Hickory Historic District encompasses the last remaining older stately homes in the city.

Small towns often named their streets after early settlers or national heroes. In Denton, this occurs in the offshoot residential streets. This chapter highlights the history and stories of these pioneers and the streets named in their honor.

DENTON COUNTY
by Otis Grenwood Welch

There's no country on earth
Can equal our state
If people will work
And patiently wait,

Till the iron horse comes
With his immigrant train,
To bear back our cotton,
Our wool and our grain.

The climate and water,
The timber and land,
Need only the touch
Of the laborer's hand

To make Denton County
In all that is great
The garden of Texas
The great Empire state.

And Denton a city
Of worldwide renown
Lewisville, Pilot Point
And Elizabethtown.

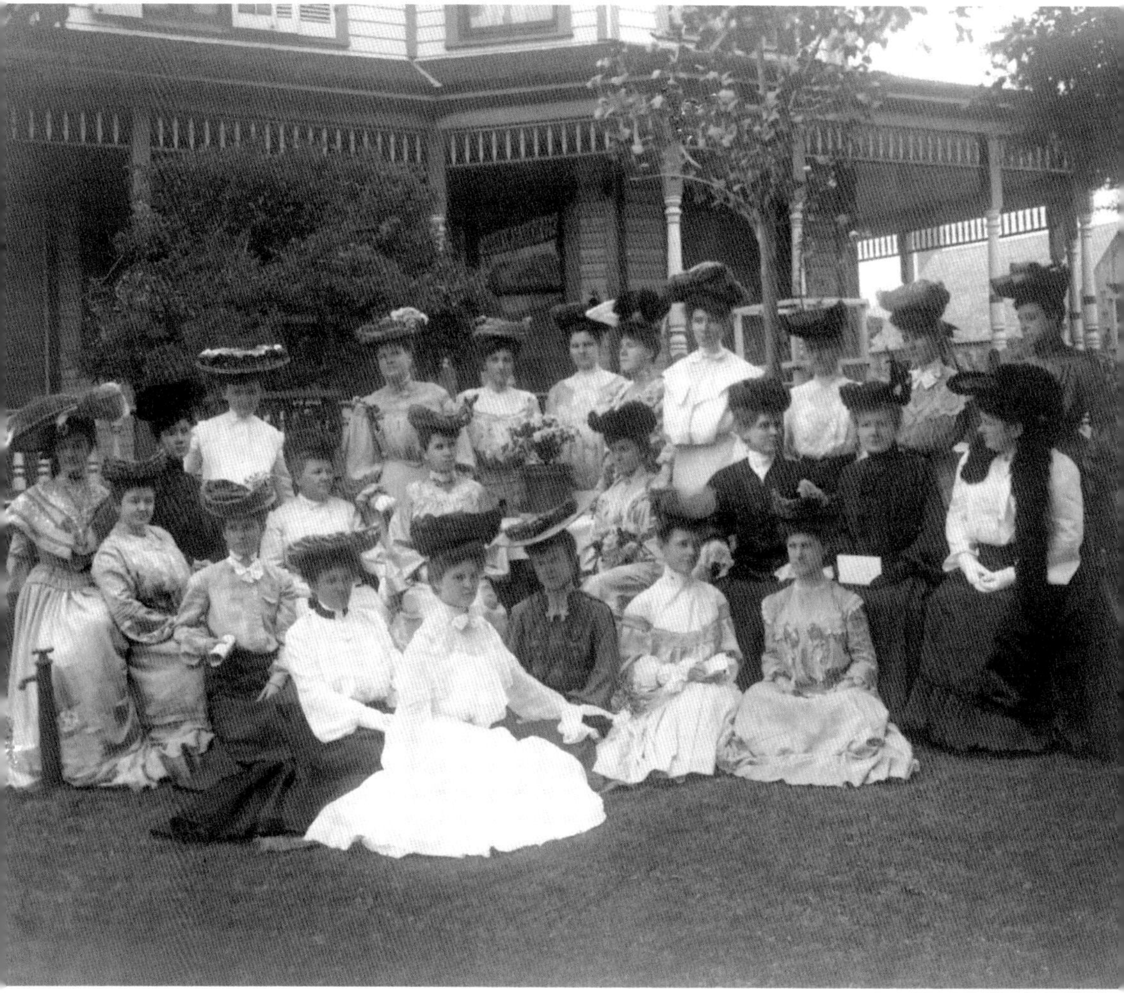

Ladies of the Club

The Ariel Club, established in 1891, is Denton's oldest club for women. It focuses on charity, education, and literary pursuits. These 1904 Ariel Club members, dressed in flowing dresses and fancy hats, are seated on the lawn of the home of Mrs. John C. Coit. Their surnames are found throughout Denton's history. Many of their families have streets named for them, including the following: Williams, Mounts, Wright, Hann, Brooks, Allen, Smith, Long, Coit, Carroll, and Edwards. Married to legendary men, these women were legends themselves through their volunteer activities and community advocacy. (Courtesy of DRC.)

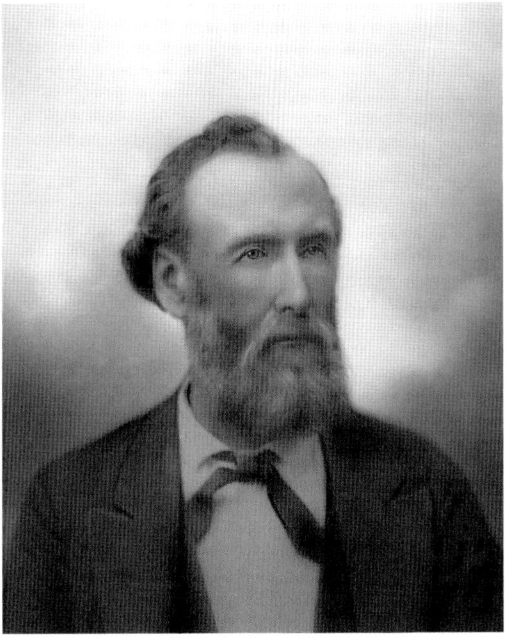

Father of Denton
After opening his law office in 1852 in Denton County, Otis Greenwood Welch (1822–1880) served as legal advisor in the formation of the city of Denton. Welch was captain of Company I First Choctaw and Chickasaw Mounted Rifles in 1861 and later transferred to the 29th Texas Cavalry. After the war, Colonel Welch resumed practicing law on the Denton Square. (Courtesy of IOOF.)

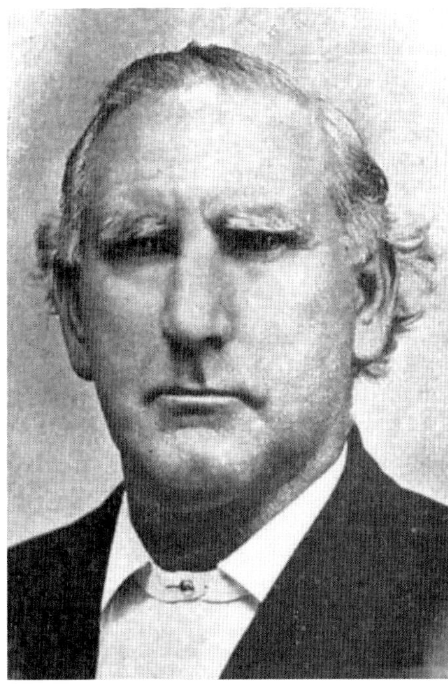

Carroll Boulevard's Namesake
Joseph Alexander Carroll (1832–1891) came to Denton in 1854; three years later, he drew the map for the town lots. He became a lawyer, served in the Civil War in the 29th Texas Cavalry, and returned home to resume his law practice. In 1876, he was elected 10th District court judge (currently the 16th District). Carroll served as mayor of Denton and charter regent of Texas Normal College. He was president of Exchange National Bank until his death. (Courtesy of IOOF.)

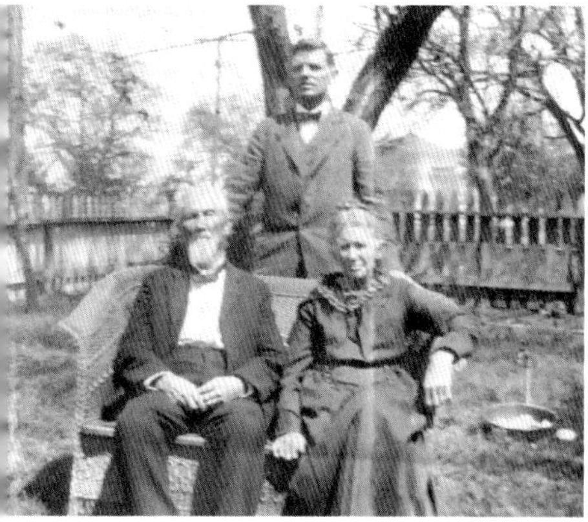

Sheriff and Merchant

As Denton County sheriff, Charles Alexander Williams (1832–1922) auctioned off Denton town lots in 1857. He was one of the first men to enlist in the Confederate army, serving as a private with the 18th Texas Cavalry. After the war, he was elected to a second term as sheriff (1866–1867). Williams and his wife, Virginia (d. 1926), are shown here on the occasion of their 50th wedding anniversary with their son, Will, standing behind them. Williams operated the Williams Dry Goods Store for 45 years, walking to work every day until his death at age 90. (Courtesy of DPL.)

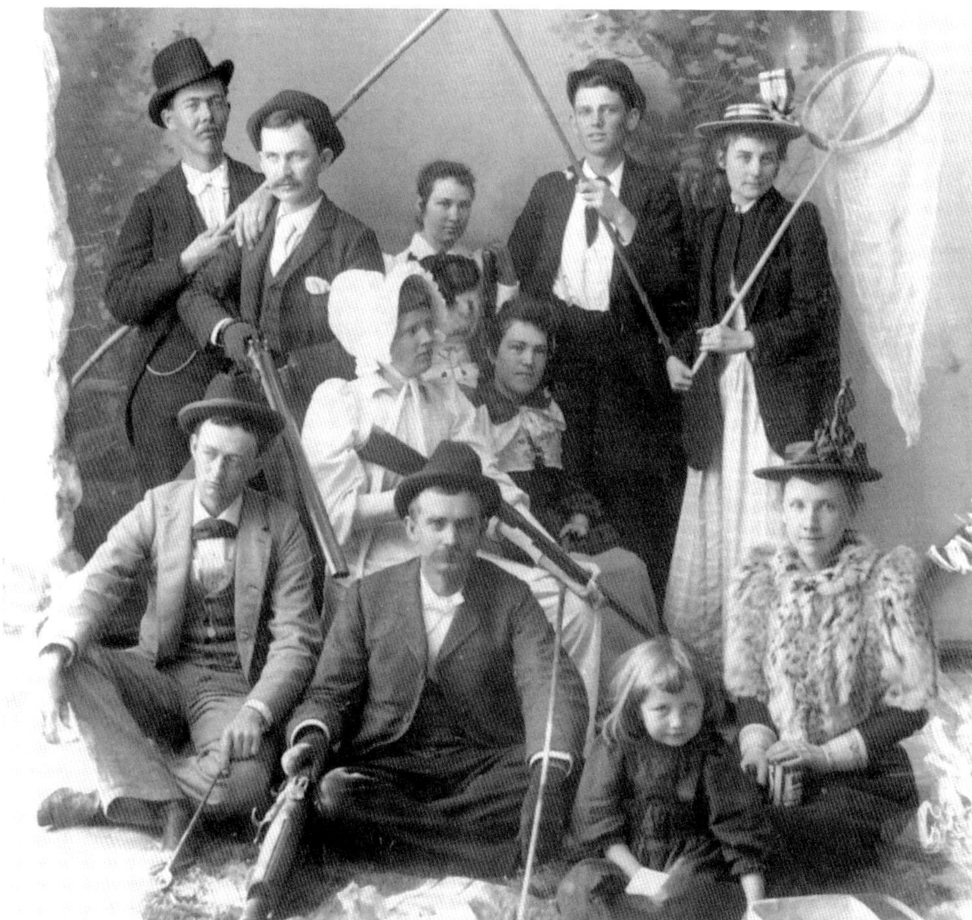

Prominent Families

Many prominent Denton families attended the Williams family picnic in Decatur, including the people posing for this photograph. They are, from left to right, as follows: (first row) John Douglas, J.P. "Pink" Magee, Bertha Saufley, and Effie Collins (Mrs. Ted) Ponder; (second row) Lee Williams and Effie Wright; (third row) Dr. Priestly Lipscomb, Joe A. Long, Lula Blewett, Will Williams, and Lenora Hann. (Courtesy of DPL.)

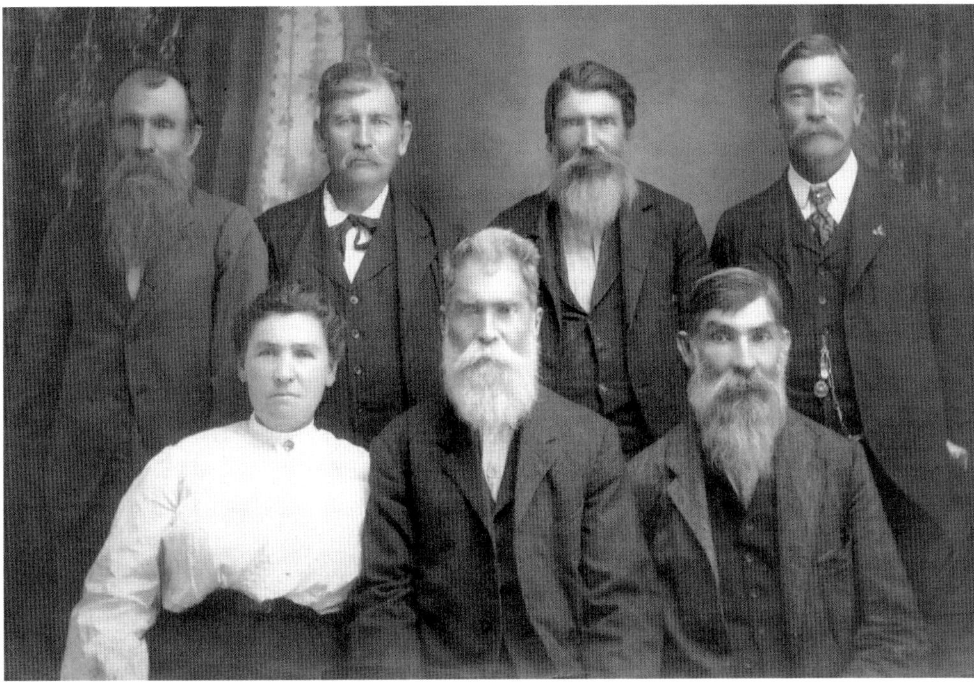

Molded from Pioneer Clay
The influential pioneer family of James Madison Daugherty was instrumental in the settlement, law and order, and commerce of the city. James Daugherty, the patriarch, was a rancher and lawyer. He is not pictured here. His sons and daughter are, from left to right, (first row) Mary Edleman, William Ausburn (lawyer), and Daniel Boone (Civil War soldier and potter); (second row) Christopher Columbus (Civil War soldier, sheriff, and merchant), Thomas W. (Civil War soldier, merchant, banker, and lawyer), Matthew (Civil War soldier, sheriff, and county judge), and James Monroe (rancher and banker). (Courtesy of DCOHC.)

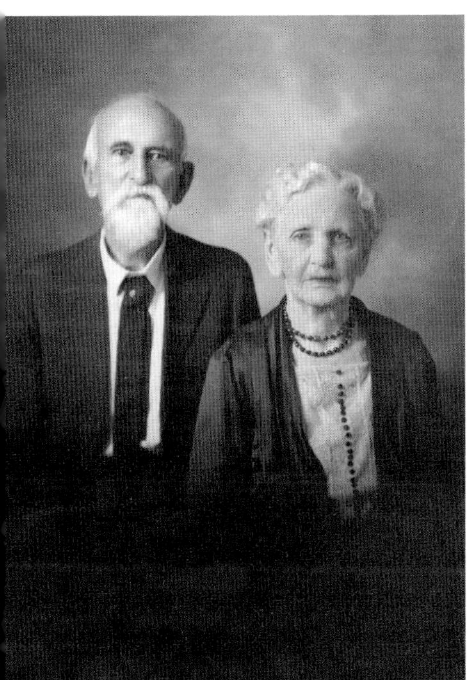

Bell Avenue Namesakes
Charles C. Bell (1840–1930) came to Denton in 1867 and operated Professor Bell's Male and Female Academy, a "promising institution," for two years in the Masonic lodge hall. Bell's institution was also known as an academy, a high school, a male and female college, and, sometimes, a seminary. By the end of the 1860s, Bell quit teaching and opened a lumber business. He played an instrumental role in planning the two universities. A main artery on the north side of Denton, Bell Avenue, is named for his family. Pictured in the 1920s are C.C. and Elmira Elizabeth Inge Bell (1840–1938). (Courtesy of DPL.)

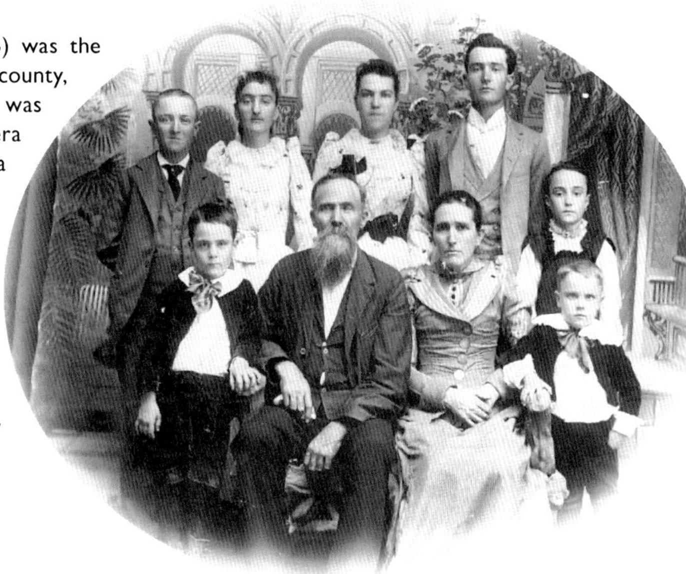

The Wright Stuff

William Crow Wright (1837–1906) was the owner of the largest ranch in the county, the Chain Seven Ranch, and he was the proprietor of the Wright Opera House. Wright, the patriarch of a large family, poses here with his wife and children. Shown are, from left to right, (first row) Whitney Crow, William Crow, Julia Ann Gober (wife), and Gober Camp; (second row) James Gillenwater, Mary Myrtle, Effie Fay Branche, William Wesley, and Eulallie Carruthers. (Courtesy of DCOHC.)

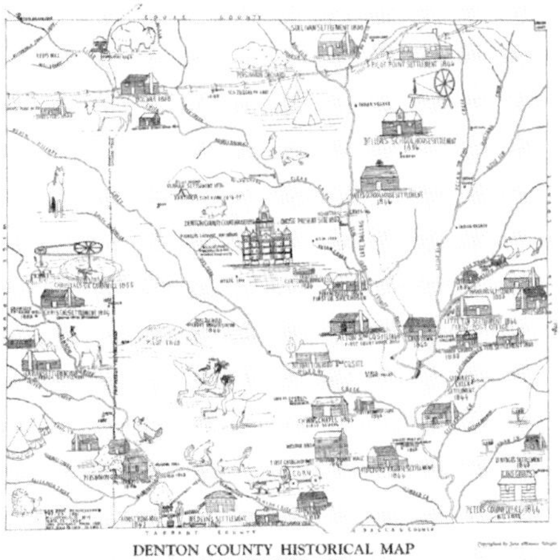

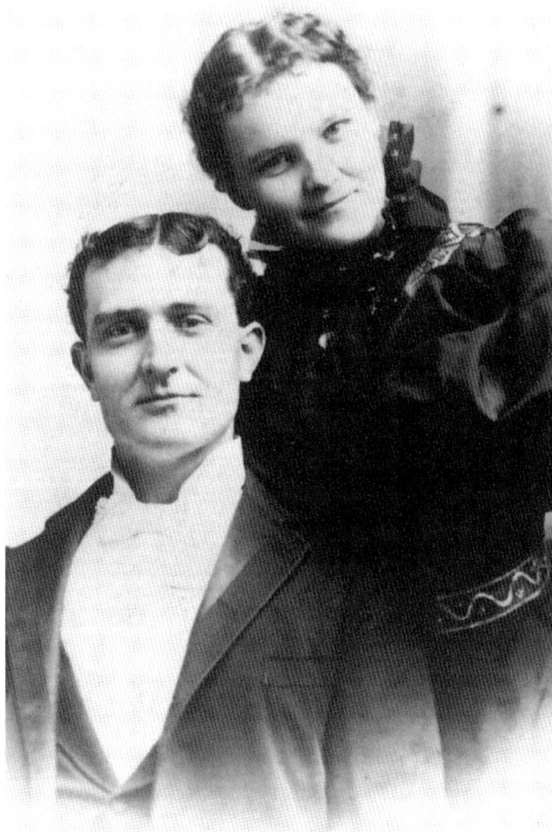

Mapping the Town

In 1936, her hobby of mapmaking enabled Sena Alleen Mounts Wright (1875–1952) to draw a historical map of the industrial and agricultural resources of Denton County for the Texas Centennial. Illustrated with line drawings, the map above shows major county waterways, towns, landmarks, roads, and railways. Sena Mounts is pictured at right with her husband, William Wesley Wright. (Courtesy of DCOHC.)

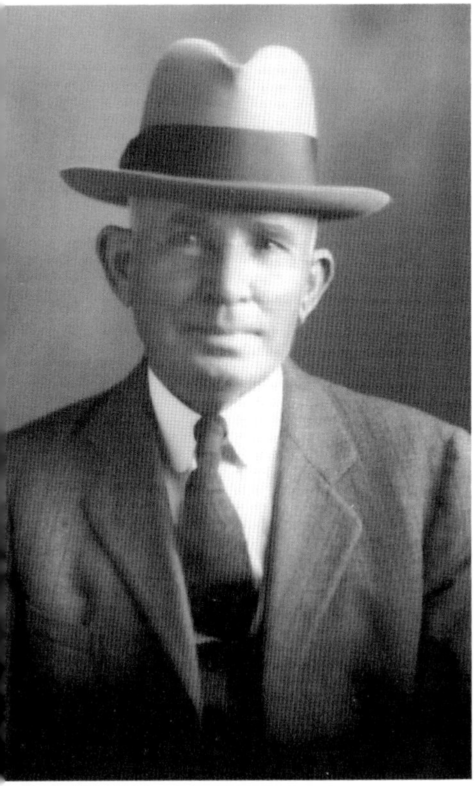

Christal Lights

James Russell "Jim" Christal (1859–1936) lost his father and older brother in Denton's first unsolved murders. His mother, Emily, persuaded her brother, Burk Burnett, to permit Christal to grow up on his cattle ranch, named 6666. Christal returned to Denton after the loss of his lower right leg prevented him from riding horses. He started the Golden Hoof Ranch and, later, built a home on Oak Street. Christal became the first county tax assessor, president of Exchange National Bank, and served on the original North Texas Normal board. An avid letter writer, Christal made friends with newsmakers of his time. He corresponded with Thomas Edison, explaining that he was building a house that would be the first all-electric home on Oak Street. He received a package containing one of the first light fixtures from the Edison Lighting Company, with a card from Edison wishing him happiness with his lights. Christal overcame his physical handicap as he ranched, wrote letters, and provided leadership in Denton. (Courtesy of Annetta Ramsay and Randy Hunt.)

Furniture and Funerals

John B. Schmitz (1858–1941) opened two complementary businesses: his furniture enterprise, in addition to selling standard pieces, also provided caskets for the funeral home for which he performed mortuary services. Schmitz, who was instrumental in attracting Denton's large German settlement, helped bring two railroad lines to Denton, organize the first fire department, establish the College of Industrial Arts, and served as a school board member. He ran unsuccessfully for state treasurer, state comptroller, governor, lieutenant governor, and congressman. Although he was never elected to office, Schmitz's political loyalty was rewarded when Theodore Roosevelt appointed him Denton postmaster. (Courtesy of DCOHC.)

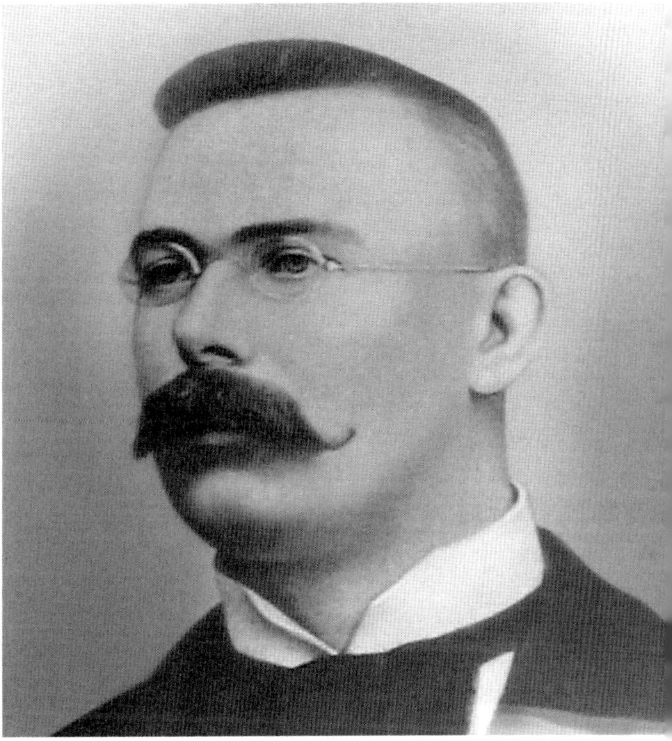

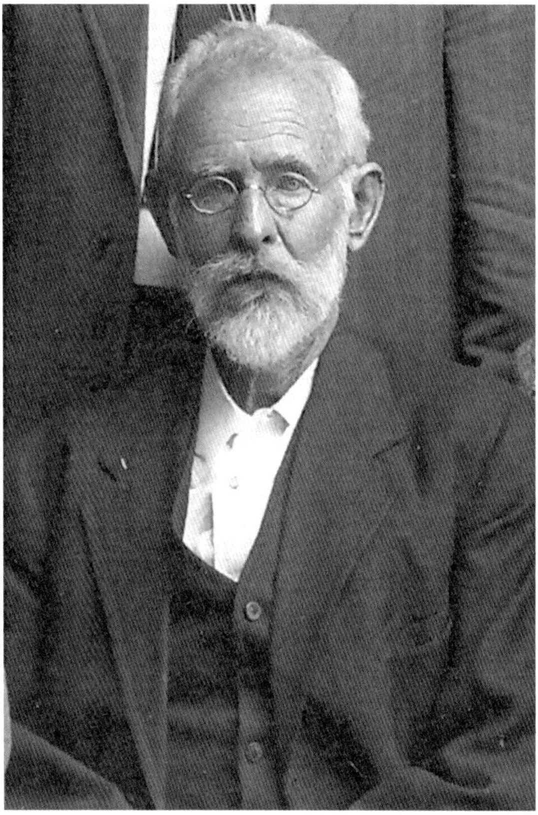

Sheriff Who Employed an Outlaw

William Franklin "Uncle Billy" Egan (1834–1921) served in the Texas 29th Cavalry with other Denton volunteers during the Civil War. After the war, Egan returned home and worked in a dry-goods store until he was elected sheriff and tax collector. Egan had once employed young Sam Bass as a hired hand. Sheriff Egan was among the men who tracked Bass during his outlaw days. During one of these forays, Bass allegedly snuck up on a sleeping Egan and whispered, "Hello, Uncle Billy" before escaping. (Courtesy of DCOHC.)

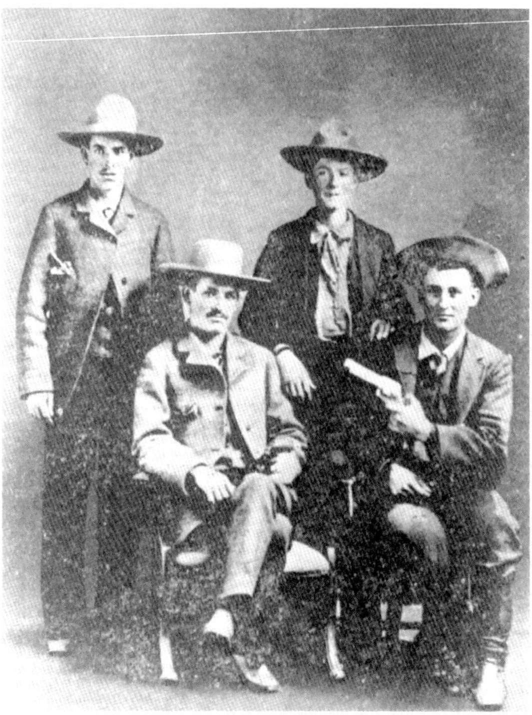

Robin Hood of the Cross Timbers

Sam Bass (1851–1878), "Texas' Beloved Bandit," came to Denton around 1870. He worked for Sheriff Egan, caring for livestock and hauling freight. Bass bought a fast sorrel mare that became known as the "Denton Mare." He began racing and gambling and formed an outlaw gang. In 1877, the Sam Bass Gang held up a Union Pacific train, netting $60,000 cash. After dividing the loot, Bass came back to Denton County. He led a crime spree of robbing stagecoaches and trains while hiding out in the thickets of rural Denton County. The fate of Bass's share fueled speculation about hidden gold in "Sam Bass' Cave" on Pilot Knob. Texas Rangers and railway-hired Pinkerton men killed Bass in a gun battle in Round Rock on his 27th birthday. This photograph, taken in the summer of 1876, shows Bass (standing, left) with Joe Collins (seated, left), John E. Gardner (standing, right), and Joel Collins (seated, right). (Courtesy of DRC.)

CHAPTER TWO

Superstars of Business and Philanthropy

The raising of extraordinarily large sums of money, given voluntarily and freely by millions of our fellow Americans, is a unique American tradition. Philanthropy, charity, giving voluntarily and freely . . . call it what you like.

—John F. Kennedy

Denton was a localized agrarian economy in its early days, but the coming of the railroads afforded the opportunity to expand beyond county lines. Saloons, hardware stores, furniture and funeral parlors, drug emporiums, icehouses, grain mills, grocery stores, and restaurants dotted the Square. Later, businesses opened beyond the Square, servicing the city's ever-growing population. The spread of the town into undeveloped acreage along and around the major highways resulted in a greater demand for services to these neighborhoods with conveniently located stores. Shopping downtown became less popular as mom-and-pop businesses moved away from the city's core. Smaller industrial manufacturing and food and beverage processing concerns, eateries, apparel and household goods stores, and banks and savings-and-loan institutions opened closer to the new neighborhoods.

Some industrialization occurred, offering job opportunities in the fields of commercial and residential building; building product supply; printing and publishing; food, grain, and dairy processing; bottling; and greenhouses and nurseries. The development of lakes and water reservoirs provided favorable conditions to open parks, picnic and playground areas, boating and fishing facilities, and other water-related entertainment, as well as the construction of lakeshore and summer housing.

Denton became a popular destination for visitors. Tourists' courts, motels, automobile dealerships, and gas and automobile service stations popped up on the main arteries of town.

Fraternal organizations and women's clubs were active in community affairs, scouting activities were offered to future community leaders, the chamber of commerce and junior chamber of commerce promoted local businesses, and garden clubs encouraged Denton residents to beautify their homes, businesses, streets, and parks.

With success came discretionary income and a willingness on the part of townsfolk to assist those less fortunate. Individuals and businesses forged alliances to form fundraising foundations and nonprofit agencies. The citizenry of Denton subscribed to Henry Ford's opinion that "the highest use of capital is not to make more money but to make money do more for the betterment of life."

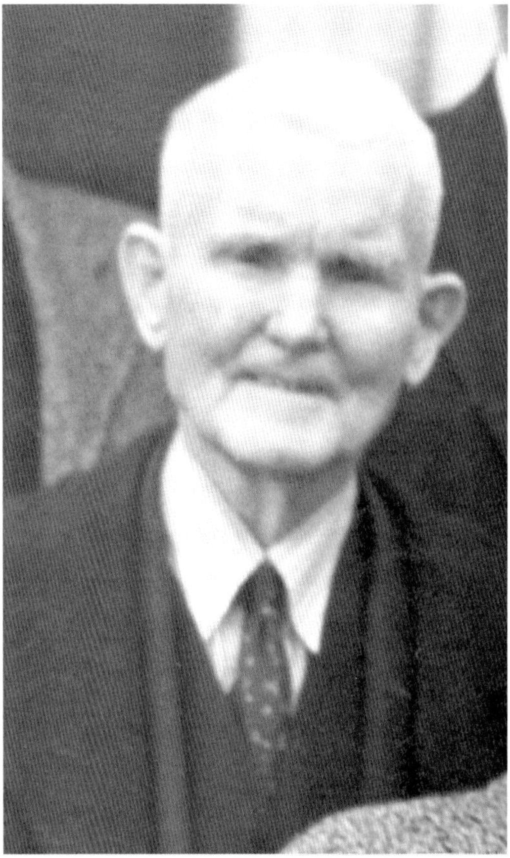

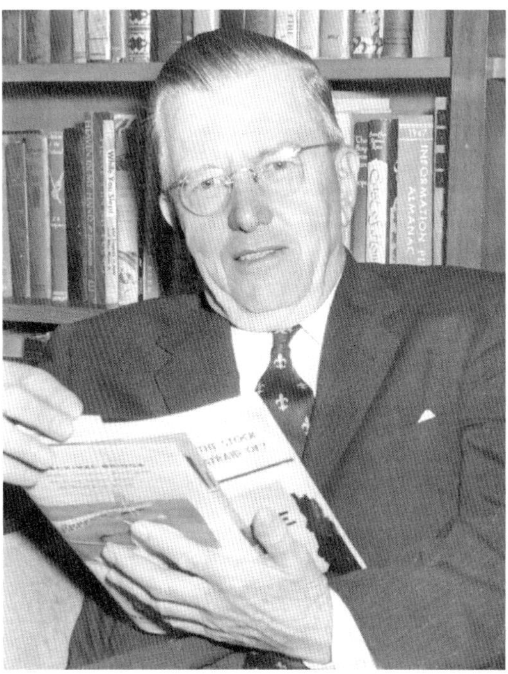

Sharp Businessmen

James Newton Rayzor (1858–1938) came to Denton in 1882 and established himself in several business ventures, including the Alliance Mill, Alliance Ice Company, and Rayzor Brothers Ice Company. He served as president of the chamber of commerce, was active in the Masonic lodge, and helped establish the College of Industrial Arts. Rayzor (above) served as deacon at First Baptist Church for 44 years and authored books about religion, history, and traveling to Europe and the Holy Land. His son, Jesse Newton (1895–1970), founded Commercial Petroleum & Transport Company, the world's largest inland water carrier. Newton (below) never forgot his Denton roots, giving land for Denia Park, Selwyn School, the Kiwanis children's clinic, and three schools, and donating funds for carillon bells for the First Baptist Church. (Both, courtesy of DCOHC.)

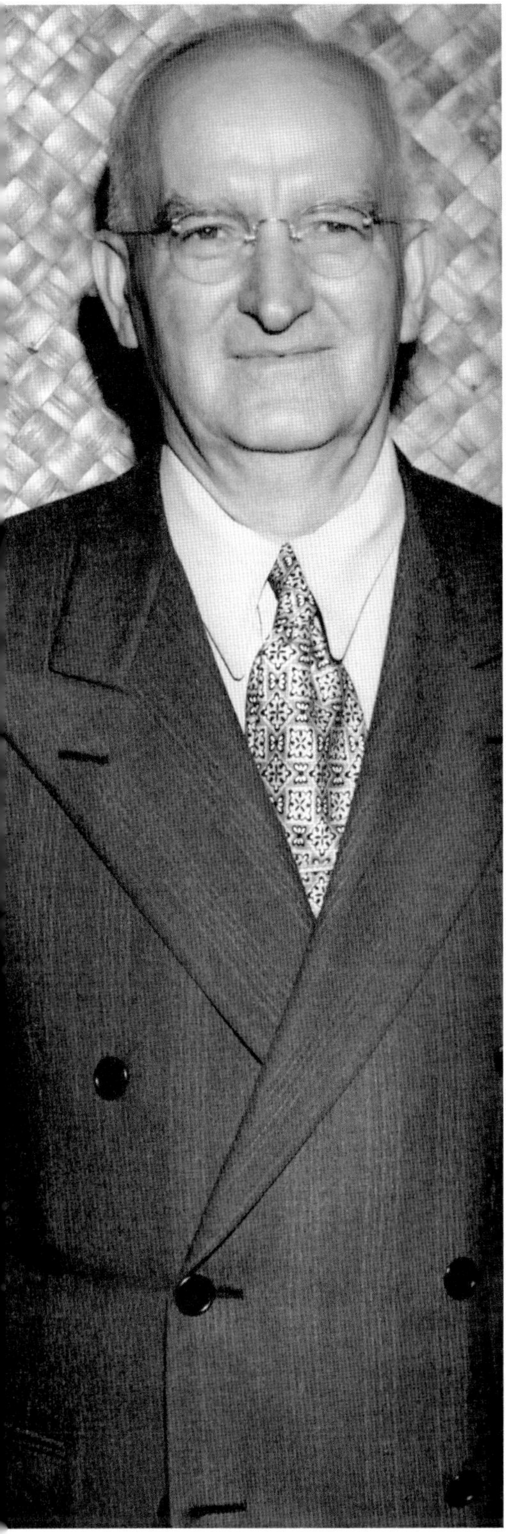

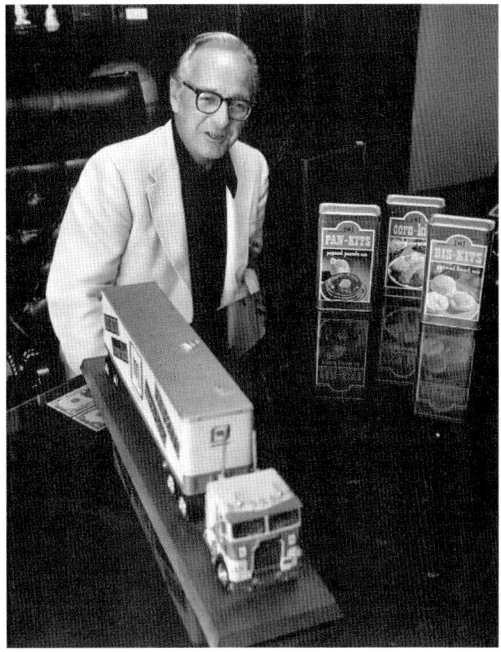

Managing Morrison Milling

A well-respected local businessman and donor to charitable causes, Edward Walter Morrison Sr. (1893–1972) (left), purchased Alliance Milling from the Rayzor family. He changed the name to Morrison Milling and managed the award-winning milling operation until his son, Edward Jr. (1940–2008) (above), succeeded him. The business has been sold, but the iconic grain storage elevators bearing the Morrison name stand as a monument to these two community leaders and philanthropists. (Both, courtesy of DRC.)

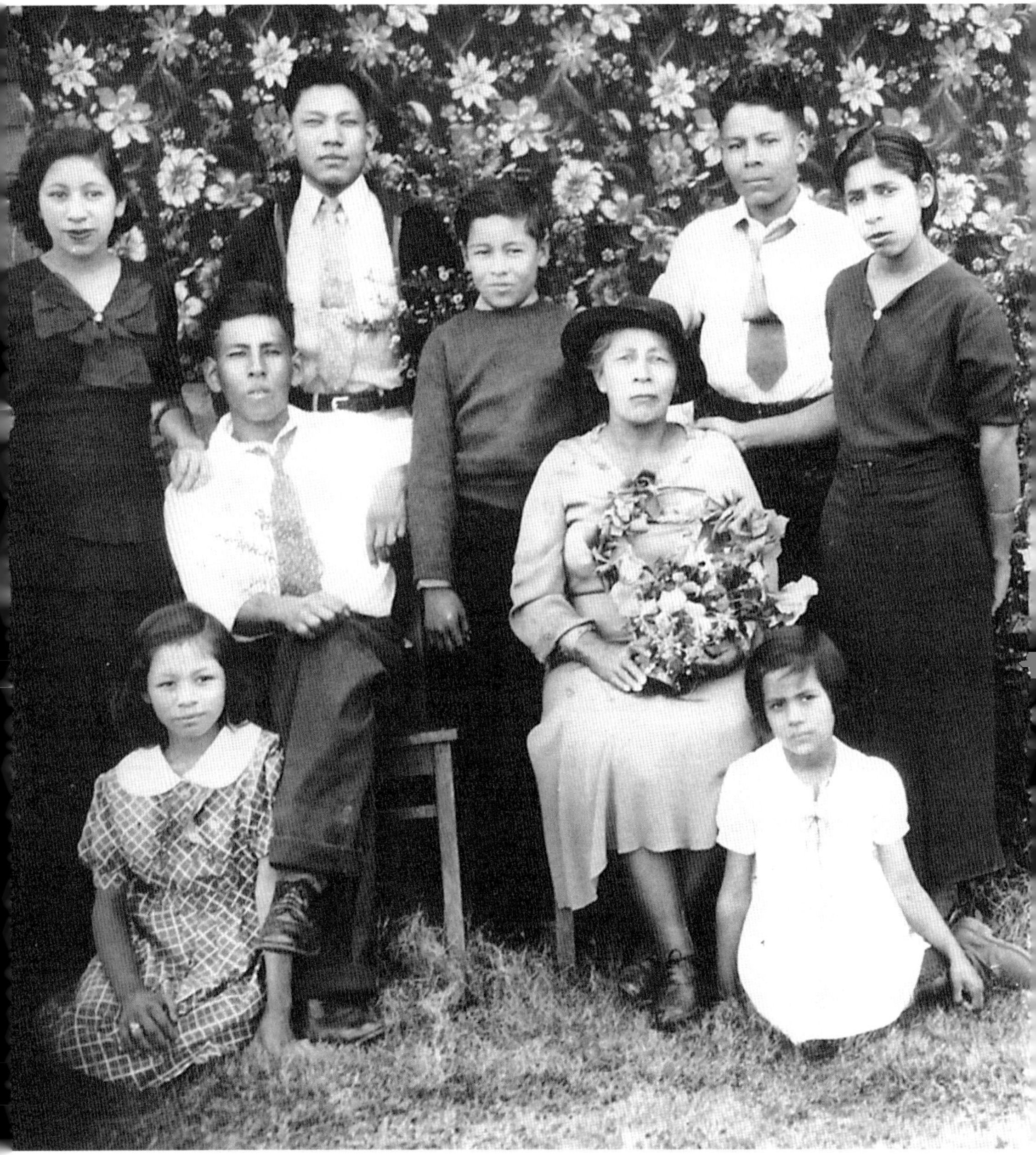

Villanueva Family

Antonio "Tony" Villanueva arrived in Denton from Mexico in 1903, a widower with a young daughter, Ramona. He married a young widow, Marguerita Avila (1885–1974), and they had nine children. Their family was among the four Hispanic families listed in the 1920 census. He worked for Juan Menchaca at his restaurant and operated a hot tamale stand on the Denton Square. This 1936 photograph of Marguerita and the Villanueva children was taken at the Villanueva home on Withers Street. Pictured from left to right are (first row) Delores and Josephine; (second row) Tony Jr., Sam, and Marguerita; (third row) Margaret, Ben, Braley, and Ramona. Not shown are Tony Sr., Trina, and Joseph. Sons Ben, Sam, and Braley, and daughter Margaret served in the military in World War II. (Courtesy of DCOHC.)

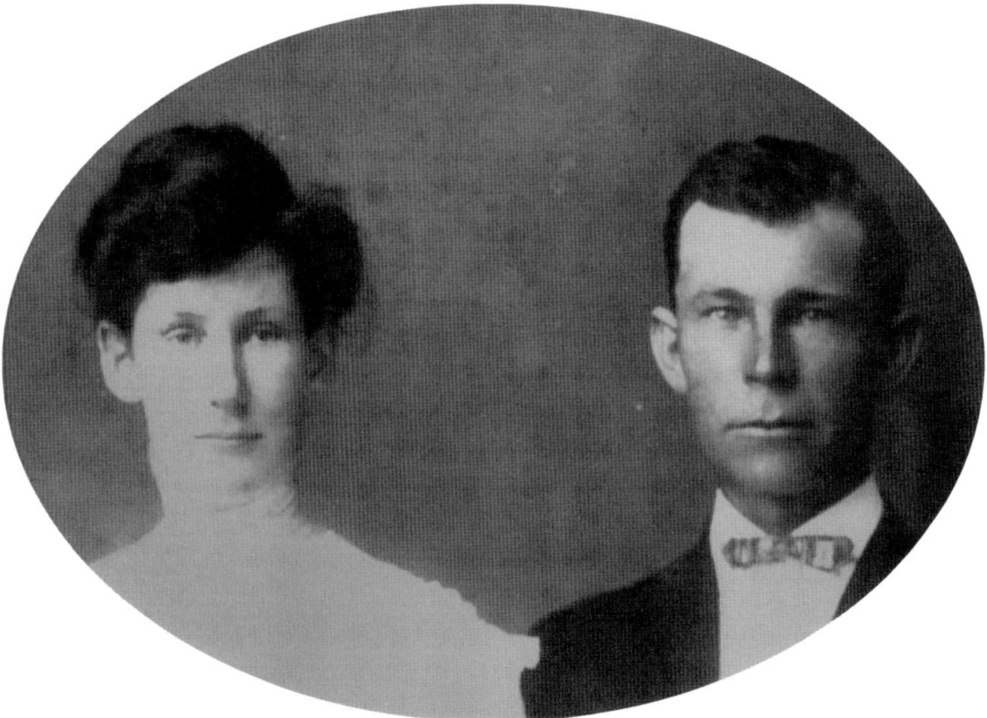

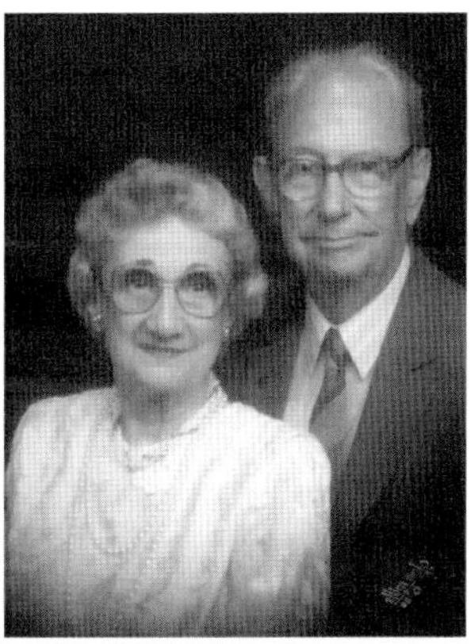

Everything's Coming Up Roses

Shown in the top photograph are Robert Lee "R.L." Selby Sr. (1869–1955) and his wife, Mary (1881–1962). They started one of the largest nursery and greenhouse businesses in the county in 1910. In the top left photograph are R.L. Selby Jr. (1913–1992) and his wife, Lewis Marie (1918–2009). They operated a flower shop on North Locust Street from 1943 until 1977, selling roses, gladiolas, and other flowers from the greenhouses. The oldest son, George (1908–2007), and his wife, Velma (1910–2003), are shown at bottom. They owned the wholesale nursery that supplied not only the flower shop, but also shops all over Texas, with millions of blooms. (Above, courtesy of DCOHC; top left, courtesy of Steve Selby; bottom left, courtesy of Dick Selby.)

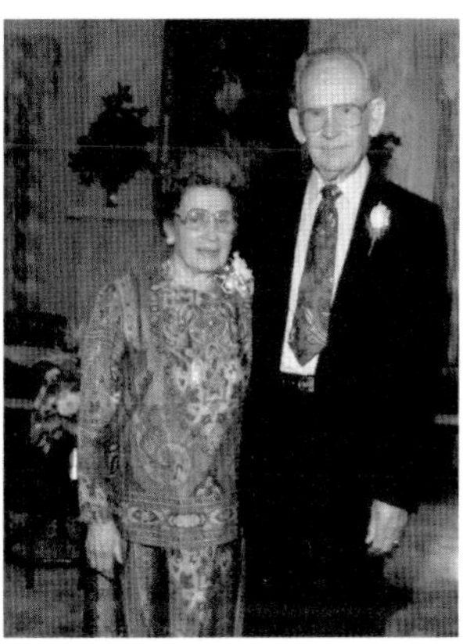

Real Estate Developer

R. Joe Skiles (1912–1981), lawyer and state representative, built one of the first residential neighborhoods in an area north of Denton that was deemed by many as too far from town and not feasible due to the heavy clay soil. It was nicknamed "Idiot's Hill." Ironically, lawyers, college professors, pilots, and doctors bought homes there, confirming to some Dentonites the truth of that nickname. Skiles later developed another neighborhood in south Denton, called Southridge. Many visitors to that development get lost in the unique design of a major street that spirals like a corkscrew, with connecting streets crossing the main artery. Skiles was honored with the first Otis Fowler Award for community service. R. Joe Skiles Park in Southridge was named after him. (Courtesy of DRC.)

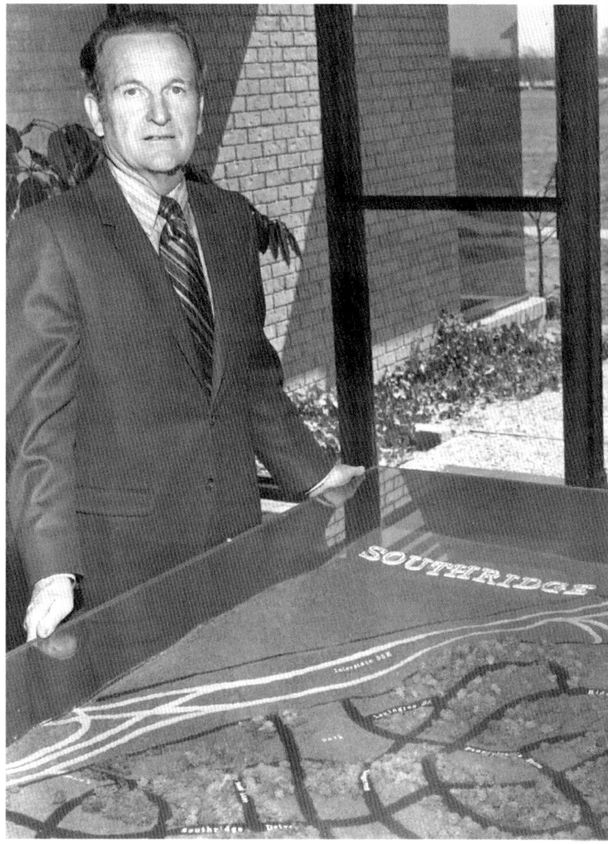

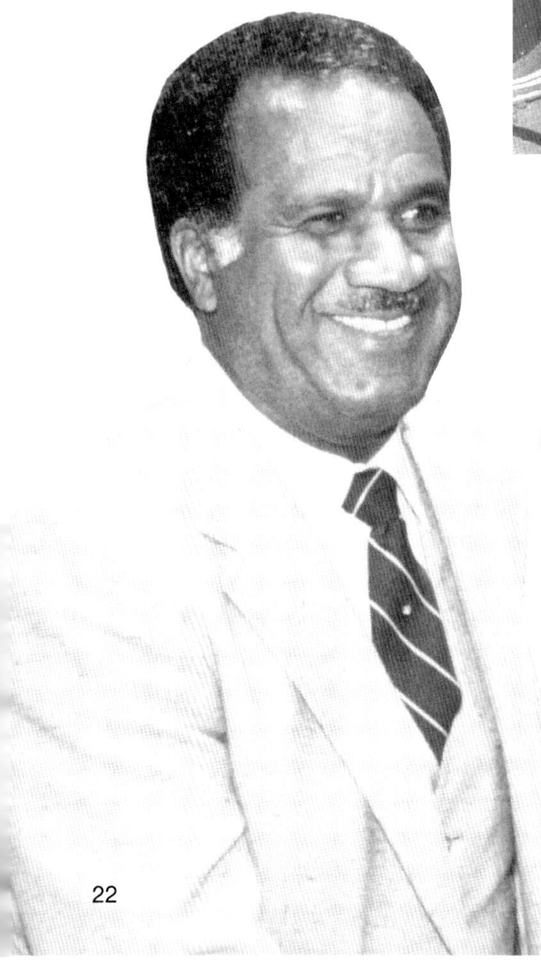

Entrepreneurial Ventures

After graduating from Prairie View A&M University, Fred Hill served in the Army, returning to Denton to apply his leadership and management skills to several entrepreneurial ventures. In addition to distinction as a local businessman, Hill has given back to the community, serving as president of the school board, founding member of Denton Black Chamber, member of the Denton Chamber, and board member of Denton Area Teachers Credit Union, Denton Regional Medical Center, Mt. Pilgrim CME Church, and Access Bank. (Courtesy of DCOHC.)

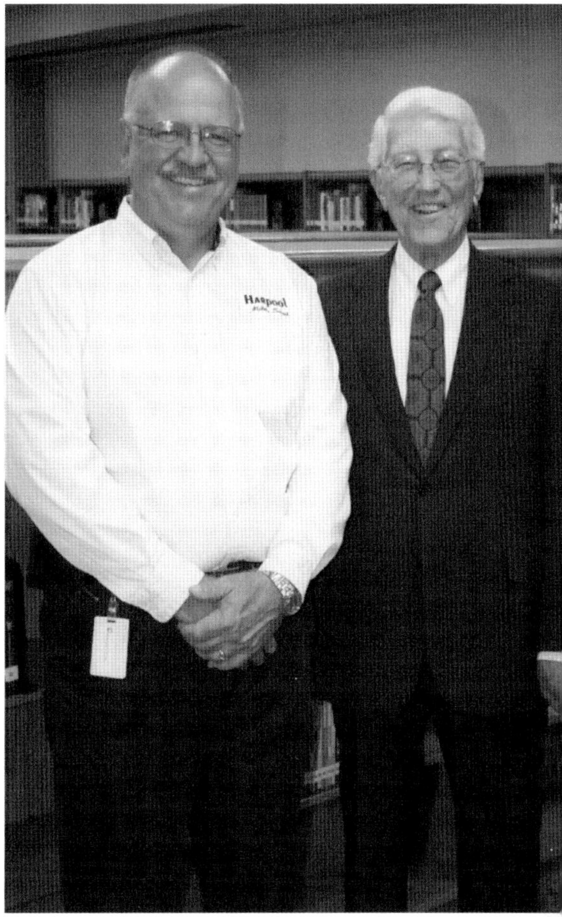

In the Beginning, a Seed

Robert Thomas "R.T." Harpool Sr. (1883–1947) moved his family to Denton in 1928. R.T. and his son Tom opened Harpool Seed, Inc., in 1939. They later opened Harpool Fertilizer. All three of R.T.'s sons were involved in the seed business in some capacity. The sons were Tom (1918–2009) (in suit and tie at right), Walter S. "Pinky" (1922–2007) (below left), and Albert (1920–2001) (below right). Al served in the military and returned to Denton to become a successful businessman. Pinky was a World War II flight instructor and an avid supporter of many civic functions. Tom served as chamber president, was on the Denton State School board, and was instrumental in obtaining Ray Roberts Lake. Tom Harpool (right) is pictured with Michael Vance, former principal of Tom Harpool Middle School, named in Harpool's honor. (Right, courtesy of *Cross Timbers Gazette;* below left, courtesy of DCOHC; below right courtesy of Barbara Harpool Hall.)

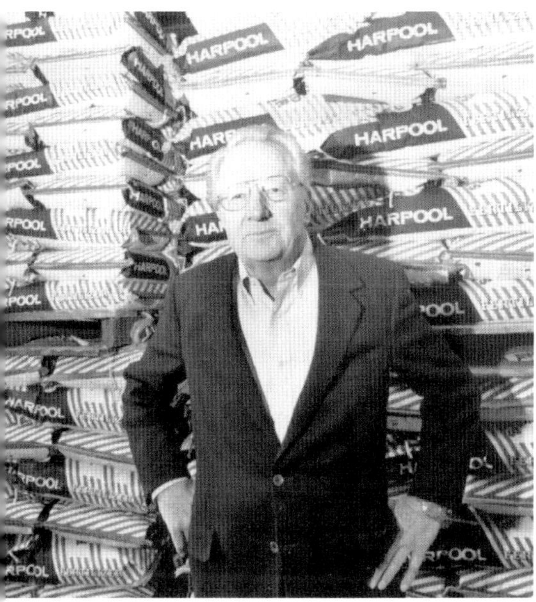

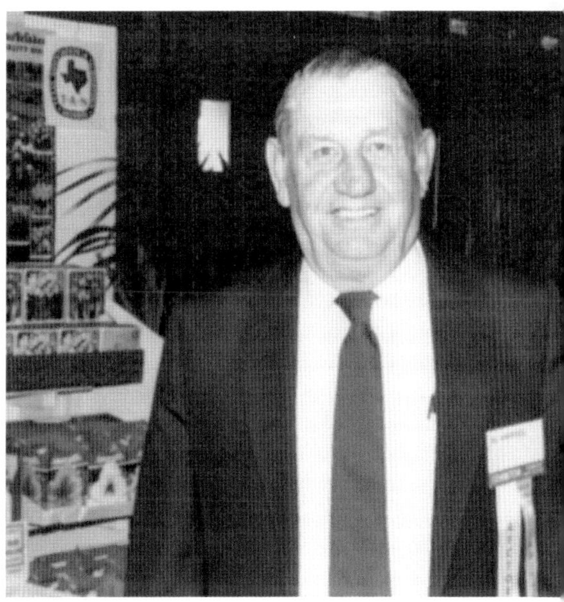

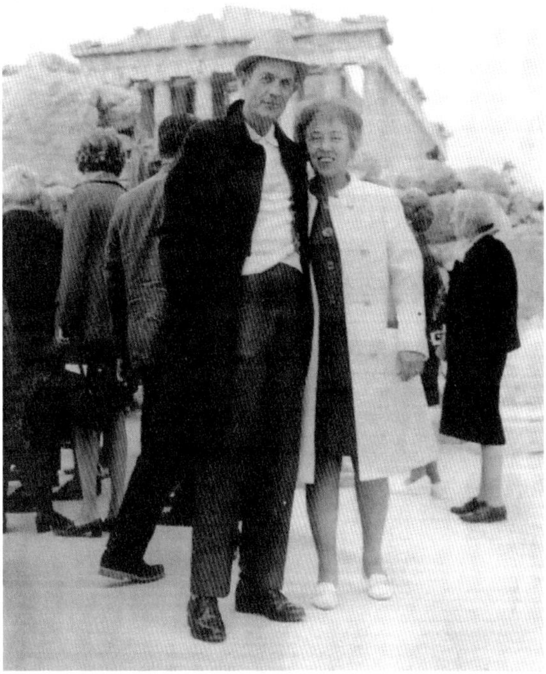

Capturing the Pitner Brand

John Michael "Doc" Pitner (1878–1952), a licensed veterinarian, founded the Pitner Sausage Packing Company in 1927. He also owned a slaughtering and processing site, which prepared the meat used in making and shipping the tasty Pitner sausage as far away as Germany. His son, Homer Melton "Doc" Pitner, joined his father's business in 1943. Doc Jr. (1914–1971) and his wife, Marjorie (1914–2007), shown in this photograph, operated the Denton Rodeo and owned and operated Roselawn Memorial Park. Their two daughters, Patsy Kelsoe and Linda Riley, are actively involved in the family business, displaying the same loving care that their parents showed to bereaved families. (Courtesy of Patsy Kelsoe.)

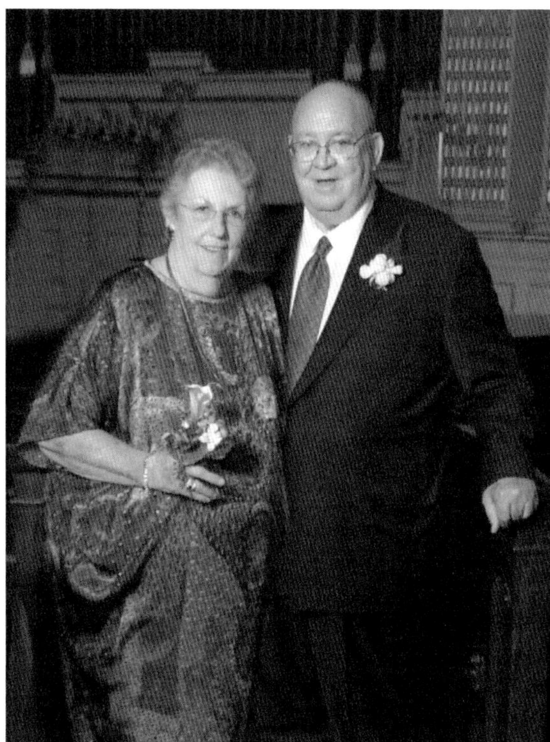

Salute to the LaGrones

Troy LaGrone (1934–2004), a fifth-generation Texan, joined Ben E. Keith Company as a clerk in 1953 and moved through the ranks to become its president. During his 47-year career, Ben E. Keith Beers grew to become the largest Anheuser-Busch distributor in the country. Troy and Sarah LaGrone (1934–2004) were known for their generosity of both time and financial support, devoting their boundless energy to many community activities and educational institutions. The Denton Independent School District named the Sarah and Troy LaGrone Advanced Technology Complex in their honor in 2006. (Courtesy of Monte B Photography.)

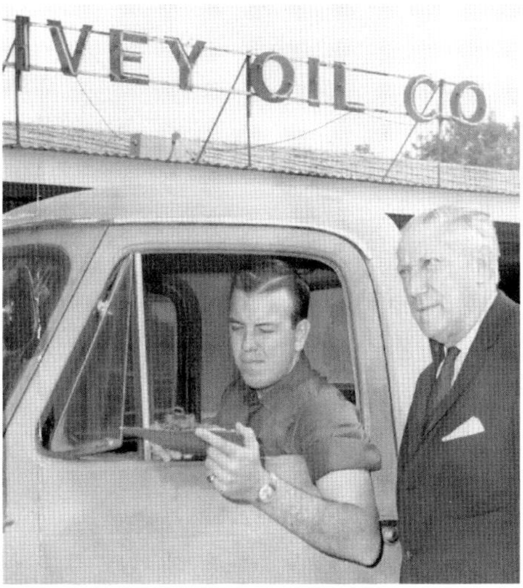

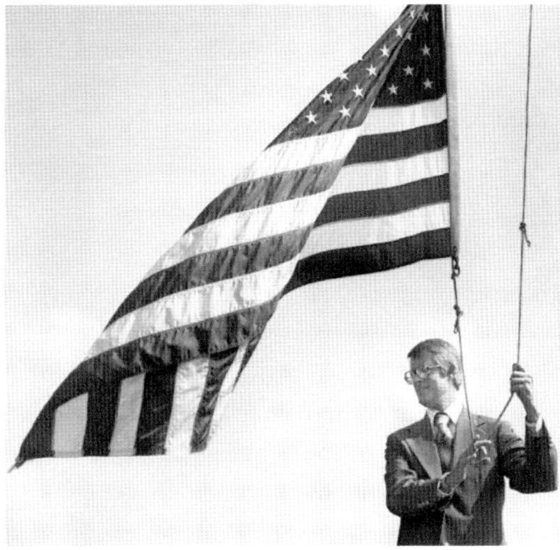

Climbing to Success

Benjamin Curtis Ivey Sr. (1898–1969) owned automobile dealerships and the Sinclair distributorship in the 1930s and 1940s. In the 1920s, when a customer bought a car from Ivey, he would teach them how to drive. Ivey's list of civic achievements is significantly supported by his philosophy that "anything that is good for the community is good for everybody." In the photograph at left, Ben Ivey Sr. (in suit and tie in the photograph at left) is checking on deliveries with company truck driver Jim Lehmberg. Pictured at right raising the American flag, Ivey's son Benjamin Curtis Jr. (1935–1996) became president of Ben Ivey Oil Company. In addition to numerous civic interests, including serving on the city council and acting as mayor pro tem, he had a particular interest in Denton State School. Both father and son were awarded the Otis Fowler Award. (Both, courtesy of DRC.)

The Utter Side of Denton

Bill Utter Sr. (1916–2006) dropped out of high school to help his family make ends meet. Utter opened his first Ford dealership in downtown Denton in 1956 and later expanded his business to Interstate 35. He received Denton's Small Business Person of the Year Award and Ford's Distinguished Quality Achievement Award. Utter was instrumental in bringing the Federal Emergency Management Agency and the Denton State School to Denton. His dealership's television advertisements humorously suggest visiting the dealership on the "utter side of Denton." (Courtesy of DCOHC.)

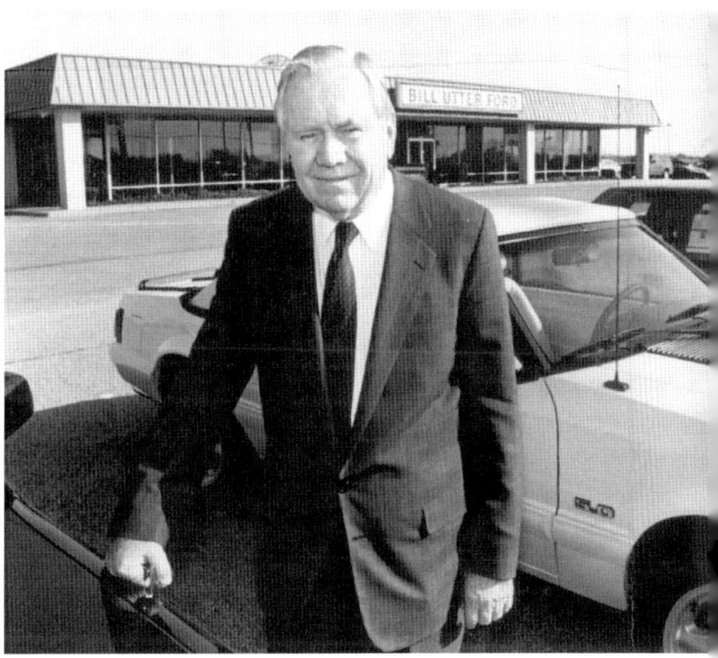

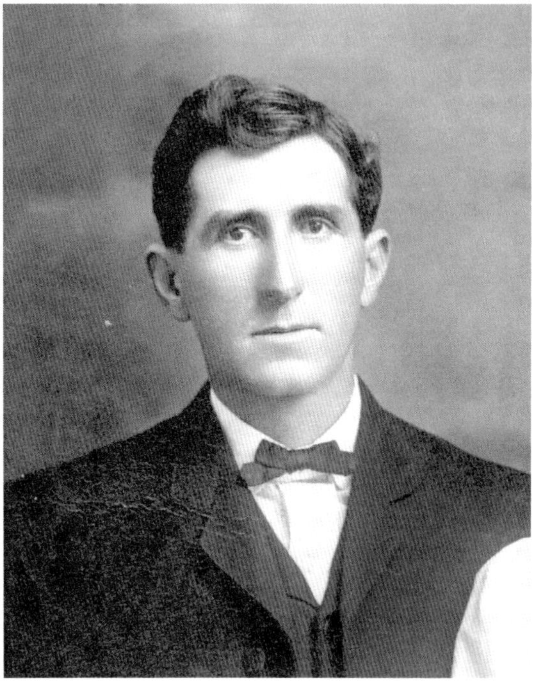

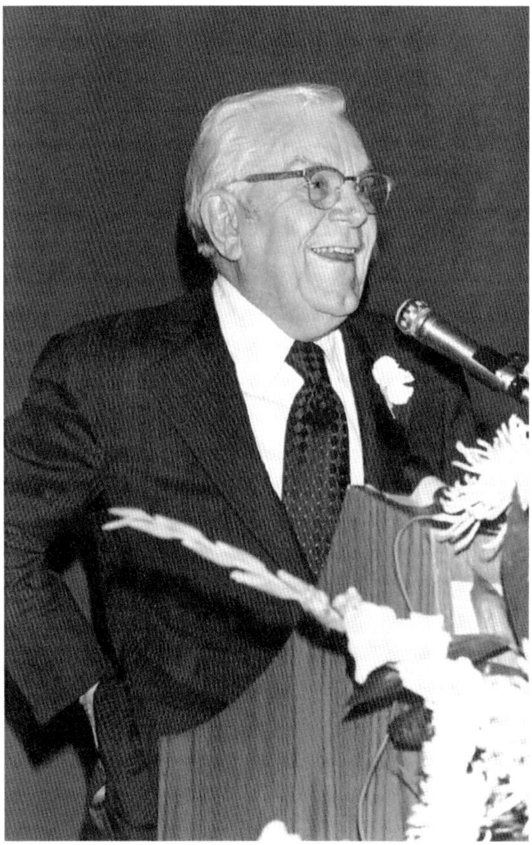

Community Bankers

During the Great Depression, First State Bank officer William Columbus "W.C." Orr Sr. (1876–1951) sent his teenage son W.C. Jr. (1912–1995) to Fort Worth on the day that there was a run on Denton's Exchange National Bank. W.C. Jr. returned with two packages of $1 bills that his father stacked in the tellers' windows. Customers were assured that there was plenty of cash and that their money was safe, thus saving a run on the bank. As one of the original incorporators of First State Bank in 1912, Orr Sr. (above) was named president in 1944 and then chairman of the board until 1951. Orr Jr. (below) joined the bank in 1948, assuming the presidency and chairmanship in 1961 and remaining in that position until 1972. Substantial expansion and growth was experienced under his leadership. Orr Jr. was a UNT distinguished alumnus and Otis Fowler Award honoree. (Above, courtesy of DCOHC; below, courtesy of DRC.)

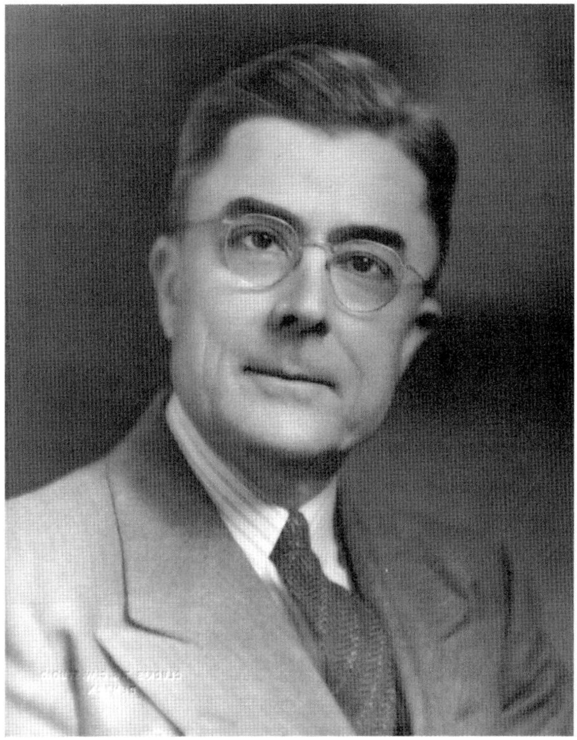

A Major Force

Fred Hawthorne Minor (1888–1976) graduated from North Texas State and the University of Texas law school before practicing law for 60 years in Denton. In 1926, he was elected to the Texas Legislature, where he remained until 1933, during which time he served as Speaker of the House. Minor served on the Denton City Council for eight years and on the board of education for 16 years. He was given the Otis Fowler Award and was named a North Texas distinguished alumnus. (Courtesy of DCofC.)

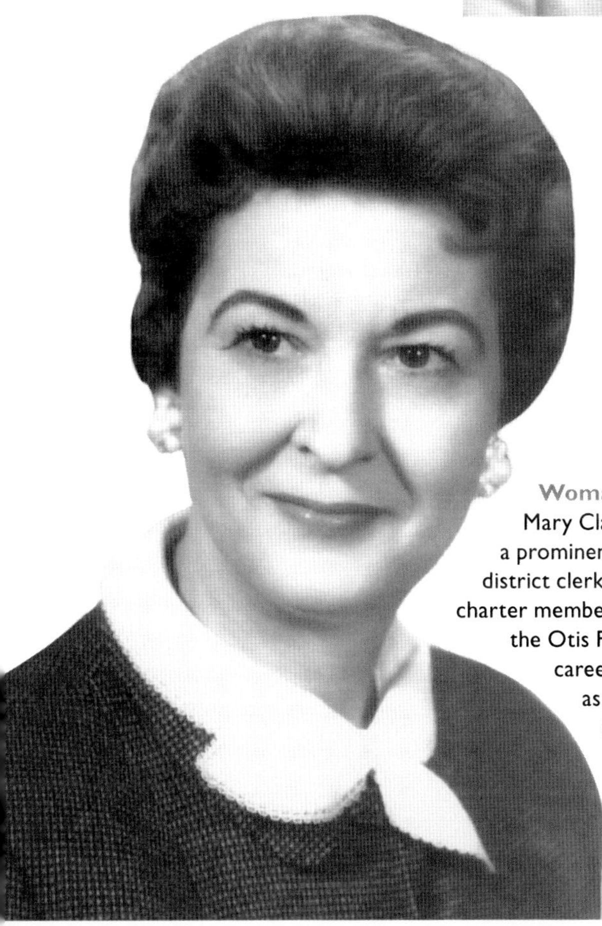

Woman REALTOR of the Year

Mary Claude Brooks Bays Gambill Gay (1917–1998), a prominent business and civic leader, served as county district clerk and on the Denton City Council. She was a charter member of the Denton Benefit League and received the Otis Fowler Award for her successful real estate career. Gay was honored locally and statewide as real estate Woman of the Year many times and remained active in the community until her death. (Courtesy of Jim Bays.)

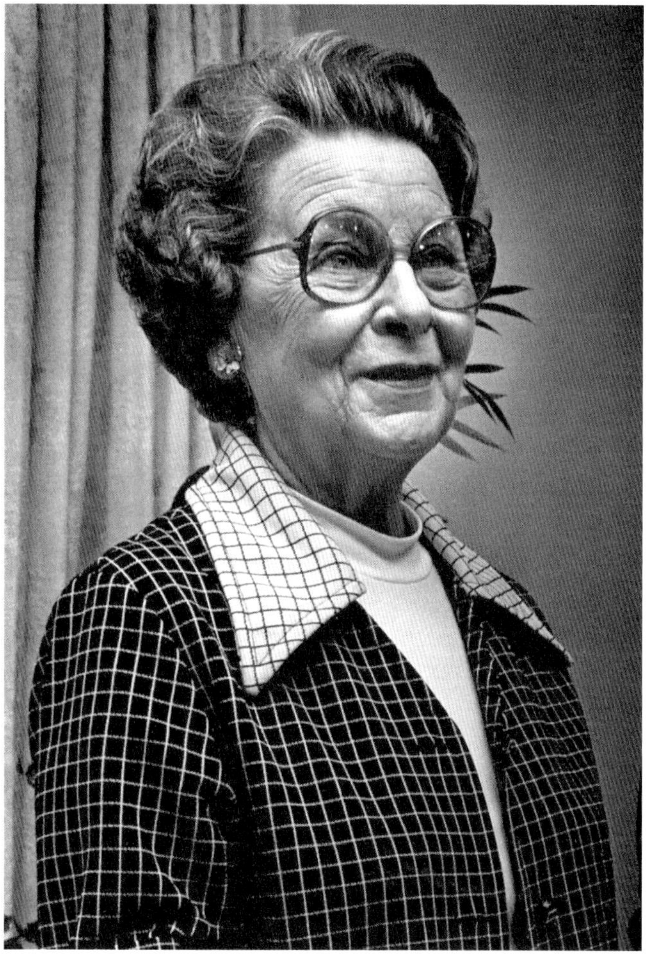

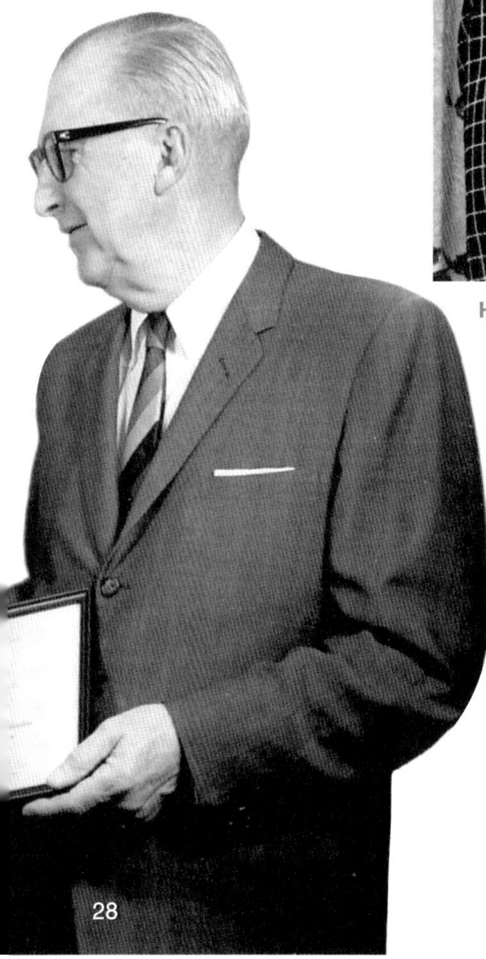

Hometown Newspaper Publishers

Riley Cross Sr. (1905–1970) and Vivian Griswold Cross (1907–1992) purchased the *Denton Record-Chronicle* in 1945, focusing on local and state news and boosting the city of Denton. During the Crosses' 25-year tenure, the newspaper received several awards from the Texas Press Association. In the late 1950s, the *Record-Chronicle* supported the racial integration of North Texas State. After suffering a heart attack, Riley Cross (left) stopped managing the newspaper. Vivian Cross (above) continued as publisher, also overseeing a local television station, until her death. (Above, courtesy of Kay Copeland; left, courtesy of DRC.)

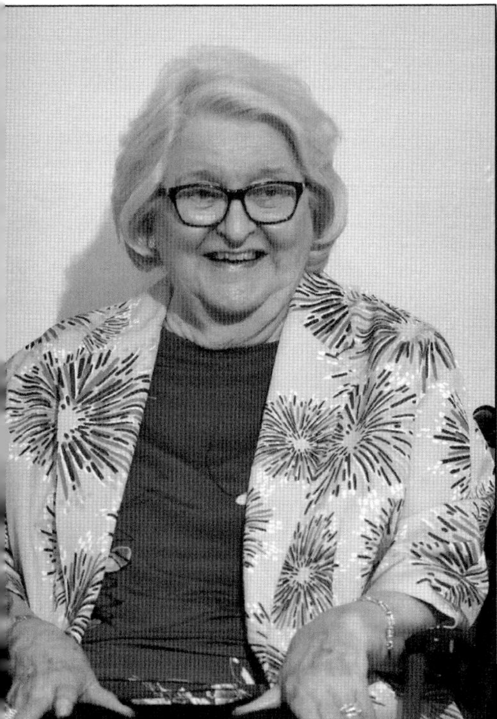

The Legacy Continues

Fred William Patterson (below, right) and Patsy Cross Patterson (left) purchased control of the *Denton Record-Chronicle* in the early 1990s, retaining its hometown focus. The Pattersons have held leadership roles in Denton for more than 60 years, promoting the city, its events, organizations, and schools. They have raised millions of dollars for the Campus Theatre, the Bayless-Selby House Museum, and the local universities. They have been recognized for their efforts as recipients of the Community Arts Recognition Award, Otis Fowler Award, and TWU Founders Award. The Pattersons remain a major part of the rich fabric of Denton life. In the below photograph, Fred Patterson poses with Roy Appleton, who went from part-time advertising salesman to general manager and president during his 43-year career with the newspaper. The Patterson-Appleton Center for Visual Arts was named in their honor. (Left, courtesy of Al Key; below, courtesy of DRC.)

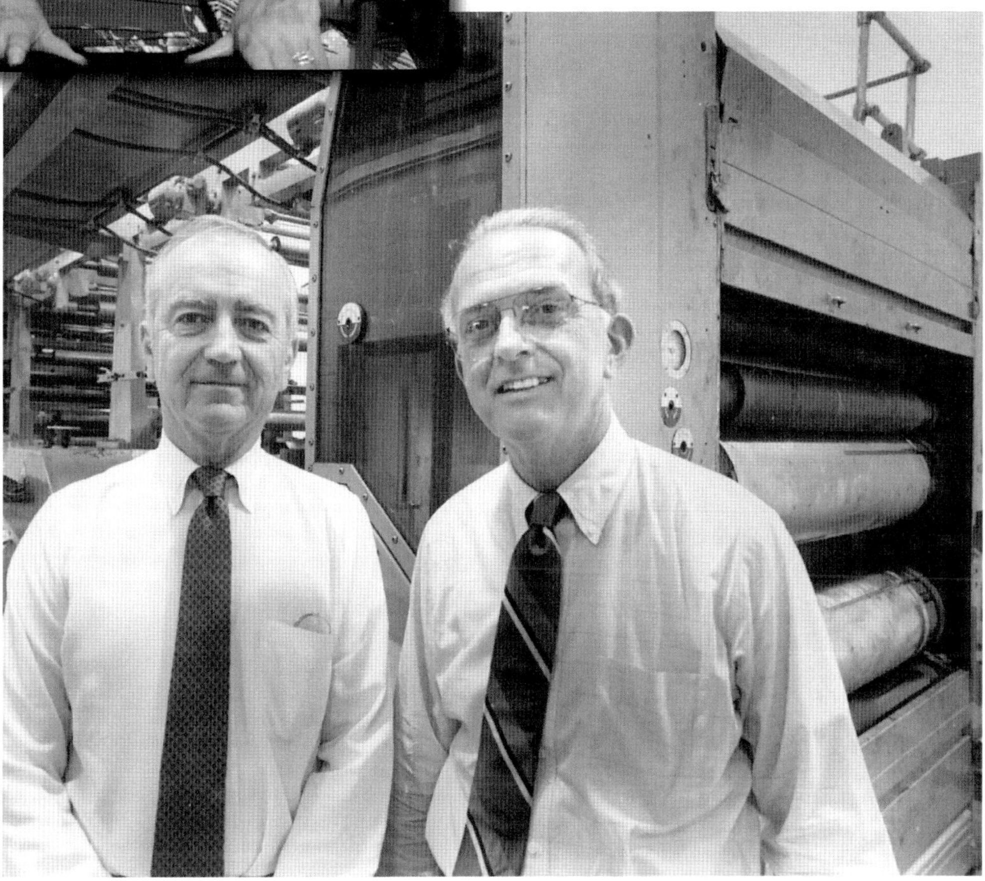

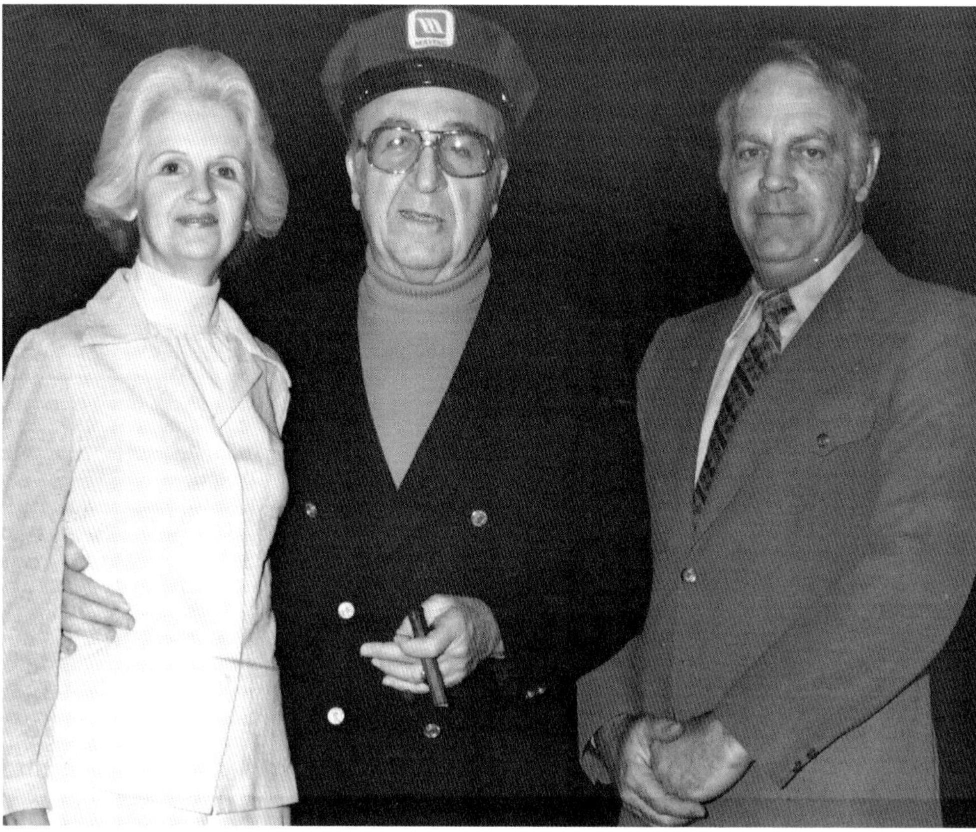

Business and Marital Merger

In 1931, F. Charles McNeill began selling appliances, and Dewey, Lee, and Essie Ball went into the furniture business on the Downtown Square. The youngest child from each family, Charles Wayne McNeill (1931–1997) and Virginia Ball, married and merged the two businesses in the 1960s. McNeill's reputation for unsurpassed customer service is the key component to the company's success in this world of big-box retailers. Here, the McNeills meet actor Jesse White (center), the Maytag repairman and "loneliest guy in town." (Courtesy of Virginia McNeill.)

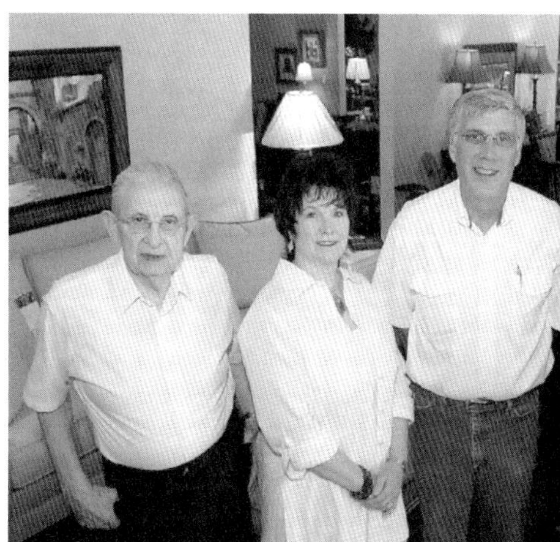

Anchor on the Square

Bill Thomas's Ethan Allen Home Interiors is at the northwest corner of Oak and Elm Streets on the site of the first Normal College. During the past 50 years, the business has expanded and remained an important anchor and an integral part of downtown Denton's economic health. Thomas was instrumental in organizing the Denton Main Street program in 1984 and is one of its biggest supporters. He was also responsible for initiating the holiday flag display program on the Square. Thomas (left) is shown here with the store's interior designer Anadara Braun-Good and his son, Craig. (Courtesy of DRC.)

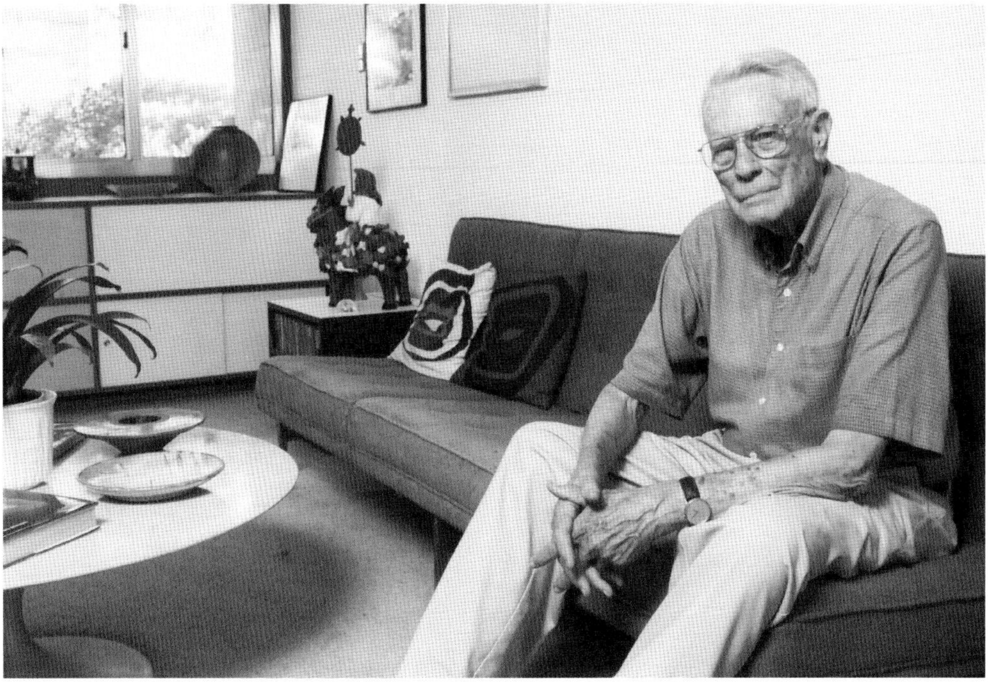

Generosity and Humility

After attending the University of Texas and serving in the US Army, Paul Voertman returned to Denton to manage his father's college bookstore, doing so for 38 years. Voertman supports many passions in the humanities, arts, and music through endowed university scholarships. He created a student art competition and donated a concert organ for the Murchison Performing Arts Center. The university named Paul Voertman Concert Hall in his honor. Voertman was named UNT distinguished alumnus in 2009. The humility of Paul Voertman is best expressed in his own words, "I'm going to do my little part." (Courtesy of DRC.)

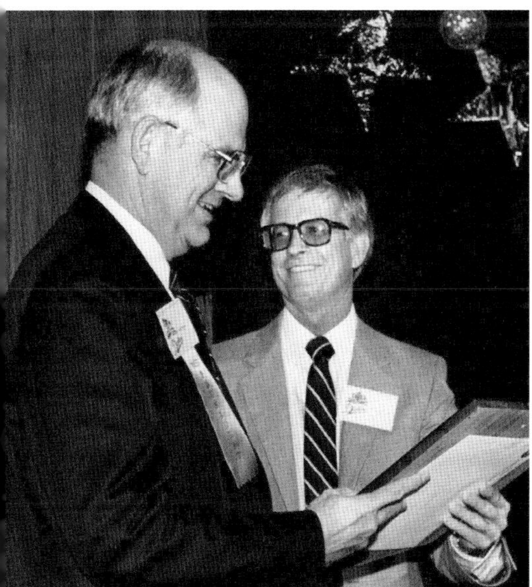

He Performed His Duty

Frank N. Martino (1929–2007) joined Russell-Newman Manufacturing as a salesman after marrying Betty Jean Newman (1929–2007). Rising through the ranks, he was named company president. His sense of business accomplishment was combined with a humble dedication to service within his profession, the community, and his church. This civic leader received the Boy Scouts Good Scout Award, the Otis Fowler Award, and the TWU Founders Award. He died while on a mission for the Mormon Church to South Africa. If there was ever a man who epitomized the tenets of the Boy Scouts—trustworthy, loyal, helpful, friendly, courteous, kind, obedient, cheerful, thrifty, brave, clean, and reverent—it was Frank Martino. Here, Martino (left) receives the Otis Fowler Award from the previous year's recipient, Ben Ivey Jr. (Courtesy of DRC.)

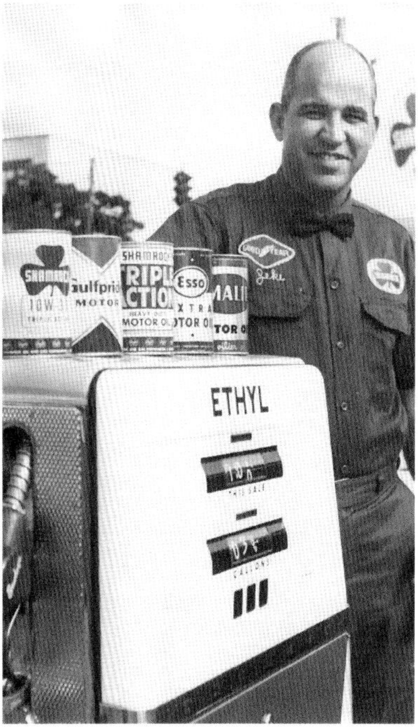

Martins Fly with Eagle Oil

Cecil Francis " Zeke" Martin (1924–2006) played football for North Texas with one of professional football's all-time greats, Ray Renfro. He then played professional football for two years in Canada. Martin was married to Bettye Lassiter Eaker (1928–2012) for 57 years. He was the president of Martin Eagle Oil Company and served as mayor of Denton. He was also the father of Little League baseball in Denton. Sharing enthusiasm for North Texas football, the Martins were awarded the North Texas Green Glory Award for their years of dedication to the university's growth. (Courtesy of DRC.)

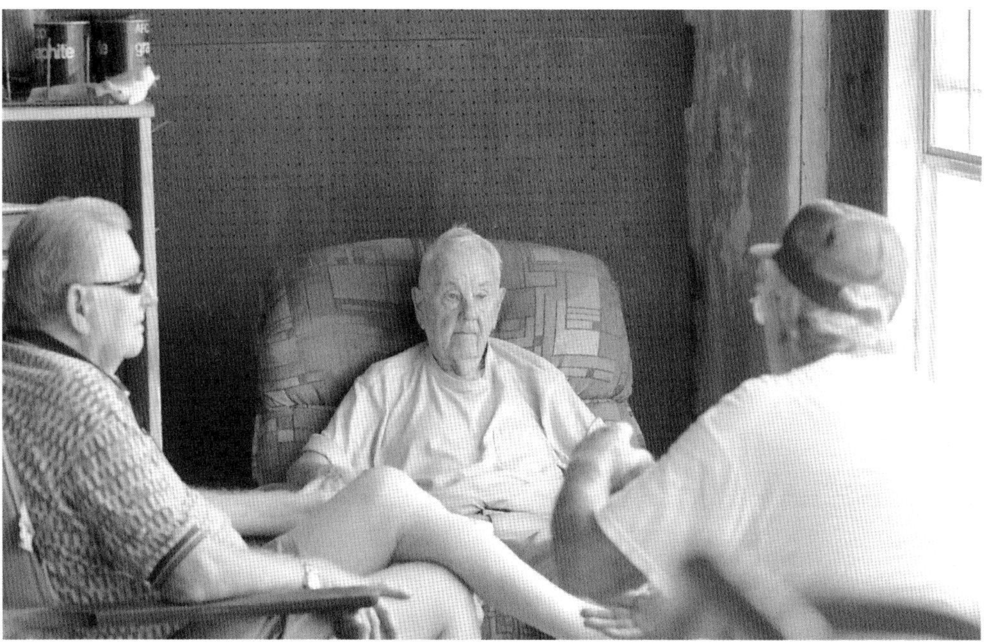

Barney's Bureaucracy

Folks in town know Jimmy Normile (center) as "Barney," because he never changed the name on his auto-supply business sign after he took over its ownership. This endearing gentleman operated Barney's Auto Supply on East Hickory Street for 53 years, sitting on an old car seat in the front of the store telling stories and garnering new gossip. If he liked a person, he would do anything for them, but he had no use for bureaucrats. He is one of the city's colorful characters who lend Denton its unique texture. (Courtesy of DRC.)

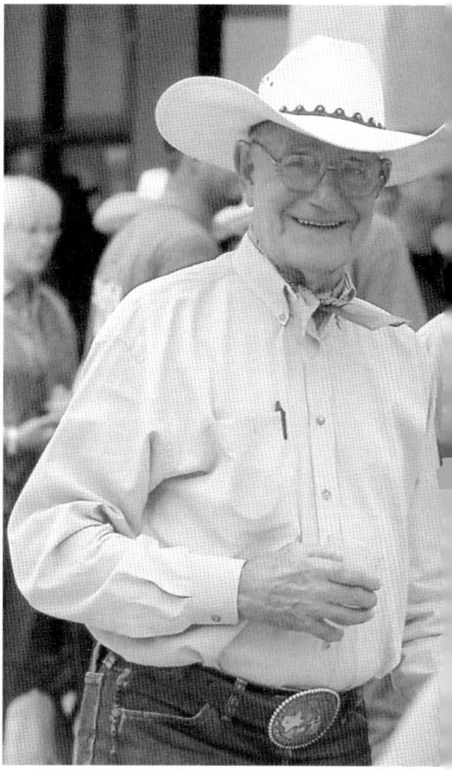

Rodeo Cowboy

Weldon Burgoon got his start in rodeo at age 11 and competed against senior ropers. He rodeoed for several years before opening a custom saddle and boot shop in Denton. Burgoon started the Denton Junior Stampede and the Denton County Youth Fair, Rodeo, and Horse Show. He served as fair and rodeo chairman, still sponsors the Mutton-Bustin' event, and helped spur on the chamber Farm and Ranch Tour. After 56 years, Burgoon can be found at his store, sharing his experiences on the rodeo circuit. Burgoon was a 2012 inductee into the Texas Rodeo Cowboy Hall of Fame. (Courtesy of Barron Ludlum Photography.)

A Man and His Horse

Rex C. Cauble (1913–2003), oil tycoon, banker, and multimillionaire rancher, was a world cutting-horse champion and honorary Texas Ranger. In addition, he owned Cutter Bill's Western Wear stores, named after his horse. Cutter Bill (1955–1982), a palomino stallion, was world champion cutting horse in 1962. Cauble lost Cutter Bill in a poker game, but the horse was returned to him. (Courtesy of DRC.)

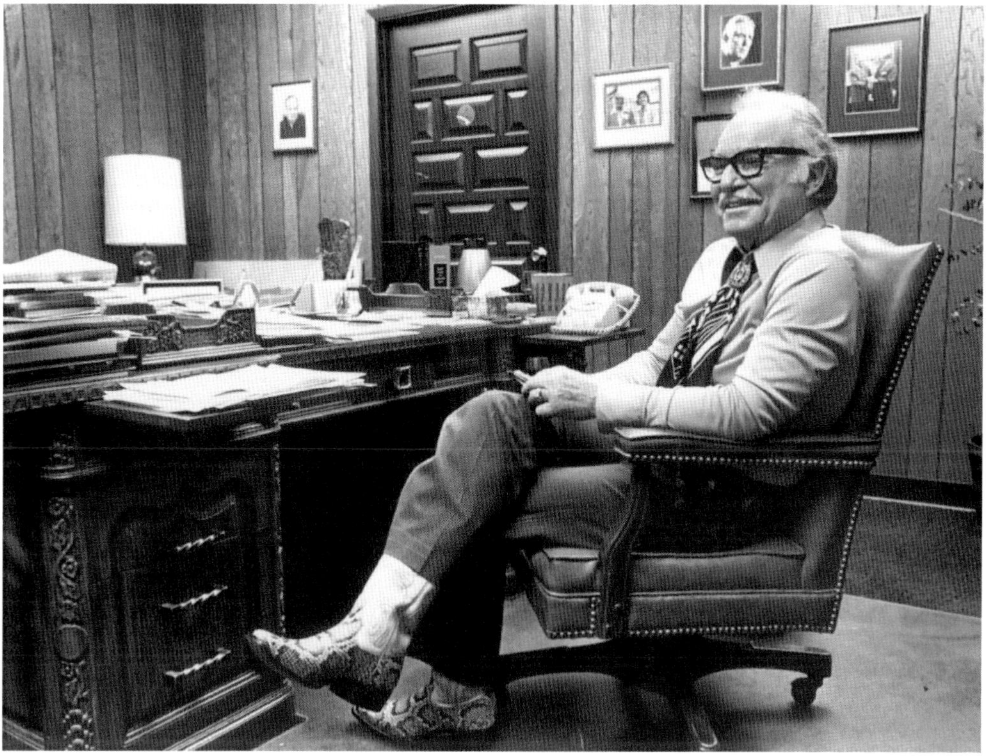

Costume Diva

Judy Smith opened her small shop on Fry Street in 1976, selling vintage clothing, accessories, and furniture. In the 1980s, she expanded her store, renting clothes as costumes. Smith is an accomplished seamstress and creates many of the costumes in the shop. Rose Costumes no longer focuses on supplying only school theater programs and Halloween rentals, for her fame has spread to a national market. Smith's Sherman Drive adopt-a-spot has become a beloved Denton landmark. (Courtesy of DRC.)

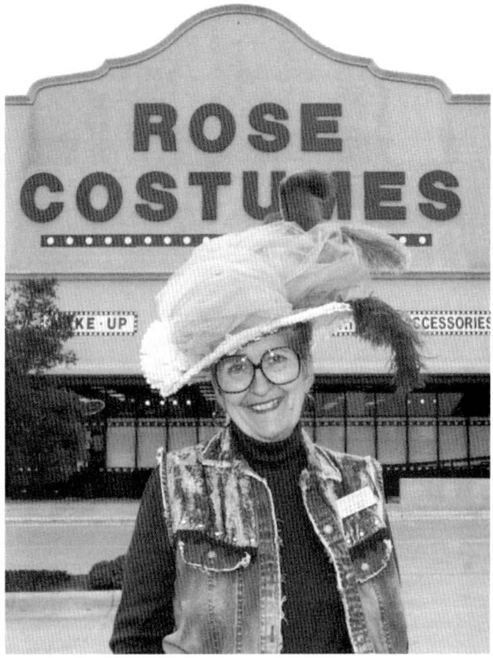

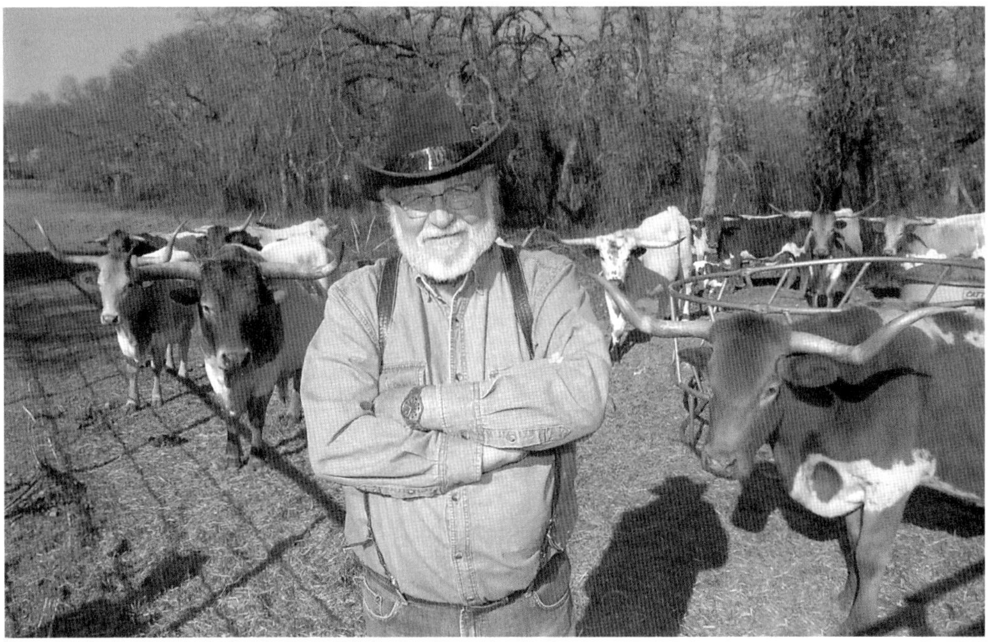

Lasting Legacy

Oscar Blankemeyer Jr. was reared on a farm in Krum before his family moved to Denton when he was eight years old. He had been an employee at Morrison Milling for 16 years before his entrepreneurial spirit sparked his venture into manufacturing and merchandising. He cofounded Lasting Products, eventually becoming one of the major producers of decorative items for Home Interiors and Gifts. Blankemeyer was awarded UNT's President's Citation in 1983, and he was made honorary alumnus in 1987. (Courtesy of Al Key.)

CHAPTER THREE

Superstars of Public, Political, and Military Service

Everyone can be great, because everyone can serve.

—Martin Luther King Jr.

Denton citizens have held civil service positions at many levels of government. The adoption of a new city charter in 1959 enabled a change from a city council–mayor form of government, in which council members select the mayor from the council members, to a city council–city manager form of local government. The council-manager structure, which establishes a representative system in which all power is concentrated in the elected council and the council hires a professionally trained manager to oversee the delivery of public services, works well for the city.

Denton residents take great pride in service to others. This chapter highlights citizens devoted to three areas: leadership in nonprofit and government work; governance on the local, state, and national scene; and service in the military. Residents have elected officials to the US Congress, the Texas Legislature, the mayor's office, and the city council. Townsfolk have served as international diplomats, been elected from business leaders as president of the chamber of commerce, held high-ranking positions in fraternal organizations, and performed their duties in times of national crisis.

Many Americans feel that the highest service one can perform for their country is military service, and Dentonites are no exception. Denton men and women have engaged in armed combat from as far back into US history as the Civil War, to the present-day Middle East conflicts.

As one might expect, these same citizens served in multiple roles throughout their lives, always in service to others. After performing their duty in the armed services during wartime, they came home to serve in leadership roles in their community. In this and following chapters, example after example of acts of courage and honor are recorded: schoolteachers who take on the challenge of state office, fighter pilots who become lawyer advocates, government employees and military men who break the race barrier to become city council members, and a woman who was respected enough by her peers to become the head of the city governing power. They are joined by two officials who recognized the life-sustaining need for water, land, and proper cultivation and preservation practices and fought to protect them through legislation and education. And, most important, are those who subjected themselves to harmful situations to protect our country from enemy forces. They are all great, because they all served.

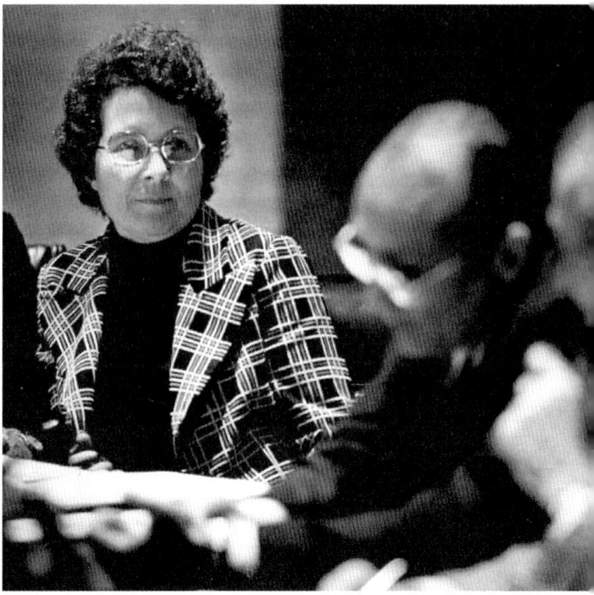

First Woman Mayor

In her capacity as Denton's first female mayor in 1976 and 1977, Elinor O. Hughes led a task force to develop a comprehensive plan to make available human services to Denton's citizens. This plan has continually evolved to provide delivery of efficient social services to those in need. Hughes also articulated the idea of uniting multiple nonprofits under one roof, making it easier for people in poverty to receive the help they need. Today, 37 years later, her dream, now called Serve Denton, has come to fruition. Leadership and innovative ideas exemplified Hughes's term as mayor, matching the desire of a community that cares for the needs of its people. (Courtesy of Elinor Hughes.)

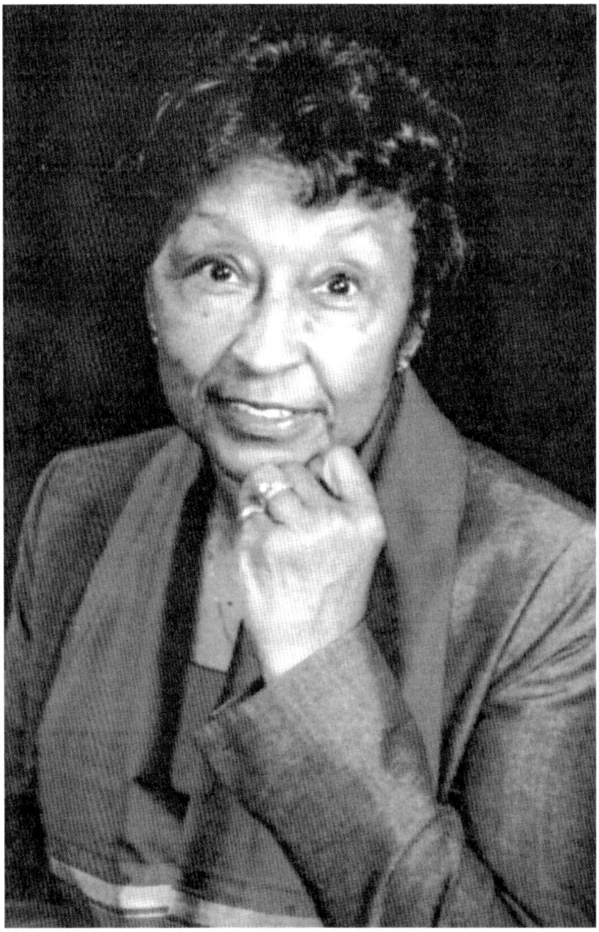

From Segregation to City Council

Linnie McAdams's humble beginnings and experiences growing up in a segregated environment honed her skills as a community activist and provided her with a highly developed sense of justice. This balanced sense was crucial to her involvement in the Denton Christian Women's Interracial Fellowship during the 1960s and 1970s and to her success in becoming the first African American woman to be elected to the city council. She served on the city council from 1984 to 1990, and as mayor pro tem for one term. (Courtesy of Linnie McAdams.)

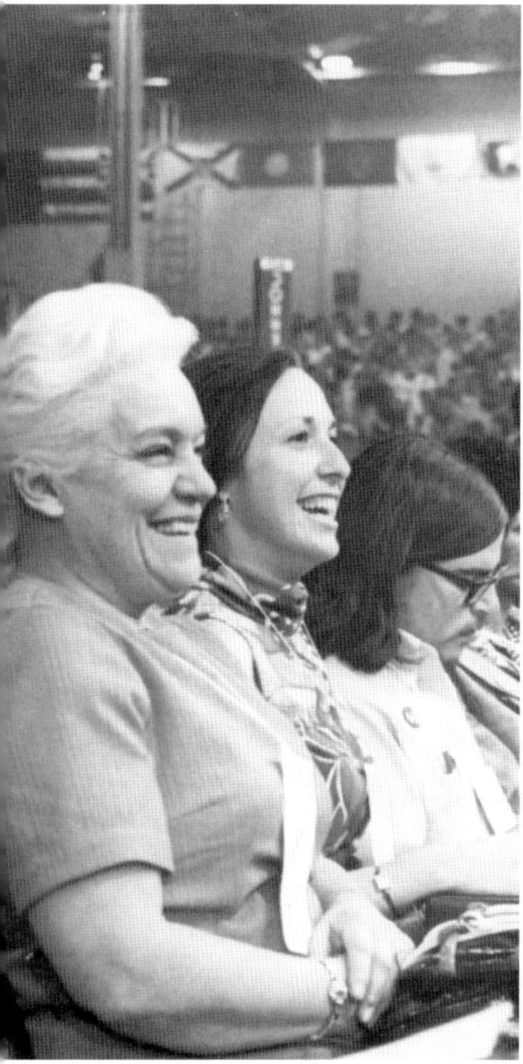

First Female City Councilwoman

Lillian Miller (1921–1974) was a stalwart in the Democratic Party. She relished involvement in political activities, whether serving on the local scene as Denton's first city councilwoman (1973–1974) or attending national party conventions. Lillian Miller Parkway is named in her honor. Miller (left) is seen here at the 1972 Democratic National Convention in Miami Beach. (Courtesy of DCOHC.)

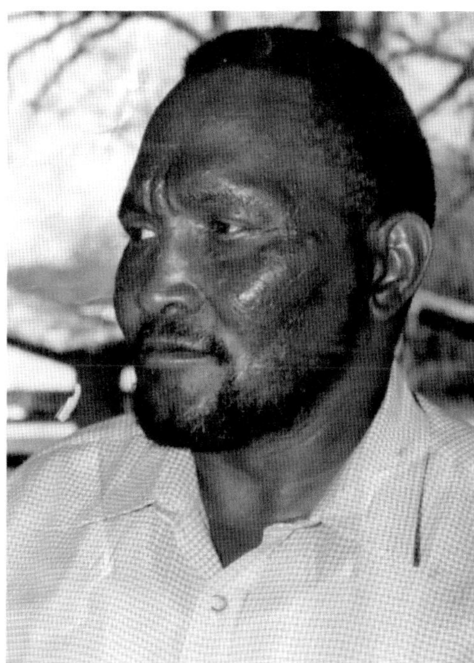

Outspoken Neighborhood Advocate

Carl Gene Young Sr. (1941–2007), three-term city councilman, was an outspoken advocate for southeast Denton and supported affordable housing and diversity in city government. Young was devoted to his constituents and was genuinely concerned with issues affecting them. Before joining the city council, Young served in the First Air Cavalry in the Vietnam War. He later organized an annual Easter Day event to honor fallen soldiers. Carl Gene Young Park is named in his honor. (Courtesy of DRC.)

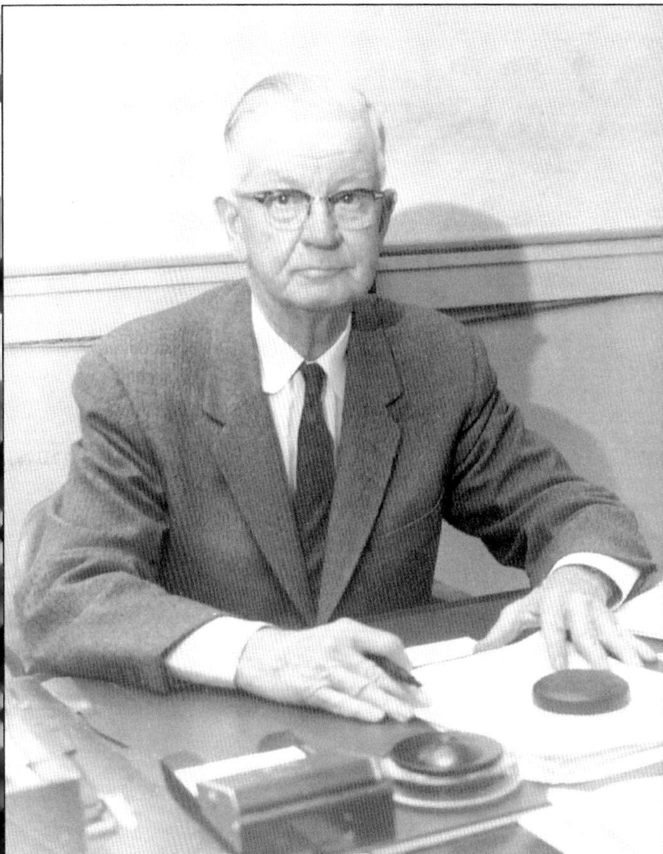

Chamber Leader and Consummate Reader. Otis L. Fowler (1886–1968), pictured at left, was the first paid manager of the Denton Chamber of Commerce, a position he held for 30 years. The chamber presents the Otis Fowler Citizen of the Year Award each year to Denton's outstanding citizen for professional achievements. Emily Fowler (1899–1971), seen below, was librarian in the sparse library that opened in the courthouse basement in 1943. She continued her career when the library moved to the city park in 1949. She oversaw the expansion of the O'Neil Ford building 20 years later and was honored upon retirement with having the library named after her. (Left, courtesy of DRC; below, courtesy of DPL.)

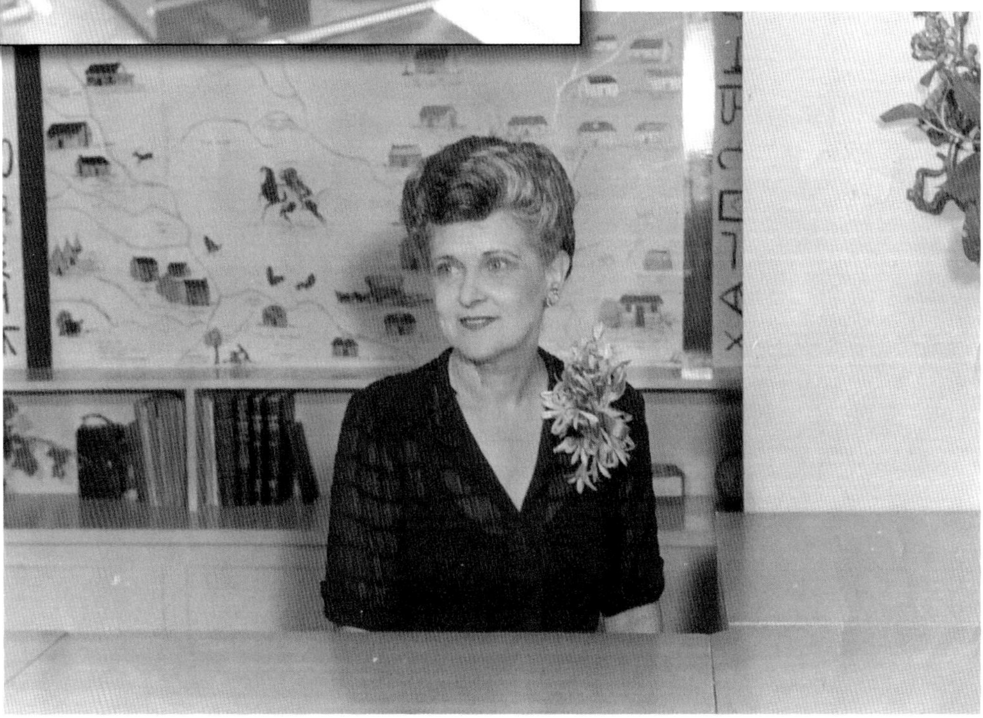

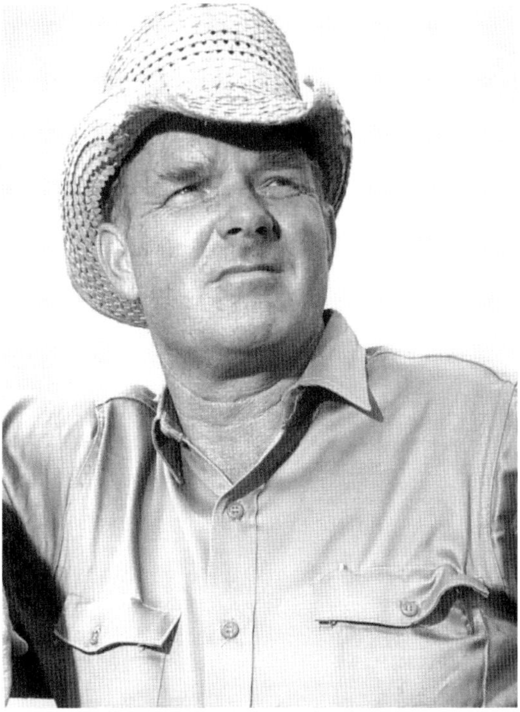

Champion of Universities, Farmers, and Ranchers

After graduation from North Texas State, Alonzo Wesley Jamison Jr. (1918–2011) earned a bronze star during World War II serving in an anti-aircraft unit. He served a short time on the North Texas history faculty while continuing his 20-year military career in the Army Reserves. Jamison was a member of the Texas House of Representatives for 14 years, focusing on improved legislative changes for farmers and ranchers. Jamison later joined the TWU history and government faculty, retiring as department chairman. (Courtesy of DRC.)

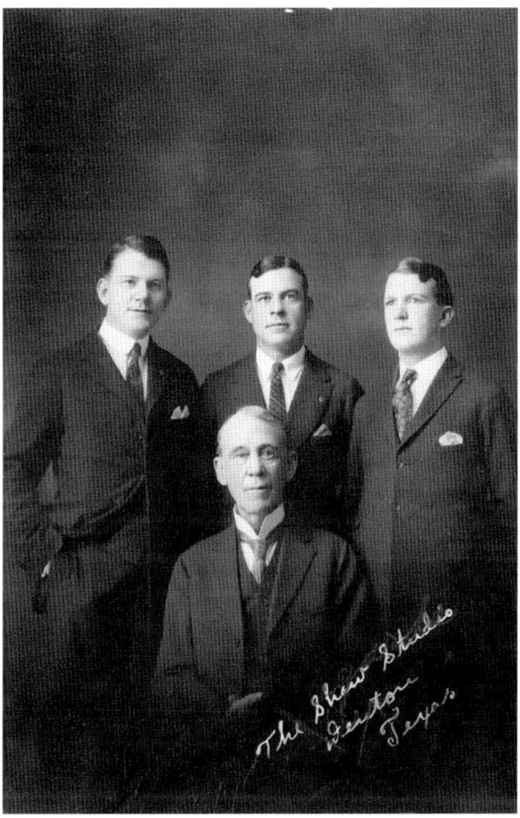

Local and Foreign Service

Alvin Clark Owsley (1856–1938) was a teacher for Denton County before receiving his law license. He participated in the founding of Texas Normal College and served on the first board of regents. After serving three terms in the Texas Legislature, Owsley became 16th Judicial District judge for Denton. In 1934, he was appointed special chief justice of the Texas Supreme Court. Owsley was the first president of the Denton Chamber of Commerce. His son Alvin Mansfield Owsley (1888–1967) was an honored veteran and lawyer, a Texas legislator, national commander of the American Legion, and a dedicated veterans' rights advocate. Alvin Mansfield Owsley was named US minister to Romania, the Irish Free State, and Denmark before he left the diplomatic service. Alvin Clark Owsley (seated) is shown with his sons Alvin (left), Clark (center), and Henry. (Courtesy of DRC.)

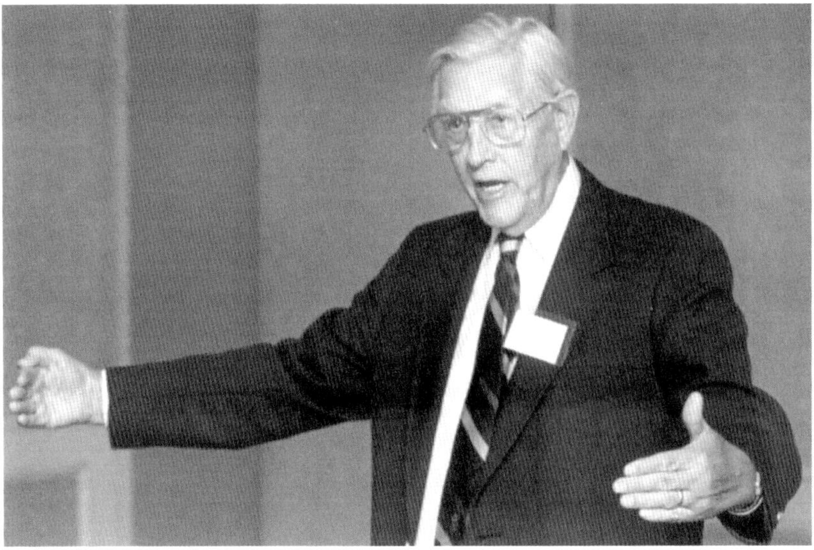

Ray Roberts Lake

Herbert Ray Roberts (1913–1992) filled the vacancy created by the death of Sam Rayburn in Texas's Fourth Congressional District in 1962. He was reelected to nine succeeding terms, returning home to Denton upon retirement. Roberts fought for water conservation throughout his career and worked diligently on the approval of construction of a new lake formed by damming up the Elm Fork of the Trinity River. When he learned that the name of the lake had been changed to Ray Roberts Lake, Roberts commented, "I'm humbled to know my name is worth a dam—and a reservoir." In the below photograph, Roberts holds a copy of *Life* magazine that featured a pictorial on the sinking of the aircraft carrier *Hornet*. Roberts was on the ship and was rescued after about two hours in shark-infested waters by a retreating destroyer. He received three battle stars in the Pacific and four in Europe. His entire life was devoted to service to community and country. (Above, courtesy of DCOHC; below, courtesy of DRC.)

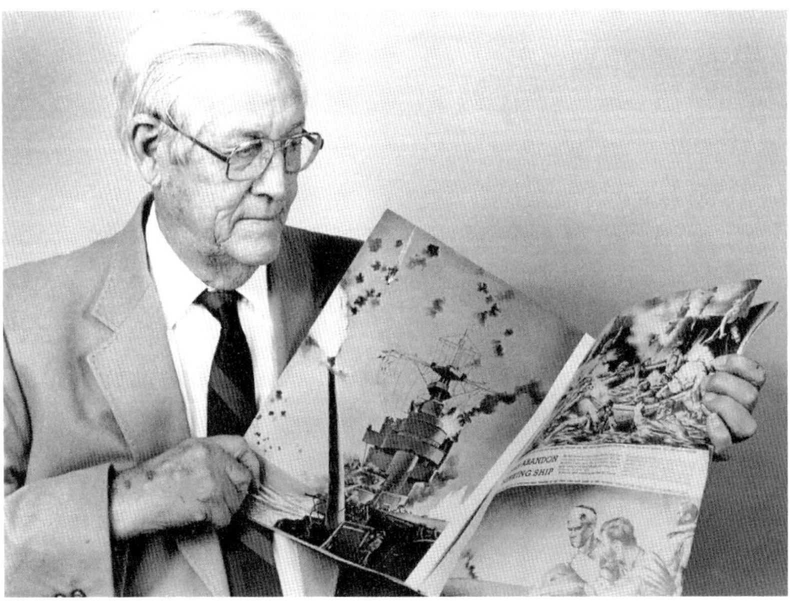

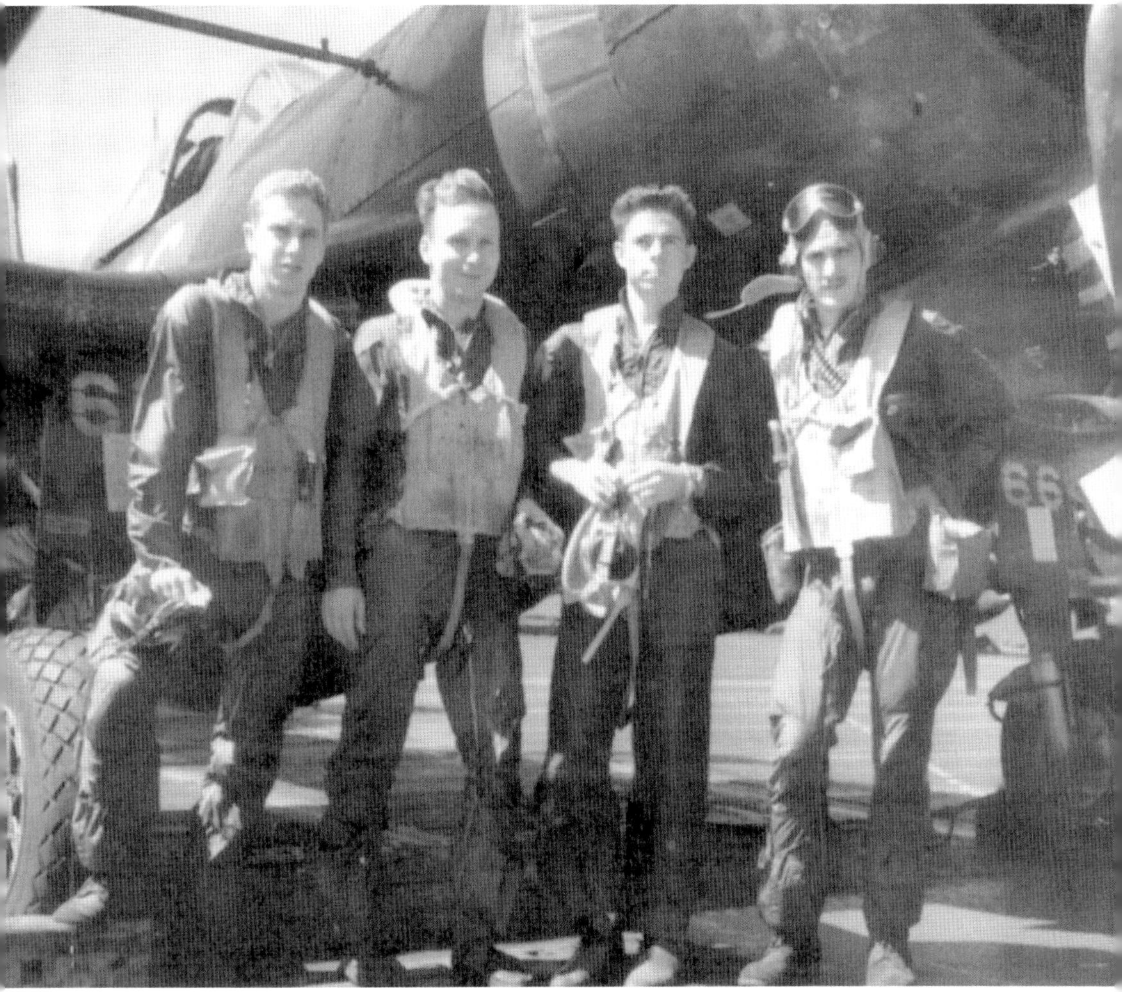

A Legend Takes Flight

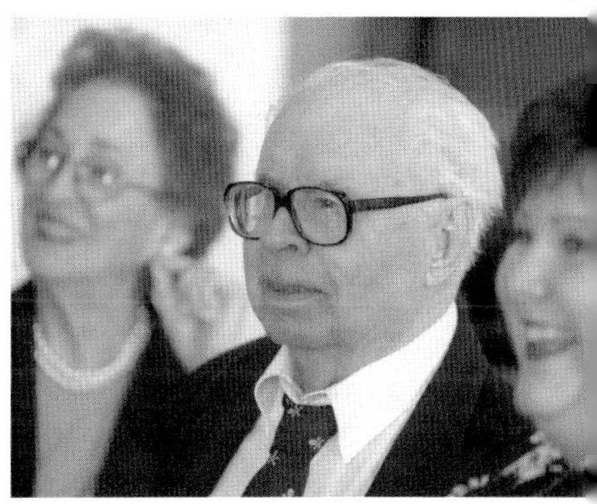

Robert Hal Jackson (1920–2008), son of Mr. and Mrs. Brent Jackson, was a fighter pilot and war hero. He flew more than 120 combat missions and was part of an attack in which US forces sank two cruisers, five destroyers, and the Japanese battleship *Yamato*. "About 10 minutes after I dropped my bomb, I saw the *Yamato* explode into a million pieces," he said. Jackson also shot down three Japanese planes. He attended North Texas State, Baylor University, and Southern Methodist University, returning to Denton to practice law for the remainder of his life. Jackson was legendary for using his astounding memory of jurors' names and details. He was famous for tricks inside and outside the courtroom. He received the Silver Star, Distinguished Flying Cross, four Air Medals, and a Navy Unit Citation. Jackson served several terms as Denton's representative in the Texas House of Representatives. In the above photograph, Jackson (third from left) stands in front of his airplane with three unidentified pilots. At right, he is shown with his wife, Barbara (left), at a Denton Bar Association ceremony honoring his years of service. (Above, courtesy of DCOHC; inset, courtesy of DRC.)

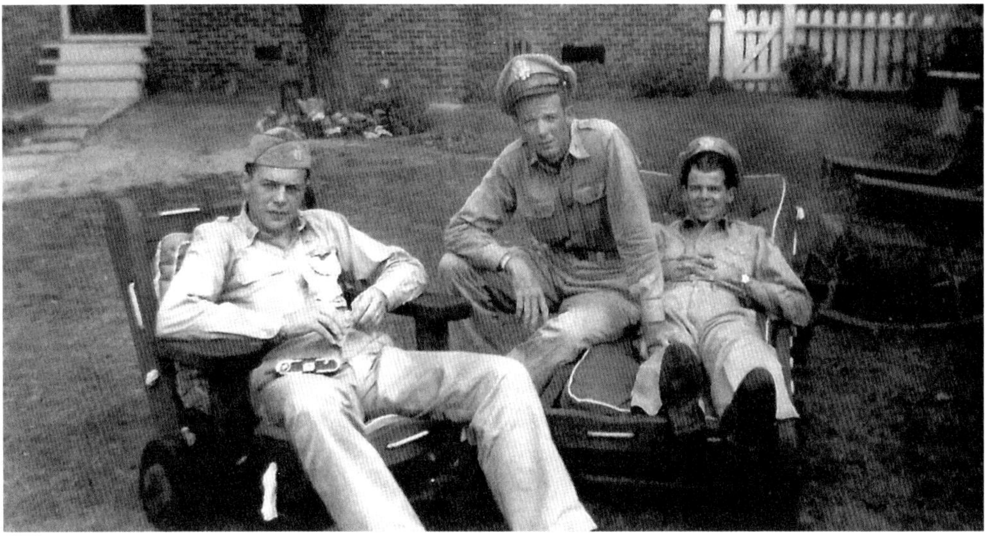

Band of Brothers

Warren P. Whitson Sr. began making Whitson's Moist Chili Seasoning at his store in Denton in 1932. His three sons, Warren P. Jr., William "Bill" (1920–2011), and John (1923–2011), joined the business as young men. During World War II, all three became pilots in the Army Air Corps. Warren and Bill served in Europe as bomber pilots, and John helped train glider pilots for the Normandy invasion. While on a bombing raid in his B-17 airplane, *Old Bill*, Bill Whitson and his crew were attacked and flew back to base with the nose of the plane shot off, the bombardier killed, and Bill and his copilot wounded. Bill Whitson received a Purple Heart and the Distinguished Flying Cross. After returning from the war, this band of brothers joined their father in the family business, Whitson Food Products and Mission Beverage Company, until the company was sold in 1968. Warren Whitson Jr. served as Denton mayor from 1962 to 1966. Bill (left), Warren (center), and John are shown in the family's backyard before their deployment. (Courtesy of Warren Whitson.)

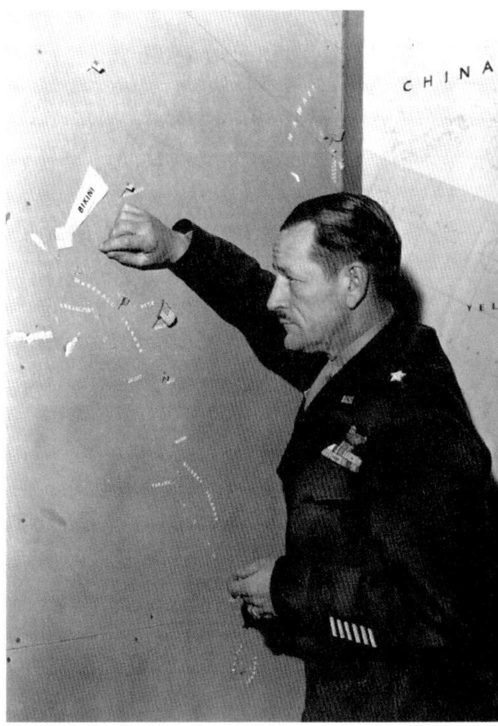

Not an Unidentified Flying Object

Roger Maxwell Ramey (1905–1963) graduated from Denton High and attended North Texas State before receiving an appointment to West Point. He served as a flight instructor, intelligence officer, and operations officer during the attack on Pearl Harbor. He later earned the Distinguished Service Cross and the Legion of Merit for his heroism during combat with the Japanese. Despite his numerous heroic and meritorious acts of courage and leadership, Ramey is remembered as being involved in an incident at Roswell Army Air Field in 1947 regarding a "flying disc" that Ramey declared to be a crashed weather balloon. He is shown in this 1946 photograph studying a map of Bikini Atoll, the site of an atomic bomb test with which he was involved. The experimental bombing transformed the Bikini Atoll into a "hell on earth." (Courtesy of the author.)

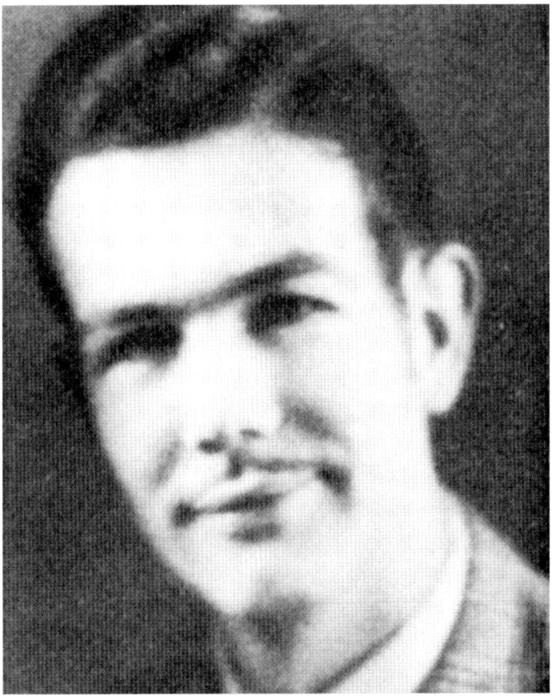

Lost at Pearl Harbor
Seaman First Class William Claude Castleberry Jr. (1916–1941) was killed aboard the battleship *Arizona* at Pearl Harbor on December 7, 1941. His body is entombed along with the other 1,177 sailors who died on "a date which will live in infamy." His parents were William Claude Castleberry and Martha Isla Castleberry. His brother Bob won the $10-million Publishers Clearing House sweepstakes prize and served three terms as Denton mayor. He created a scholarship at UNT in his deceased brother's name and at TWU in memory of their parents. This rare photograph of Claude Castleberry Jr. was taken before he entered the service. (Courtesy of DPL.)

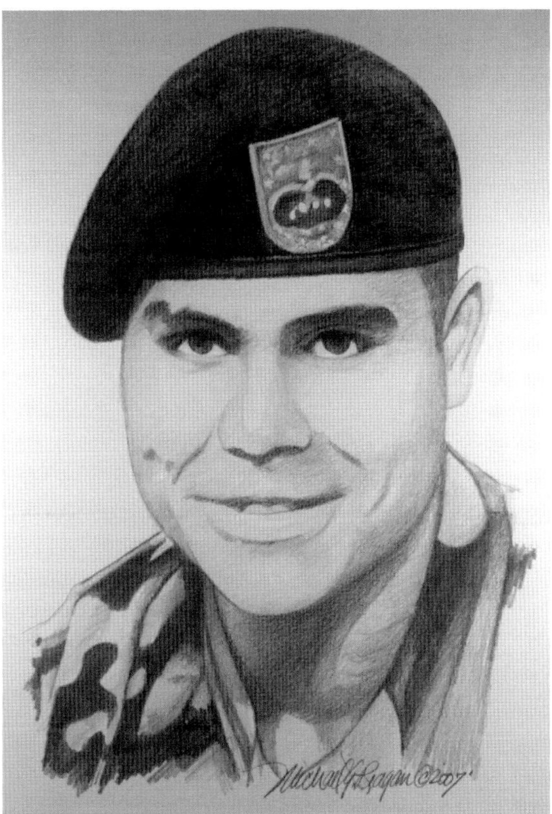

Last Full Measure of Devotion
Ernest Wayne Dallas Jr. (1983–2005) entered the US Army in 2003. After concluding his training, Dallas was assigned as a Cavalry fighting vehicle driver and deployed in 2005 with his unit, Killer Troop, in support of Operation Iraqi Freedom. Dallas was the first Denton soldier killed in Iraq. His awards and decorations include the National Defense Service Medal, Iraqi Campaign Medal, Global War on Terrorism Service Medal, Army Service Ribbon, Combat Action Badge, Bronze Star, and the Purple Heart. Denton dedicated the Spc. Ernest W. Dallas Jr. Veterans Memorial Park on November 11, 2011. (Courtesy of Michael Reagan, Fallen Heroes Portrait Project.)

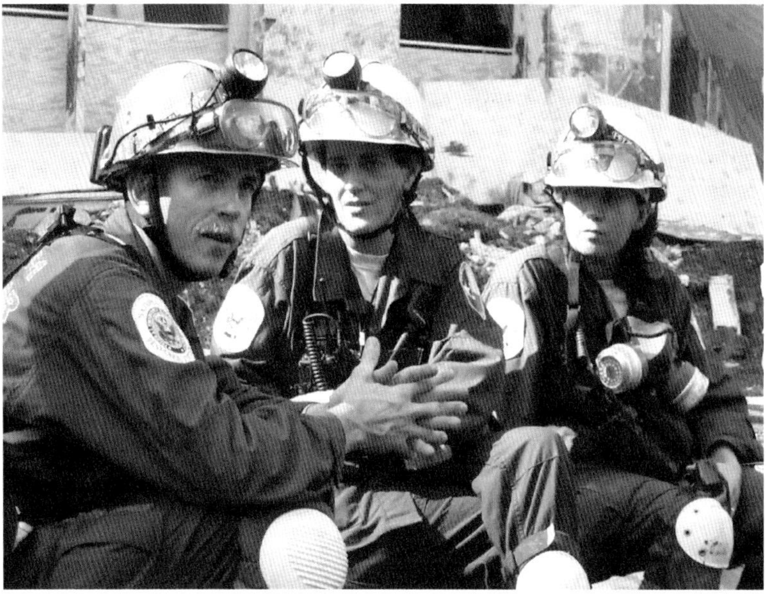

Denton Firefighters at Ground Zero

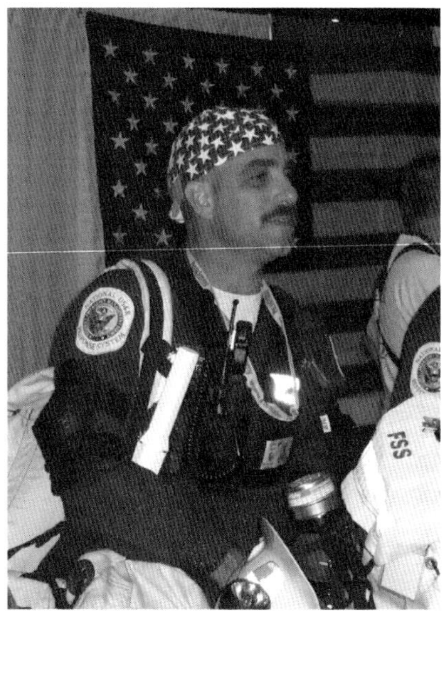

As part of Texas Task Force 1, Alan Hempstead, Jeff Dixon, and Brad Fuller assisted at Ground Zero in New York City after the terrorist attacks of 9/11. Hempstead, Battalion Chief Fuller, and firefighter/paramedic Dixon left Denton the day the towers fell in 2001. They trained with other rescue workers and finally left by plane on September 17 for Fort Dix in New Jersey, and then traveled by bus to New York City. They stayed until September 24, working through horrendous scenes of destruction and loss of life. Since the task force is a rescue team, its job was done after just seven days at the site. These three photographs, taken at Ground Zero, show Alan Hempstead (top photograph, at left) with unidentified dog handlers; Jeff Dixon (right photograph); and Brad Fuller (bottom photograph). (Courtesy of DCOHC.)

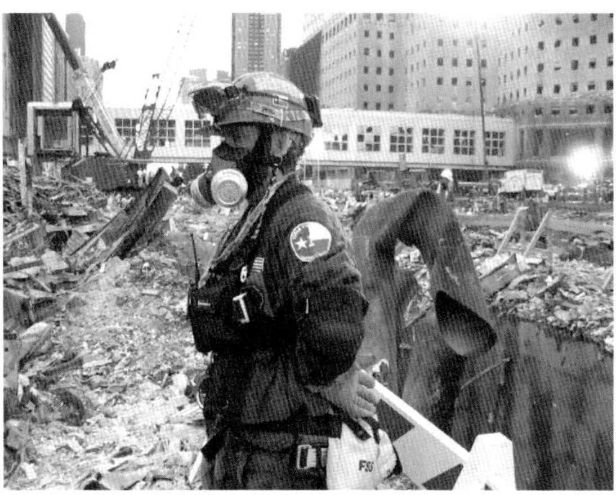

CHAPTER FOUR

Superstars of the Arts

Art has the power to change minds and change lives.
It can open dialogue between cultures and communities.

—Amy Rice

According to the National Endowment for the Arts, the term "the arts" includes the following: instrumental and vocal music; dance; drama; folk art; creative writing; architecture and allied fields; painting; sculpture; photography; graphic and craft arts; industrial design; costume and fashion design; motion pictures; television; radio; film; video; tape and sound recording; fields related to the presentation, performance, execution, and exhibition of such major art forms; all traditional arts practiced by the diverse peoples of this country; and the study and application of the arts to the human environment.

The city of Denton is fortunate to have superb talent in every genre of the arts. The two universities enhance and develop these exceptional abilities by producing students of proficiency and skill. The renowned music and drama departments of the high schools and the universities, and the onstage opportunities provided by the community theater, serve as an incubator for breeding and training actors, singers, and dancers. A fortunate by-product of this talent is the quality of entertainment enjoyed by the community's residents.

Several female artists and professors made a major contribution not only to the education of Texas Woman's University students from the 1930s to the early 1970s, but were renowned in their respective fields. Carlotta Corpron, Mabel Maxcy, Toni LaSelle, and Coreen Spellman were master technicians in watercolor and oil painting, photography, pottery, sculpture, abstract impressionism, and hand weaving, and they brought Modernism to Denton and to Texas.

The city has had two Texas poet laureates, Arthur Sampley and Karla K. Morton, and a poet laureate alternate, Gene Shuford. Award-winning journalists and photojournalists abound, and, fortunately for Denton residents, some chose to remain to inform and delight them through various media outlets. Others became nationally famous through public and commercial television broadcasting. These professionals each attribute their success to the training they received in Denton from their dedicated teachers.

Texas Poet Laureate 2010

Karla K. Morton, the first female Texas Poet Laureate in nearly 20 years, is the author of 10 award-winning poetry books. Morton wrote her poetry collection, *Redefining Beauty* during her journey battling breast cancer. She created the *Little Town, Texas Tour,* traveling across the state, sharing her poetry and love for the arts with high schools, universities, and arts organizations. This resulted in a book of children's poetry. Her latest book, *Passion-Art-Community,* features her poetry accompanied by art created by Denton residents. Morton, through her poem "Clearing the Woods," excerpted here, described Denton's naming of its streets: "As hard as it was to get here, it was harder to stay . . . but many did—the Daugherty's, the Beaty's, the Taylor's, the Wright's. And we can't forget about William Woodruff, and D.C. [*sic*] Welch, and C.C. Lacy, who plotted the roads, naming them after native trees. Years later, we will call it progress to plow down everything in our way. . . . The forest paid dearly. Hear them in the dawn as they echo in the streets—Locust, Sycamore, Oak, Hickory, Elm." Morton's courage and love of community resonates indeed throughout her poetry. (Courtesy of Walter Eagleton.)

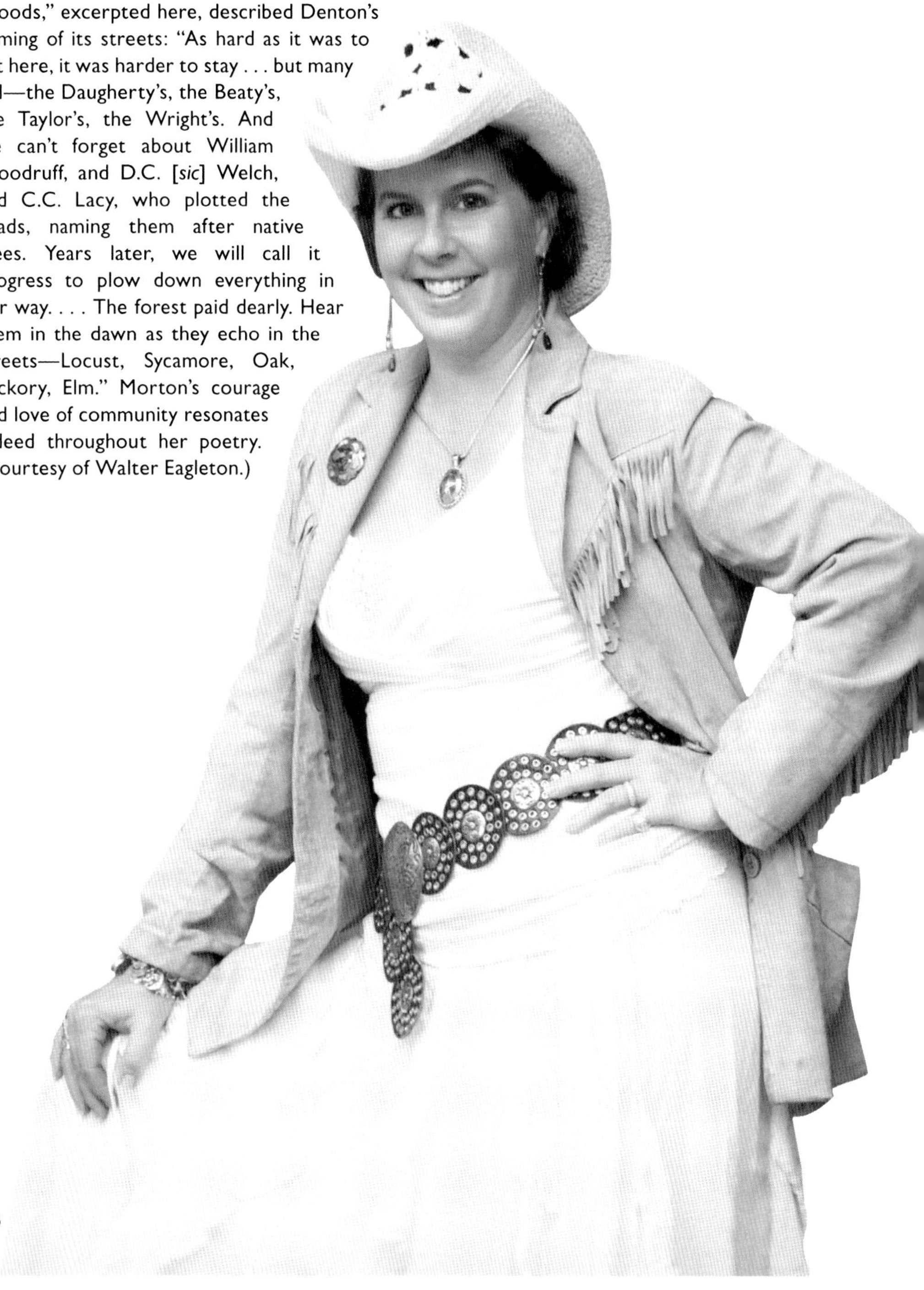

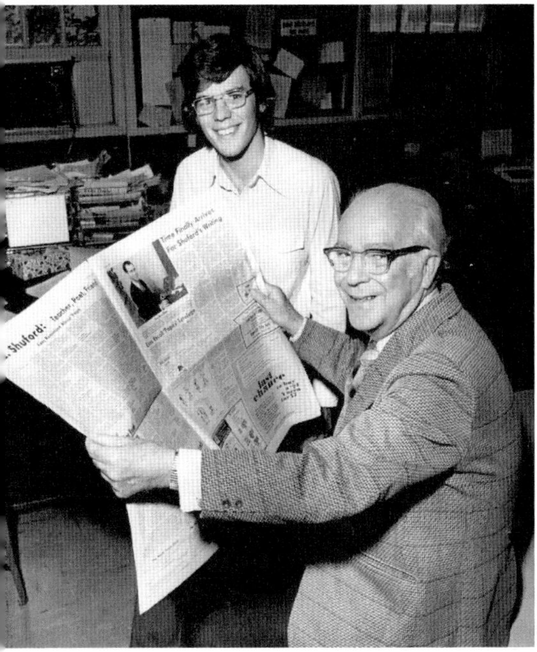

"Pop" Shuford

Cecil Eugene "Gene" Shuford (1907–1986) joined the journalism faculty at North Texas State in 1937. As the first chairman from 1945 until 1974, he is credited with establishing and building the journalism department. Former students, who called him "Pop," include television journalist Bill Moyers, Dallas columnist Steve Blow, and AP correspondent Mike Cochran. Shuford won 70 prizes from the Poetry Society of Texas and was Texas Poet Laureate alternate. He received the North Texas State President's Award for outstanding contributions to the university. Upon Shuford's retirement, his former students honored him with a special edition of the *North Texas Daily* newspaper. Here, Shuford (right) reads that edition with student Steve Blow looking on. (Courtesy of DRC.)

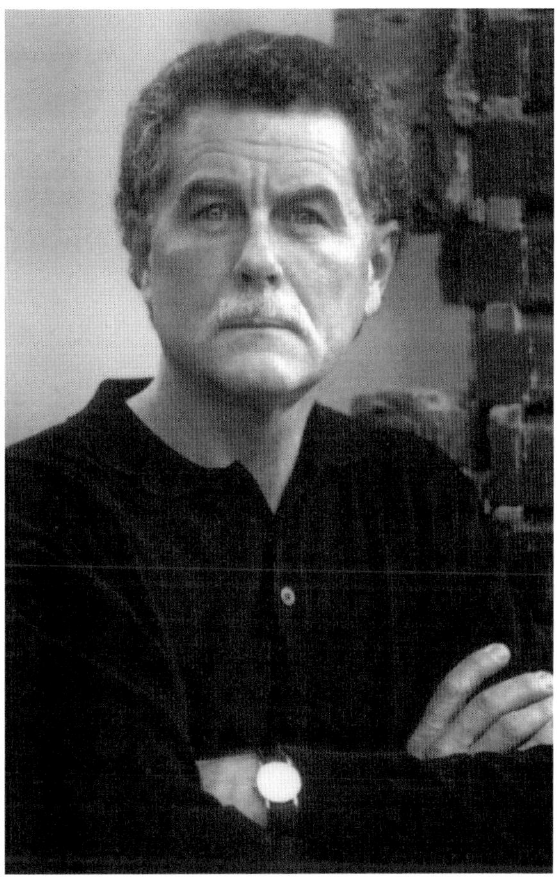

Case of the Jitters

The skills earned as North Texas State's student newspaper editor resulted in Clinton Howard Swindle (1945–2004) being named Outstanding Journalism Graduate. He gained experience writing for three newspapers before joining the *Dallas Morning News*, where he worked as a reporter and editor. The *News* won its first Pulitzer Prize and two more Pulitzers for projects that Swindle edited. Swindle authored eight nonfiction and mystery books, one of which, *Jitter Joint*, was made into a Universal Pictures movie. (Courtesy of DRC.)

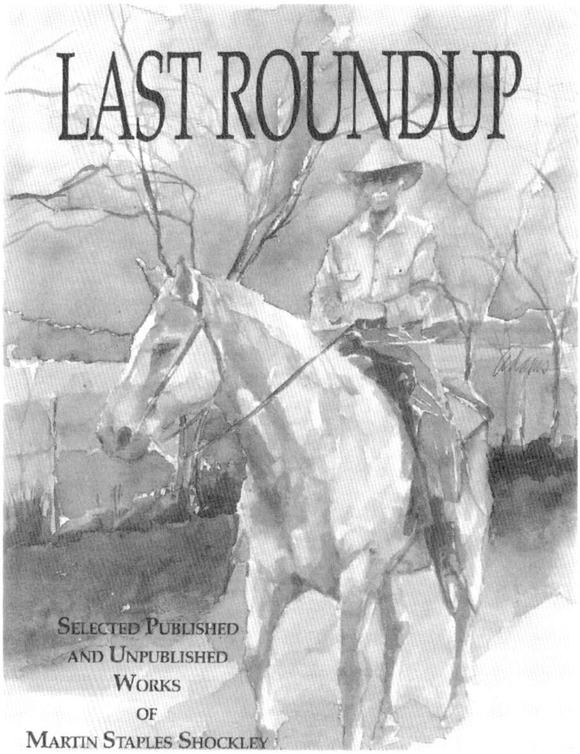

Shockley's Last Roundup
North Texas State English professor Martin Staples Shockley (1908–2003), pictured below at the podium, served as the president of the Poetry Society of Texas and the Texas Folklore Society. During his 24-year teaching career, he wrote two textbooks and published poetry, fiction, essays, and scholarly articles. Shockley's works were compiled into a book, *Last Roundup*. Virginia-born Shockley expresses his preference for Texas in the excerpt below from his poem "God's Country." (Above, courtesy of UNT; below, courtesy of DRC.)

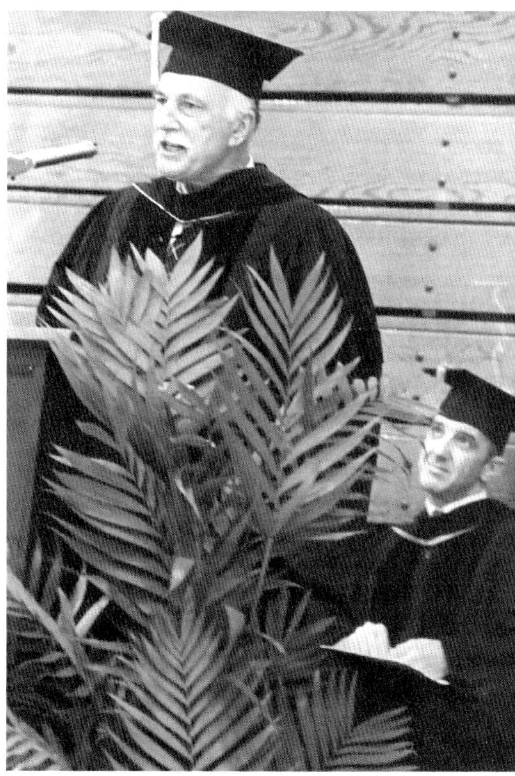

Texas is wind-blown prairies, purple hills,
bright sun, blue shadows, and clear air;
land where the longhorns roam and mustangs run,
where coyotes sing the silver stars
and golden eagles soar
from rough red rocks into a smooth blue sky.
God's country must be nice; too nice I fear.
You can have God's country; I like it here.

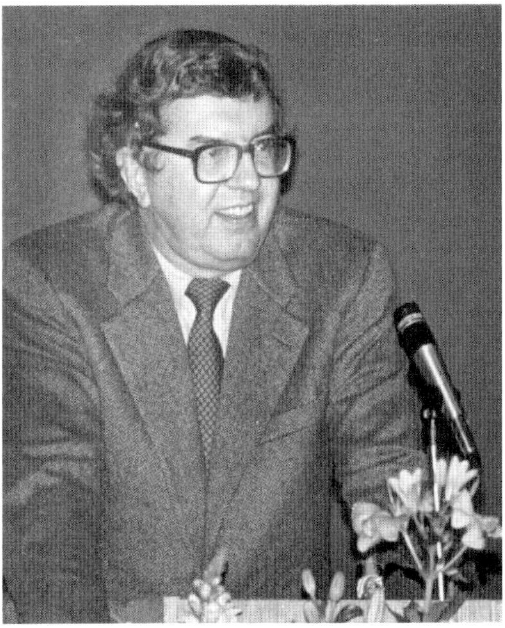

Pulitzer and Academy Awards

Prolific author and screenwriter Larry Jeff McMurtry, whose work is set predominantly in urban or frontier Texas, received degrees from North Texas State and Rice University. In addition to having written more than 45 books and seven screenplays, McMurtry taught university creative writing courses. He won the Pulitzer Prize for his novel *Lonesome Dove* and Academy Awards for his screen adaptations of Annie Proulx's short story "Brokeback Mountain" and his novel *Terms of Endearment*. One of McMurtry's English professors at North Texas was Martin Shockley. McMurtry was presented the 2014 UNT Emerald Eagle Honors for lifetime achievement in literature. (Courtesy of DCOHC.)

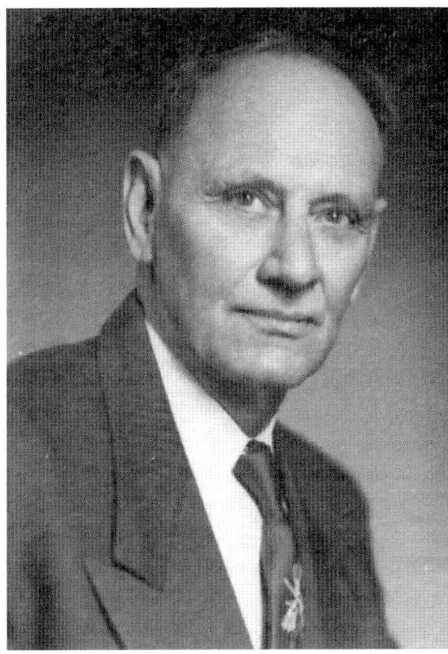

Historian Bridges the Gap

History of Denton, Texas From Its Beginning to 1960 took Clarence Allen "C.A." Bridges (1888–1979) nearly 20 years to research and write. After earning three degrees from North Texas State, Bridges remained on the faculty for 36 years. His comprehensive history of Denton's past was the first book on the subject published since Edward F. Bates's 1918 book *History and Reminiscences of Denton County* and is considered the most accurate information about the city during the 100 years he covered. (Courtesy of C.A. Bridges.)

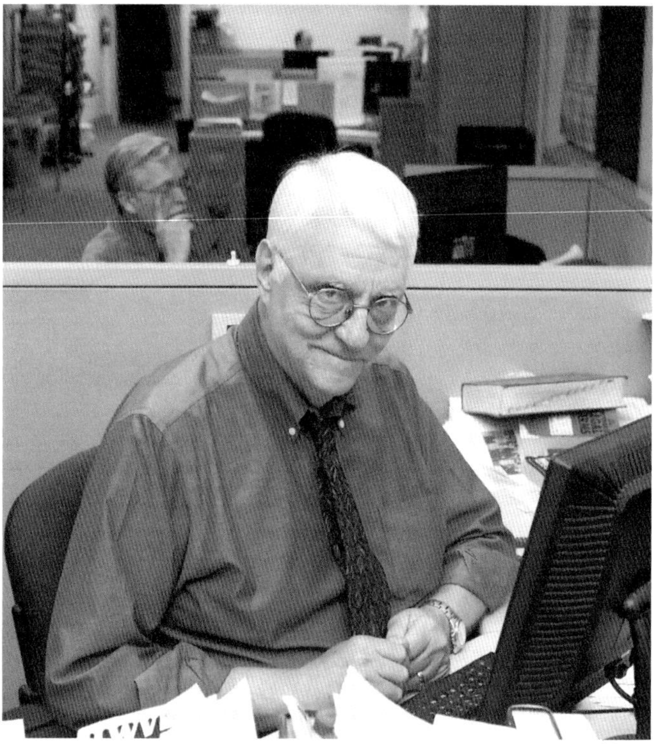

Ink-Stained Wretch
Mike Trimble, award-winning former opinion editor for the *Denton Record-Chronicle*, is a wizard with words. Trimble won the American Society of Newspaper Editors award for best editorial writing, beating out writers from the *New York Times* and the *Los Angeles Times*. In 2009, the Denton Chamber of Commerce awarded him its highest honor, the Otis Fowler Award. Trimble retired from the *Denton Record-Chronicle* after 18 years. His unique, thought-provoking columns could make his readers think, laugh, and cry. (Courtesy of DRC.)

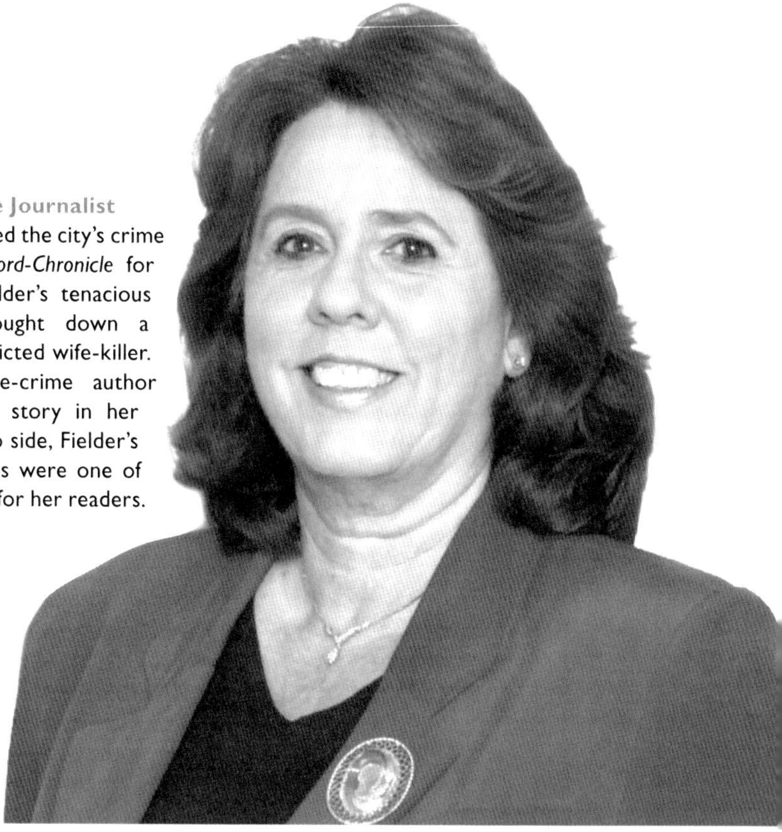

Persistent Investigative Journalist
Donna Kaye Fielder covered the city's crime beat for the *Denton Record-Chronicle* for more than 33 years. Fielder's tenacious investigative stories brought down a corrupt sheriff and a convicted wife-killer. This award-winning, true-crime author documented the murder story in her book *Ladykiller*. On the flip side, Fielder's humorous Sunday columns were one of the highlights of the week for her readers. (Courtesy of DRC.)

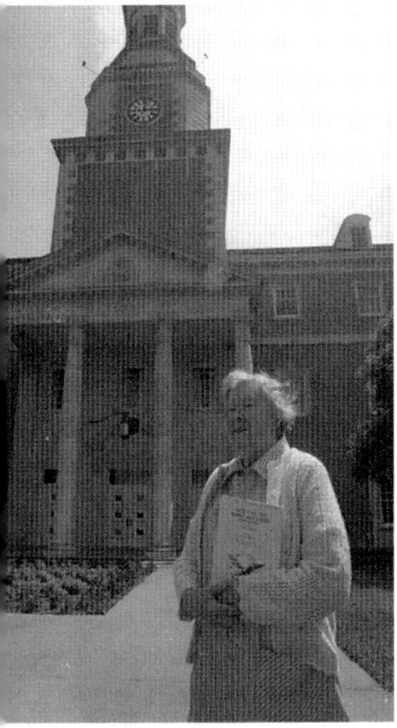

Glory to the Green

Julia Smith (1905–1989), Denton native and graduate from North Texas Normal, composed the college alma mater "Glory to the Green and White" while a student at the school. After completing her education at Juilliard and New York University, Smith wrote one of her more famous operettas, *Cynthia Parker*, which premiered at North Texas. She was recognized as one of the 10 outstanding composers in the United States for her time. Smith is standing in front of the Alfred F. and Johanna H. Hurley Administration Building, listening to the college alma mater being played on the carillon bells. (Courtesy of UNT.)

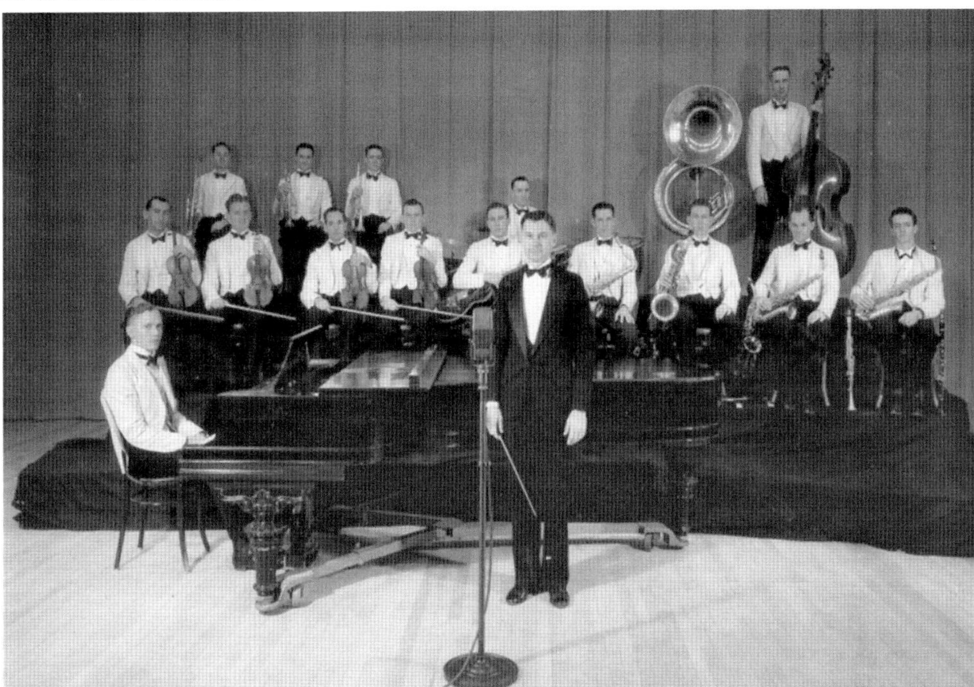

Star Maker

Floyd Freeman "'Fessor" Graham (1902–1974) left his job at Denton High to become the orchestra conductor at North Texas State College. His Aces of Collegeland Band, formed in 1927, performed Saturday Night Stage Shows featuring future movie stars and singers Ann Sheridan, Joan Blondell, Nancy Gates, Louise Tobin, and Pat Boone. The Aces band was the forerunner to the One O'Clock Lab Band. Graham laid the groundwork at North Texas for what became the first degree in jazz studies offered by a major academic university. In 1958, the student body established the 'Fessor Graham Award, the highest honor bestowed by the students on a faculty member. (Courtesy of Pati Haworth.)

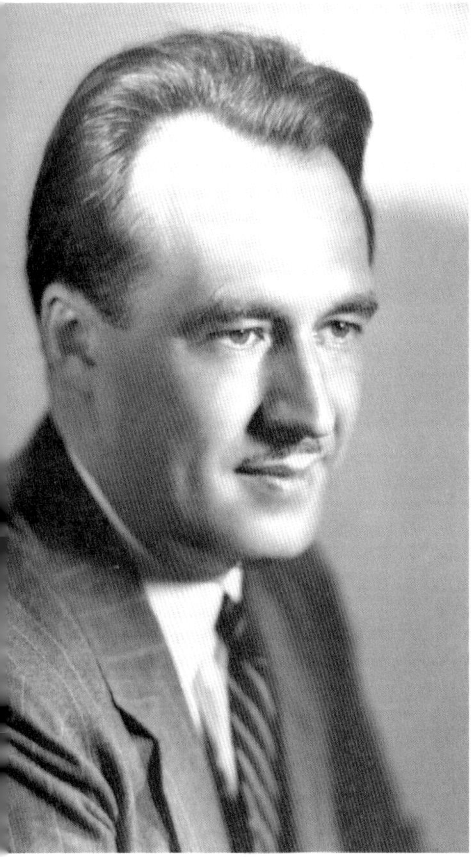

The Fruit of the Lips

Wilford Conwell Bain (1908–1997), department head of the music school at North Texas Teachers College, implemented several initiatives when the school began offering music degrees in music education, applied music, theory, and band. In 1938, Bain organized the college's first a cappella choir, which was heard on WFAA in Dallas. In 1939, under Bain's leadership, North Texas was admitted to the National Association of Schools of Music as an associate member, the first such accreditation for the college in a discipline other than teacher training. (Courtesy of DPL.)

Syncopated Rhythm

In 1963, the music program once again championed innovation in musical technique with the establishment of the Electronic Music Center, formed by faculty composer Merrill Leroy Ellis (1916–1981). Ellis brought a Moog synthesizer to North Texas, the first college to own one. The Merrill Ellis Intermedia Theater was opened in 1983, and the program was renamed the Center for Experimental Music and Intermedia. Its key components involve experimentation with electroacoustic composition and the incorporation of various intermedia, such as dance and visual-projection systems. (Courtesy of UNT.)

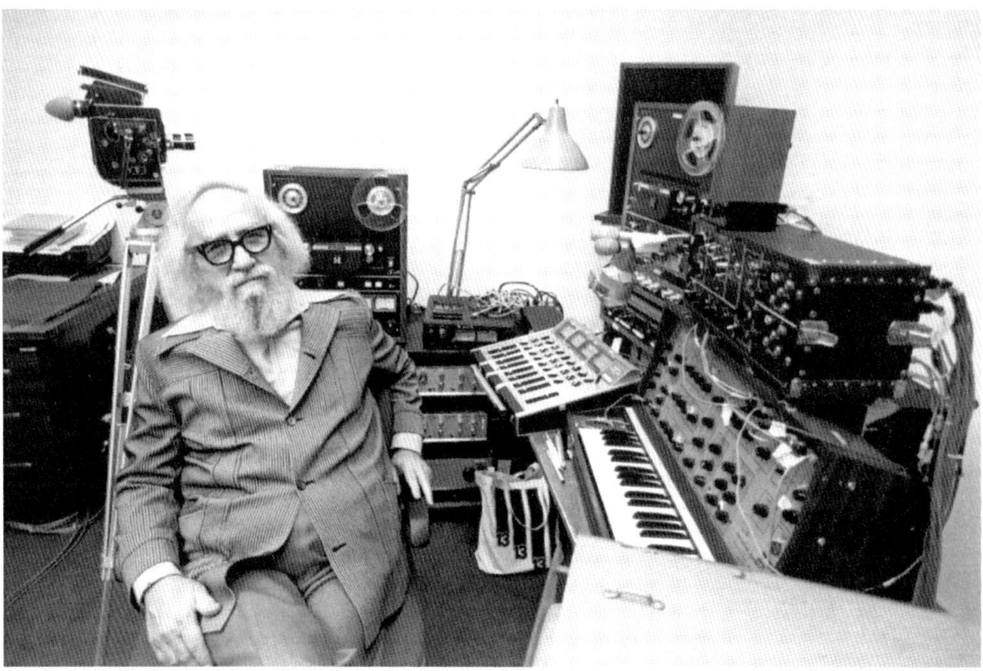

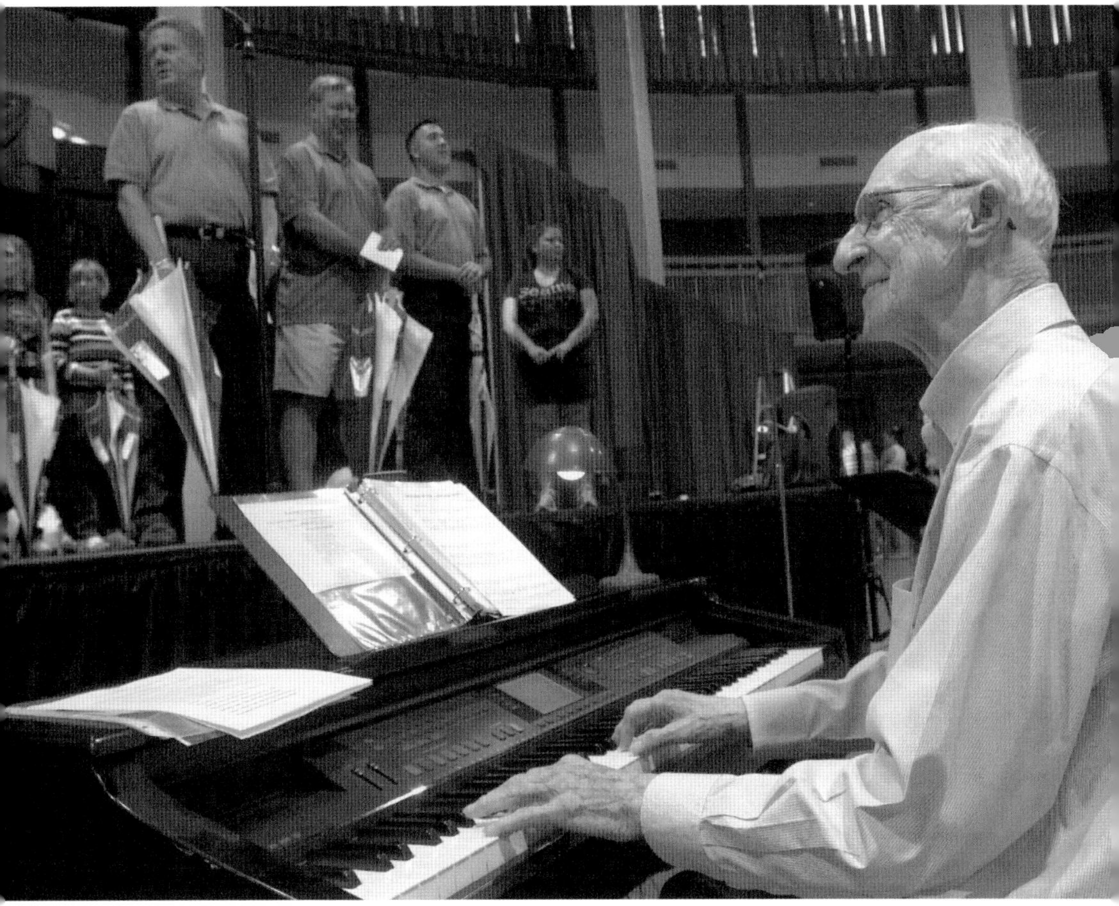

Denton's Piano Man

Robert J. "Bob" Rogers (1921–2013), pianist and professor emeritus of music at UNT, volunteer extraordinaire, philanthropist, educator, and mentor, was a fixture in the Denton community. An alumnus of North Texas, Juilliard, and Columbia, Rogers returned to North Texas in 1948 to teach piano pedagogy and applied piano until he retired in 1984. Rogers's legacy of service and volunteerism is unprecedented. He volunteered as accompanist at countless fundraisers and campus events raising millions of dollars and giving scholarships to students. (Courtesy of DRC.)

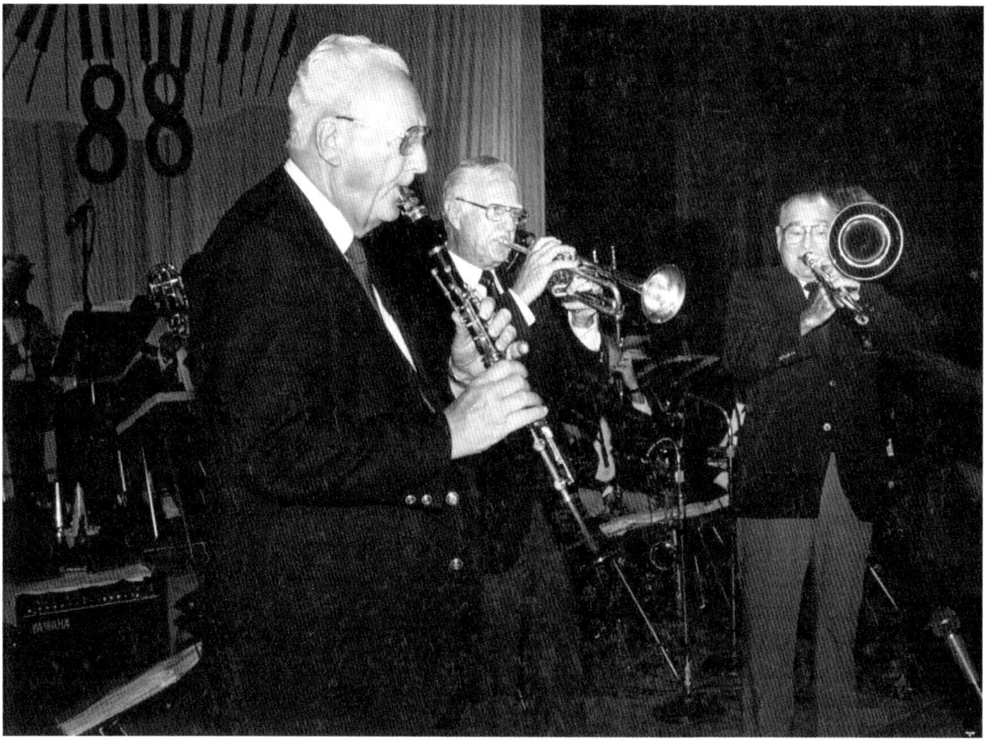

Good Time for Jazz

Morris Eugene "Gene" Hall (1913–1993) graduated from North Texas State in 1944 and played with numerous bands and worked in radio. Hall began teaching at his alma mater in 1947, creating the Two O'Clock Laboratory Dance Band, named for the time it met. He established the first collegiate jazz degree, although it was referred to as a "dance band" major because of objections to the word "jazz." In 1959, Hall developed a jazz program at Michigan State University. He received the International Association of Jazz Educators' Hall of Fame Award in 1981. Hall (left) is shown playing with other members of the Golden Eagles Jazz Band. (Courtesy of UNT.)

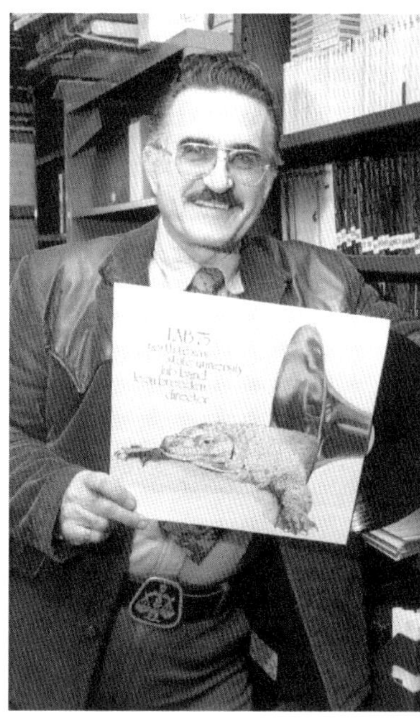

One O'Clock Lab Band

Leon Breeden (1921–2010), renowned multi-instrumentalist and arranger, succeeded Gene Hall as the head of the jazz program and moved the practice time up an hour, giving it the name it has today, the One O'Clock Lab Band. Under Breeden's leadership, the program earned nearly 50 national awards, and two band albums were nominated for Grammy Awards, the first such college band albums to be granted this honor. The One O'Clock Lab Band has shared the stage with musical greats such as Duke Ellington and Stan Getz. Breeden was chosen by the student body for the 'Fessor Graham Award in 1965. Breeden is seen here holding the album *Lab '75*, which was nominated in the Grammy big band category. (Courtesy of DRC.)

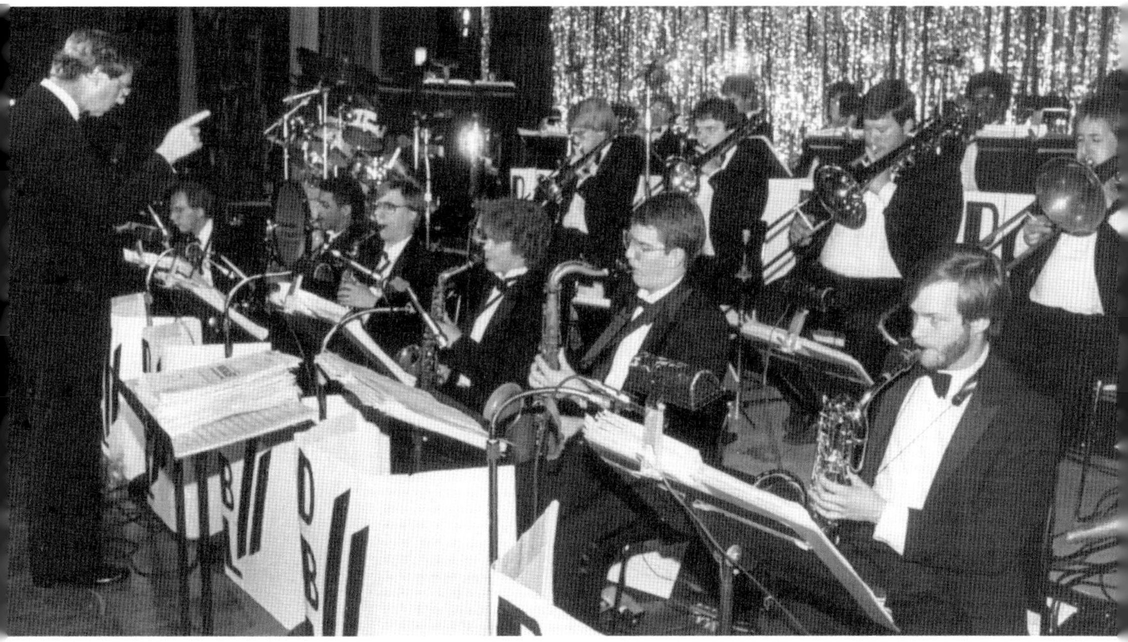

Grammy Award Nominee

Neil Slater, award-winning composer/arranger, noted jazz pianist and educator, and Grammy Award nominee, became the director of the internationally acclaimed One O'Clock Lab Band in 1981. In addition to creating more than 70 compositions for jazz ensembles, Slater has written for symphony, mixed chamber groups, a cappella choirs, and theater. During his 27-year tenure at UNT, Slater was credited with expanding the depth and breadth of its outstanding jazz studies program. (Courtesy of DCOHC.)

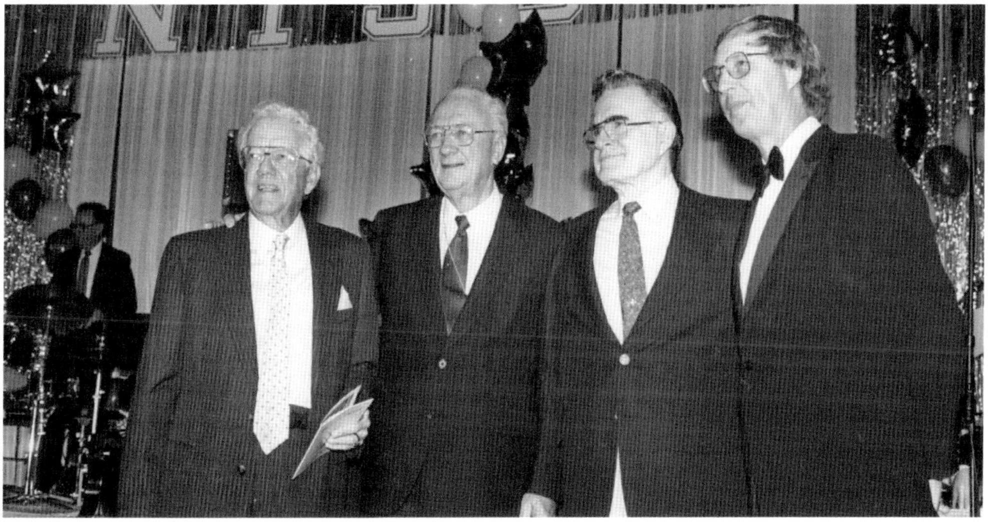

Legacy of Jazz Leaders

Gathered for this photograph on a special occasion are, from left to right, Robert L. Marquis Jr., son of North Texas's sixth president and faculty member from 1934 to 1977, and three of the past leaders of the O'Clock Lab Bands, Gene Hall, Leon Breeden, and Neil Slater. (Courtesy of UNT.)

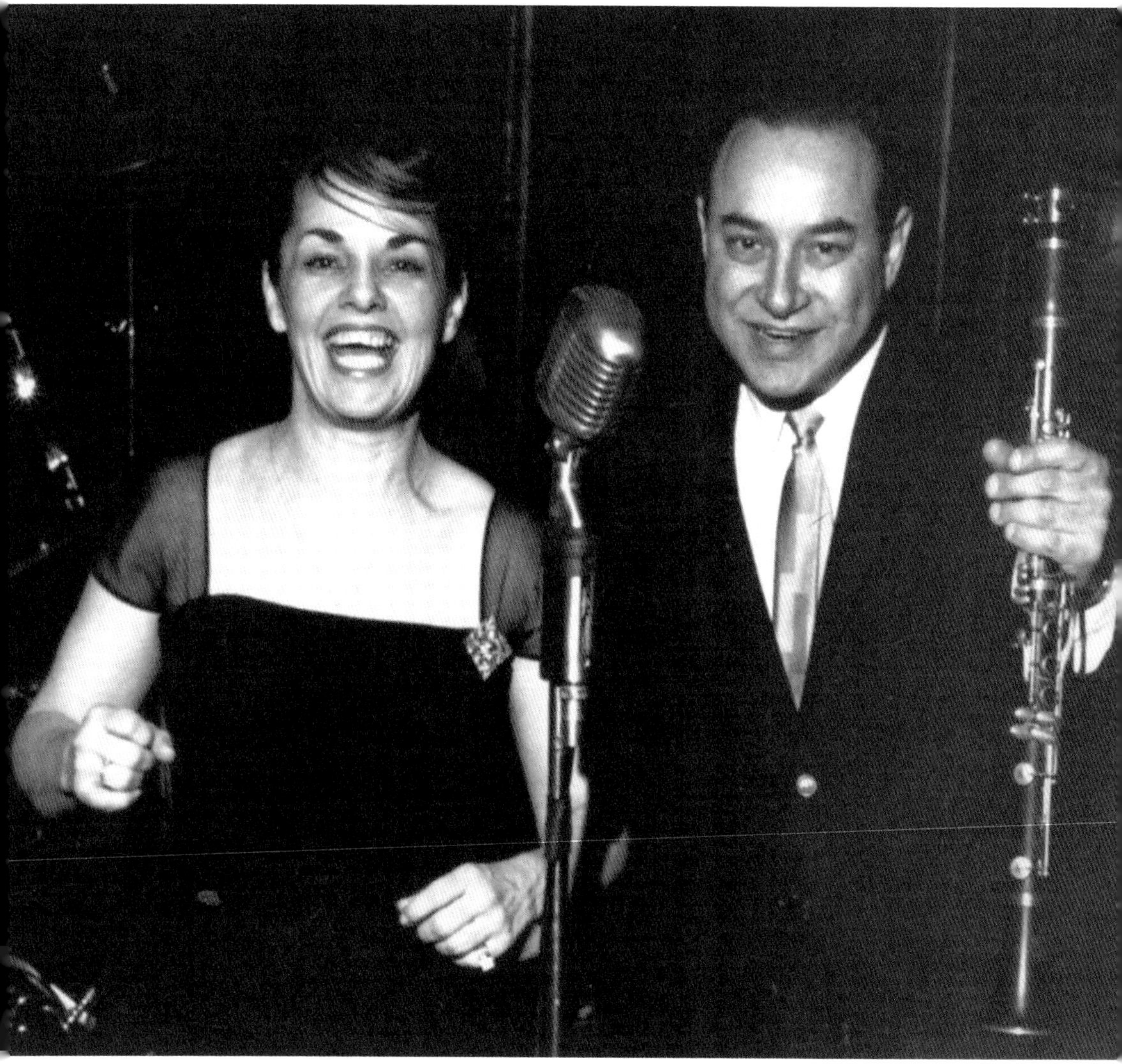

Denton's Jazz Songbird

Mary Louise Tobin grew up in Denton, singing with her 10 siblings. After winning a radio talent contest in 1932, she toured on the Interstate Theatre Circuit. Tobin married trumpet player Harry James in 1935. During the next eight years, she sang with jazz bands, including Benny Goodman's orchestra. Despite her skyrocketing career, she left Goodman to start a family. Although Tobin's touring days were essentially ended, she still performed and recorded while raising her two sons. Harry James divorced Tobin to marry Betty Grable. Singing at the 1962 Newport Jazz Festival, she met and later married clarinetist Peanuts Hucko (1918–2003). The couple is shown in this photograph. Tobin donated her archive of memorabilia of her career to Texas A&M University, Commerce. (Courtesy of DRC.)

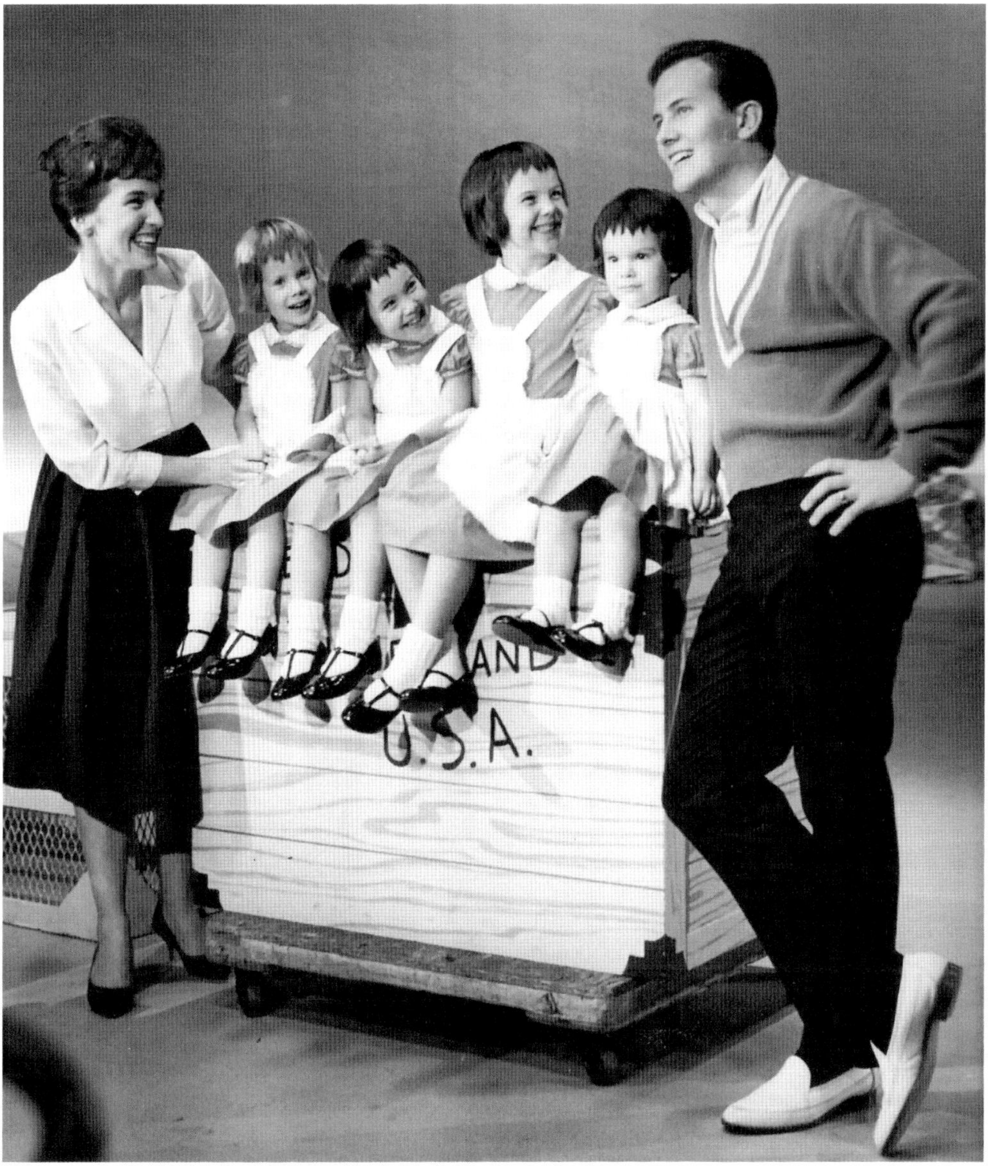

White Bucks Style Icon

Charles Eugene "Pat" Boone got his start when he attended North Texas State in 1955 to study music and drama. He performed with the Aces of Collegeland and in the Kiwanis Minstrel Shows. Boone's career included 38 No. 1 hits, 15 feature films, and a television show. He later invested in a moderately successful Denton restaurant called Pat Boone Country Inn. He remains popular among his Denton fans, who were treated to a performance by the star at the university in 2012. A young Pat Boone is shown here wearing his famous white bucks. Along with his wife, Shirley, are, from left to right, daughters Debby, Linda, Cheryl, and Laura. (Courtesy of author.)

Rock 'n' Roll Hall of Famer

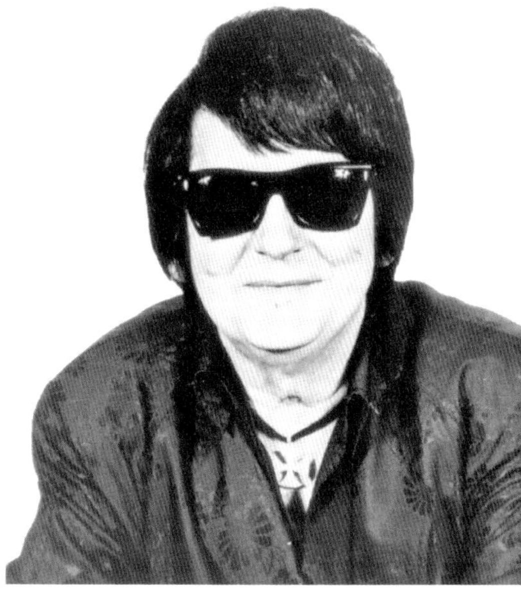

While attending North Texas State College from 1954 to 1955, Roy Kelton Orbison (1936–1988) recorded his first hit, "Ooby Dooby," a song written by fellow UNT students Wade Moore and Dick Penner, and also "Go-Go-Go." His hits included "Only the Lonely," "Blue Angel," "Running Scared," "Blue Bayou," "It's Over," "Crying," and "Oh, Pretty Woman." Elvis Presley referred to Orbison as "the greatest singer in the world." After his death, Orbison was inducted into the Rock and Roll Hall of Fame and the Rockabilly Hall of Fame, and he received a star on the Hollywood Walk of Fame. The music industry continued to give accolades to Orbison with a 1991 Grammy for Best Male Pop Vocal Performance and a Grammy Lifetime Achievement Award. Orbison was chosen posthumously to receive UNT's most prestigious honor, the Distinguished Alumnus Award, in 2013. (Courtesy of DRC.)

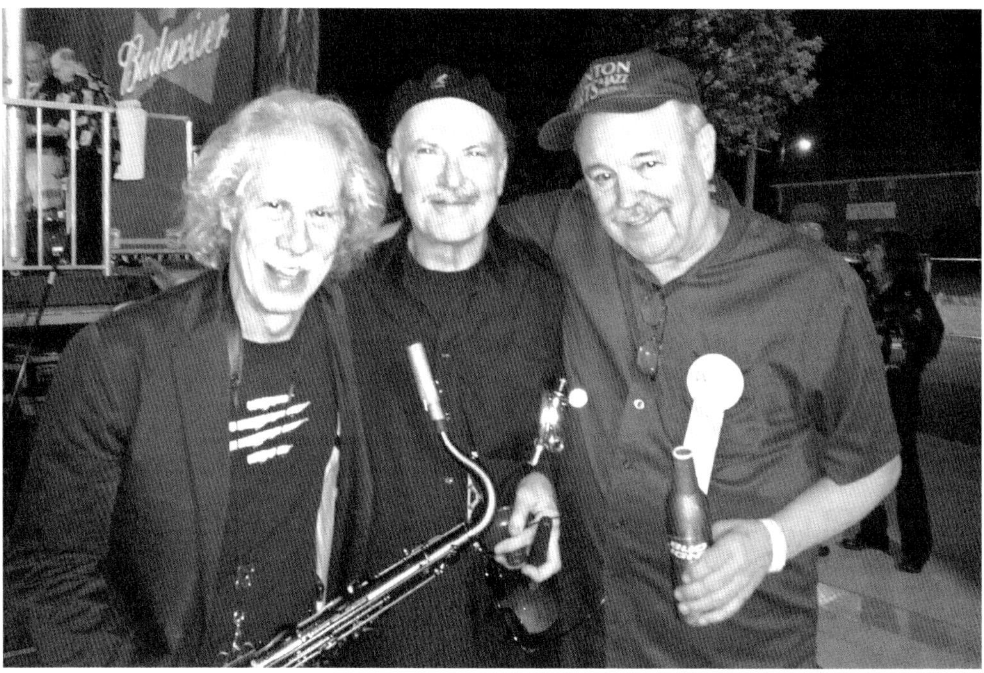

Blues Brother

One O'Clock Lab Band member and UNT graduate "Blue" Lou Marini Jr. was an original member of The Blues Brothers and the *Saturday Night Live* band. This saxophonist, arranger, composer, and noted jazz, rock, blues, and soul musician was a member of Blood, Sweat & Tears. Many of his arrangements and compositions have become favorites for the UNT lab bands. Marini (left) is shown after a performance at the Denton Arts & Jazz Festival with renowned trumpet player Steve Howard (center) and Jay Saunders, UNT trumpet professor and director of the One O'Clock Lab Band. (Courtesy of Jay Saunders.)

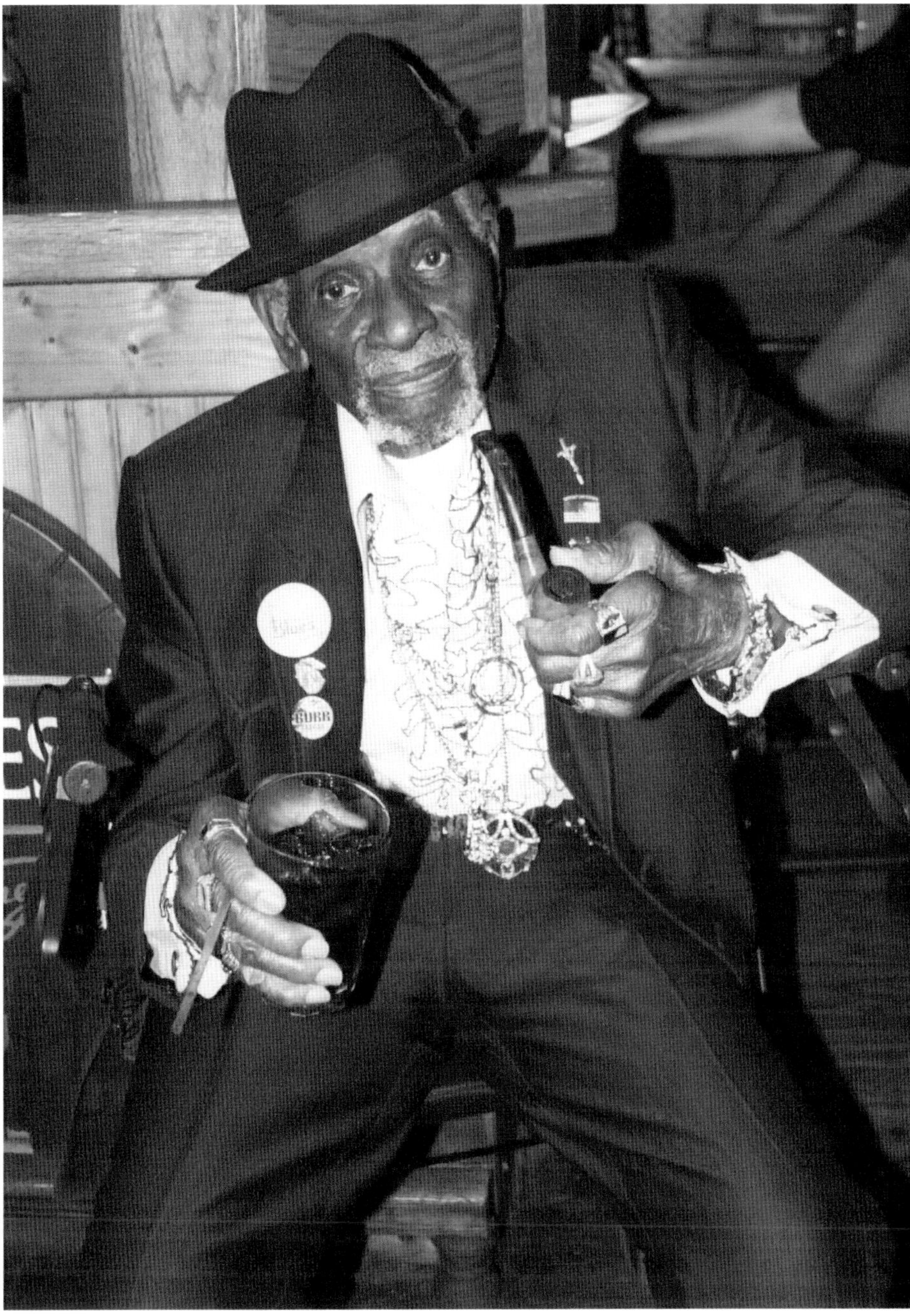

Keeping the Blues Alive
Tom "Pops" Carter (1919–2012) sang his bluesy, story-oriented songs at local Denton clubs. Carter earned his nickname from students who danced to his music at Fry Street Fair. The bluesman played jazz, hard rock, country, punk rock, and funk with legends B.B. King, Stevie Ray Vaughan, and Gatemouth Brown. In a 2008 short documentary titled *Pops Carter: Keeping the Blues Alive*, Carter said, "I believe in helping people if I can. I was taught that you can't live in this world by yourself." (Courtesy of Stephanie Will-Shipp.)

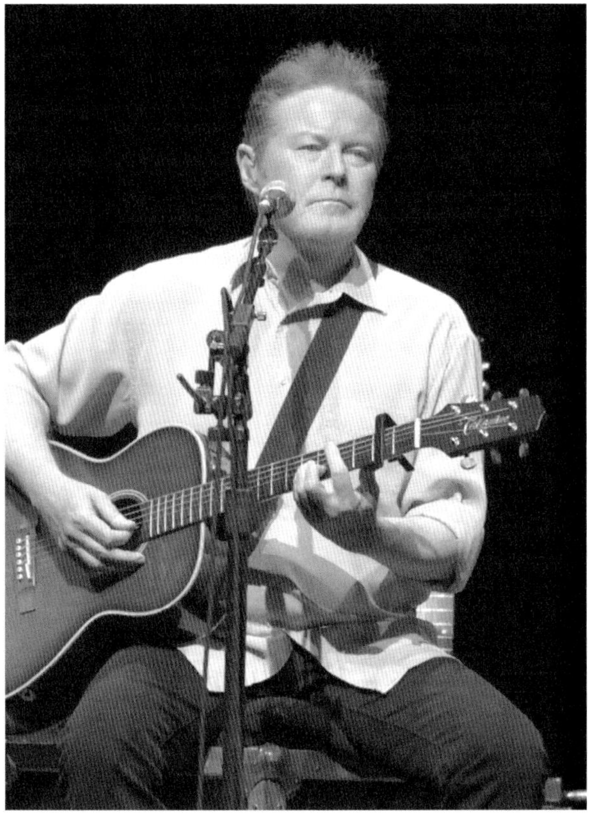

Not the Only Eagles in Town

Donald Hugh "Don" Henley attended North Texas State before forming his first band, Shiloh. In 1971, he formed the Eagles, coincidentally the same name as the college's mascot. The Eagles have five No. 1 singles, eight Grammys, five American Music Awards, and six No. 1 albums, and are considered one of the most successful musical bands of the 1970s. Henley either cowrote or sang lead vocals on many of the Eagles' songs, including "Witchy Woman," "Desperado," "Best of My Love," "One of These Nights," and "Hotel California." (Courtesy of DRC.)

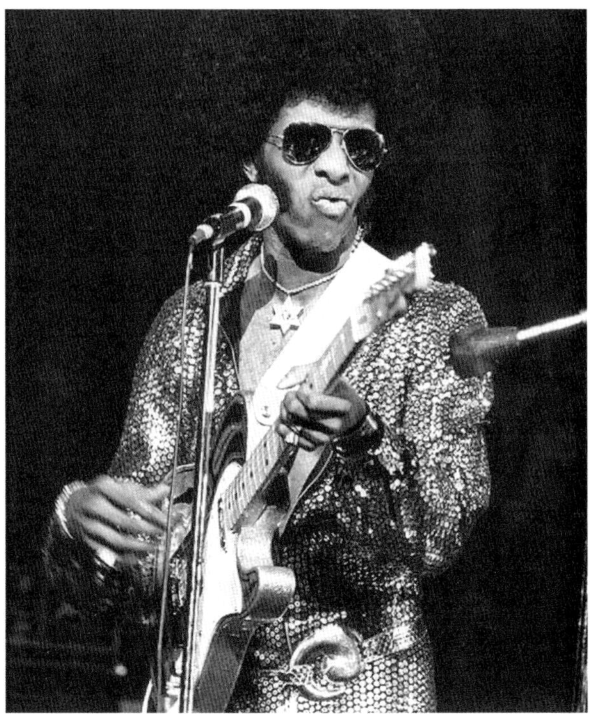

It's a Family Affair

Sylvester Stewart "Sly" Stone, rhythm and blues artist, was born in Denton and performed as Sly and the Family Stone with his sister Rose and brother Freddie. The multiracial, multigender band that Stone assembled fused funk, soul, and psychedelic rock and became one of the most influential acts ever. The San Francisco–based group released a string of hits, beginning with the 1968 album *Dance to the Music*, followed by "Everyday People," "Family Affair," "Thank You (Falettinme Be Mice Elf Agin)," and "Stand!" The group was inducted into the Rock and Roll Hall of Fame in 1993. (Courtesy of author.)

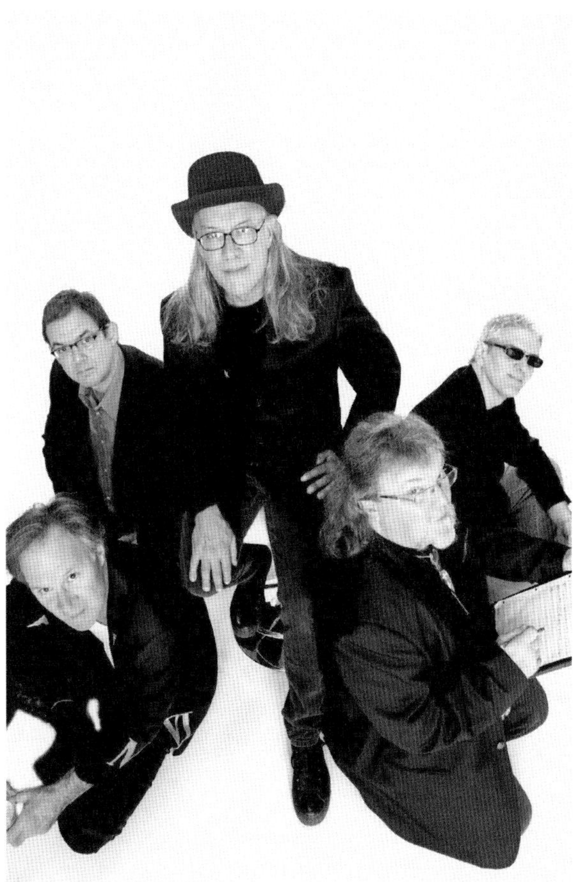

Nuclear Polka
Grammy Winning Band

Brave Combo has won two Grammys and been nominated seven times for their particular repertoire of salsa, cha-cha, blues, rock, classical music, and "nuclear polka," a mix that has earned the band international fame. It would not be a Denton event without the band's iconic chicken dance, performed every year at the Denton Arts & Jazz Festival and at the holiday Christmas-tree-lighting festival. Members of the band are, from left to right, Steve Carter, Danny O'Brien, founder Carl Finch, Jeffrey Barnes, and Alan Emert-Mansfield. (Courtesy of Ed Steele.)

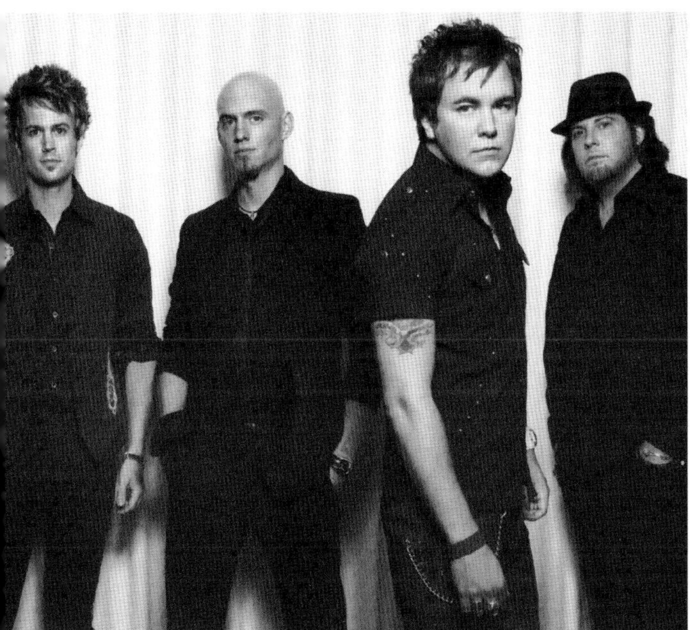

A Young Band

Members of the Eli Young Band met at UNT as students in the late 1990s. These four UNT alumni have built a career recording country albums with a hint of hard rock. They earned their first platinum record in 2011. They won Song of the Year at the 2011 Academy of Country Music Awards. The band was nominated for a 2013 Grammy Award for Best Country Duo/Group Performance and Academy of Country Music Best Song of the Year. The band members are, from left to right, Chris Thompson, Jon Jones, Mike Eli, and James Young. (Courtesy of author.)

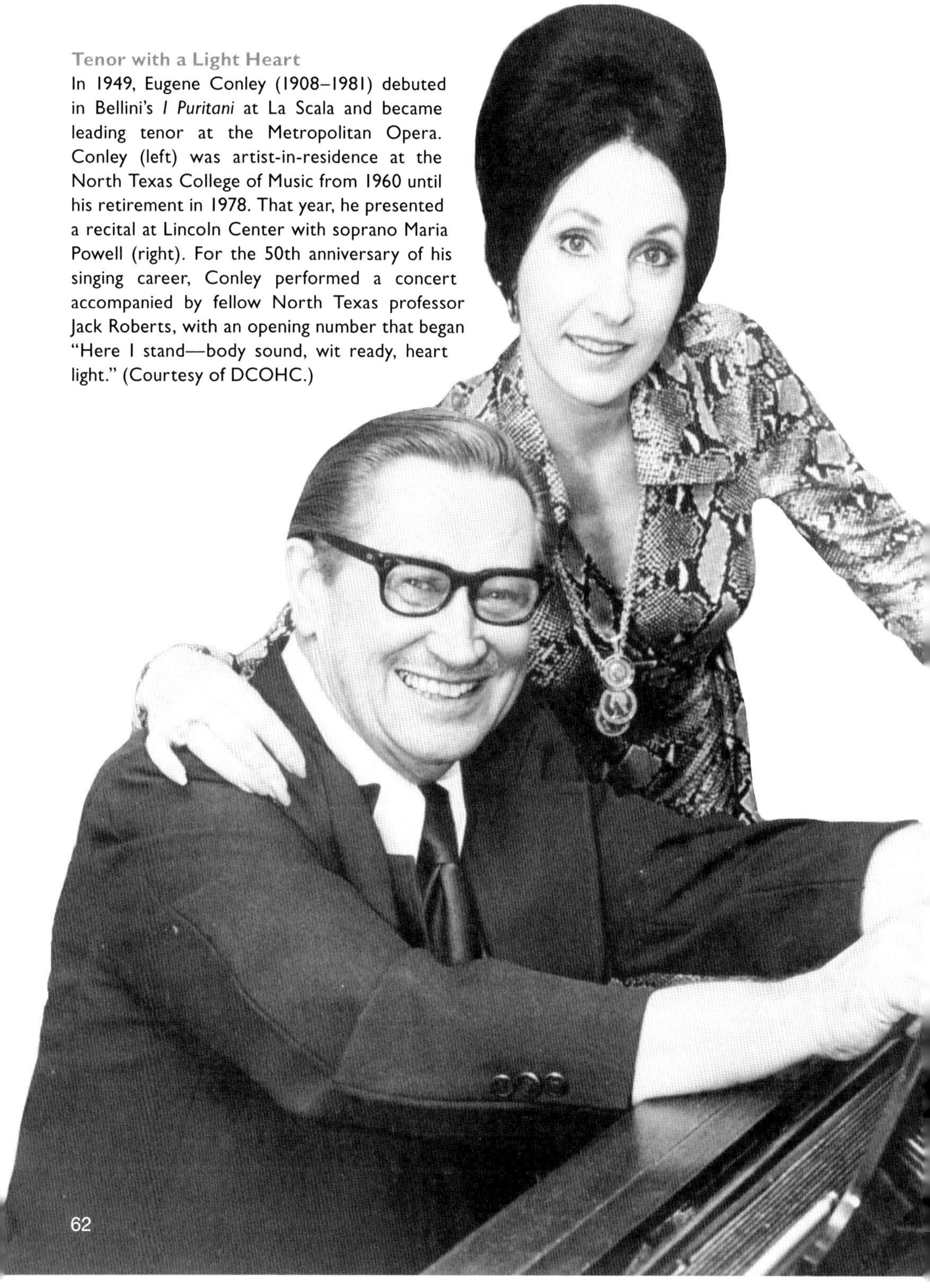

Tenor with a Light Heart
In 1949, Eugene Conley (1908–1981) debuted in Bellini's *I Puritani* at La Scala and became leading tenor at the Metropolitan Opera. Conley (left) was artist-in-residence at the North Texas College of Music from 1960 until his retirement in 1978. That year, he presented a recital at Lincoln Center with soprano Maria Powell (right). For the 50th anniversary of his singing career, Conley performed a concert accompanied by fellow North Texas professor Jack Roberts, with an opening number that began "Here I stand—body sound, wit ready, heart light." (Courtesy of DCOHC.)

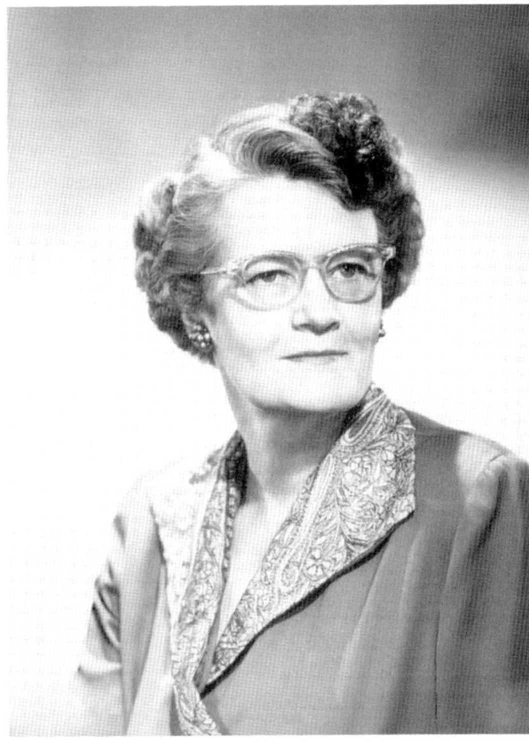

Abstract Life

Carlotta M. Corpron (1901–1988) used dim lighting and long exposures to create movement and depth in her photographs. She made strides in the realm of abstract, experimental photographs exploring unfamiliar territory in the 1940s. She was professor of art history and advertising design at TWU for 33 years before retiring in 1968. The photograph below, taken in 1944, shows a piece from her series *Nature Studies* called "Nature Dancer." (Right, courtesy of DCOHC; below, courtesy of DRC.)

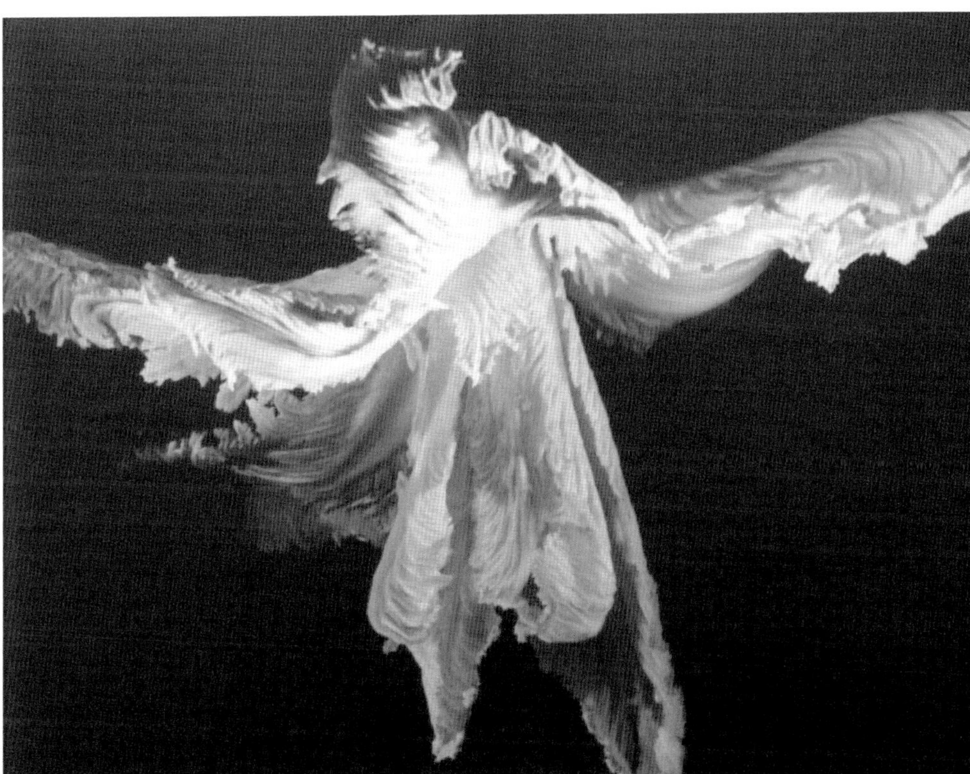

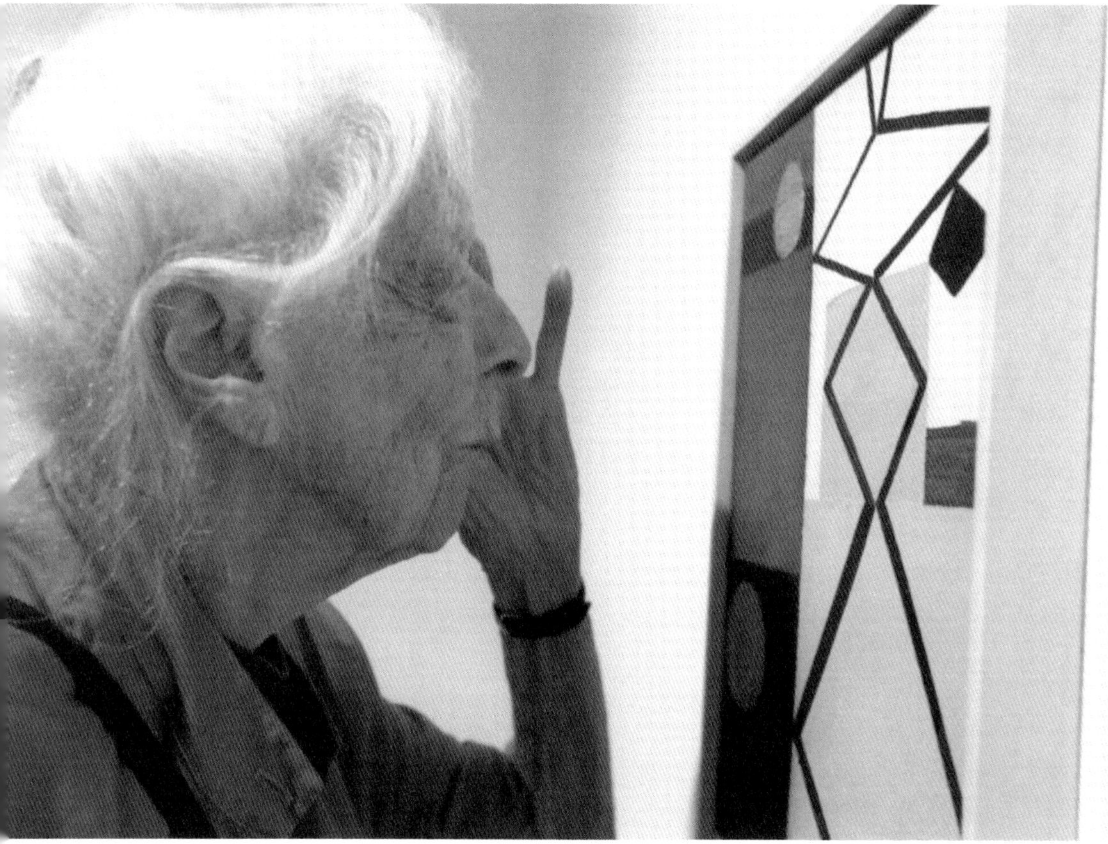

Texas Modernist

Dorothy Antoinette "Toni" LaSelle (1902–2002) was art professor at TWU from 1928 to 1972. She directed the design projects for the Little Chapel in the Woods and the memorial windows of Trinity Presbyterian Church. Her works have appeared in galleries and museums all over the United States. A pioneer of Texas Modernism, LaSelle was one of the first Texas painters to immerse herself in abstract expressionism, bringing sophistication to her elemental, typically small-scale abstractions. LaSelle, at age 99, is shown taking a close look at one of her 1949 paintings. (Courtesy of DRC.)

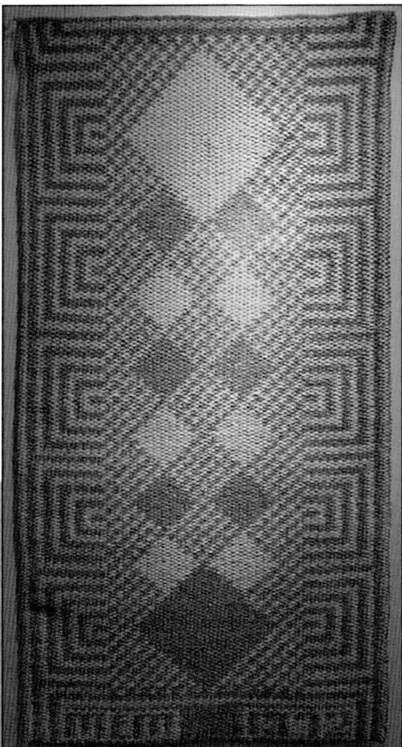

Weaving a Full Life

Mabel Ellet Maxcy (1903–2002) received a bachelor of music degree from the College of Industrial Arts, where she studied art with Mary Marshall, and a master's and doctorate from Columbia University in New York, where she taught art. She began her teaching career at Texas State College for Women in 1945, teaching pottery and ceramic sculpture and art education for 35 years. She also developed a curriculum in hand weaving that led to bachelor's and master's degrees. Maxcy and her students were responsible for organizing the Denton Handweavers Guild. The weaving shown at left, from the permanent collection of the Greater Denton Arts Council, is described as *Untitled*. (Above, courtesy of DRC; left, courtesy of GDAC.)

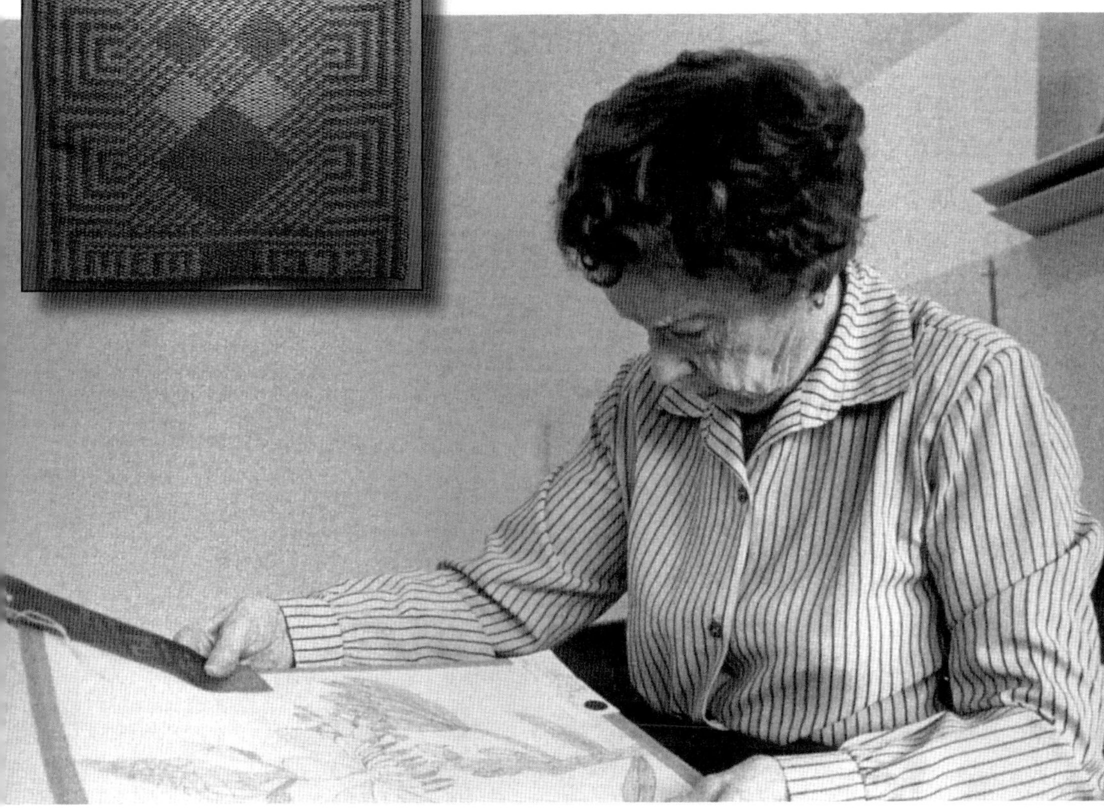

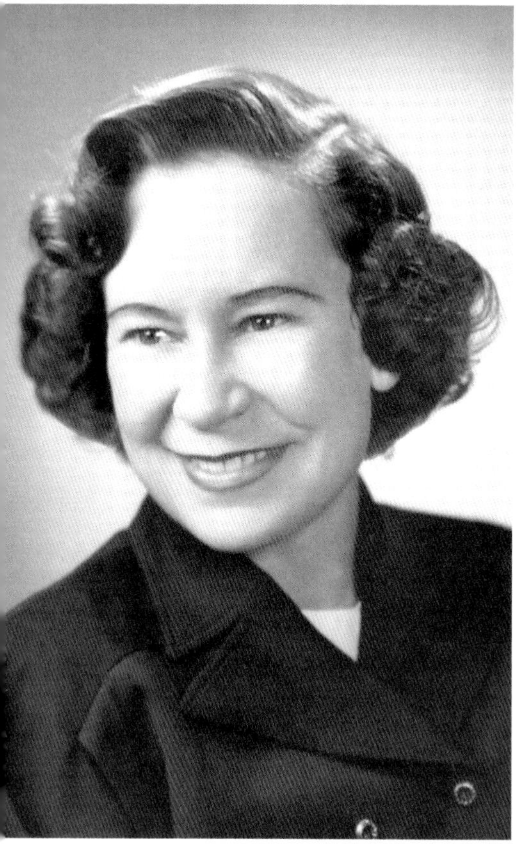

Noted Printmaker

Coreen Mary Spellman (1905–1978), oil painter, designer, illustrator, watercolorist, lithographer, and muralist, received her degrees from the Texas State College for Women, Columbia University in New York, and the University of Iowa. In 1929, Spellman taught printmaking, painting, illustration, and design at TSCW for 45 years. She also taught at the Dallas Museum of Fine Arts School. Many of her paintings depict human-made structures and industrial landscapes in a style combining realism, precisionism, and abstraction. She said of her painting, "I enjoy taking some rather obscure or unimportant subject or theme and making something fine and important out of it." Spellman's pieces are exhibited in collections of the Brooklyn Museum, Omaha's Joslyn Museum, the Dallas Museum of Art, Southern Methodist University, and the San Antonio Museum, among many others. The watercolor depicted below is *Summer Memory.* (Left, courtesy of TWU; below, courtesy of GDAC.)

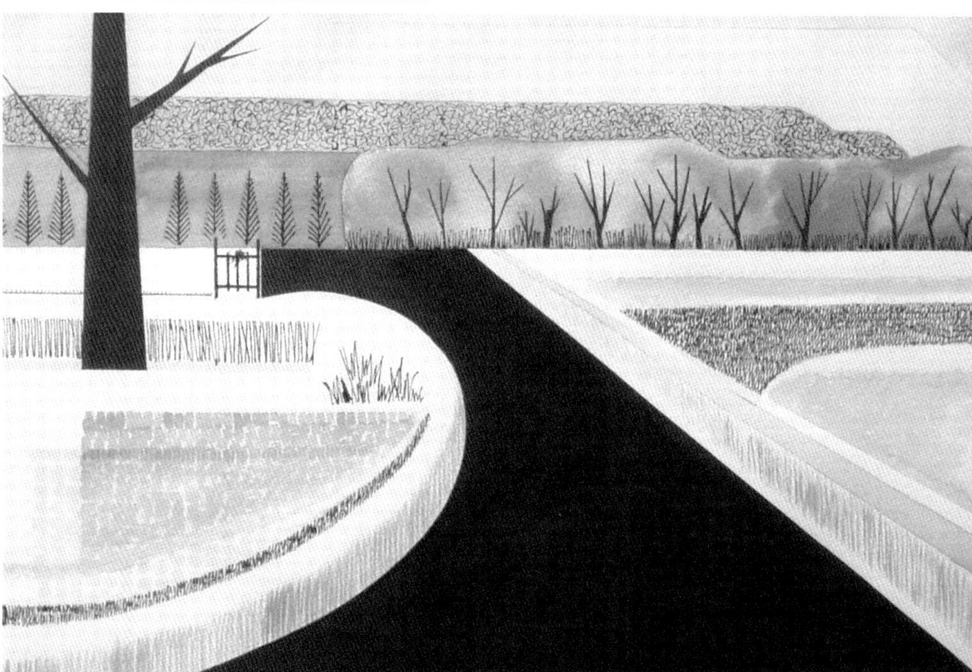

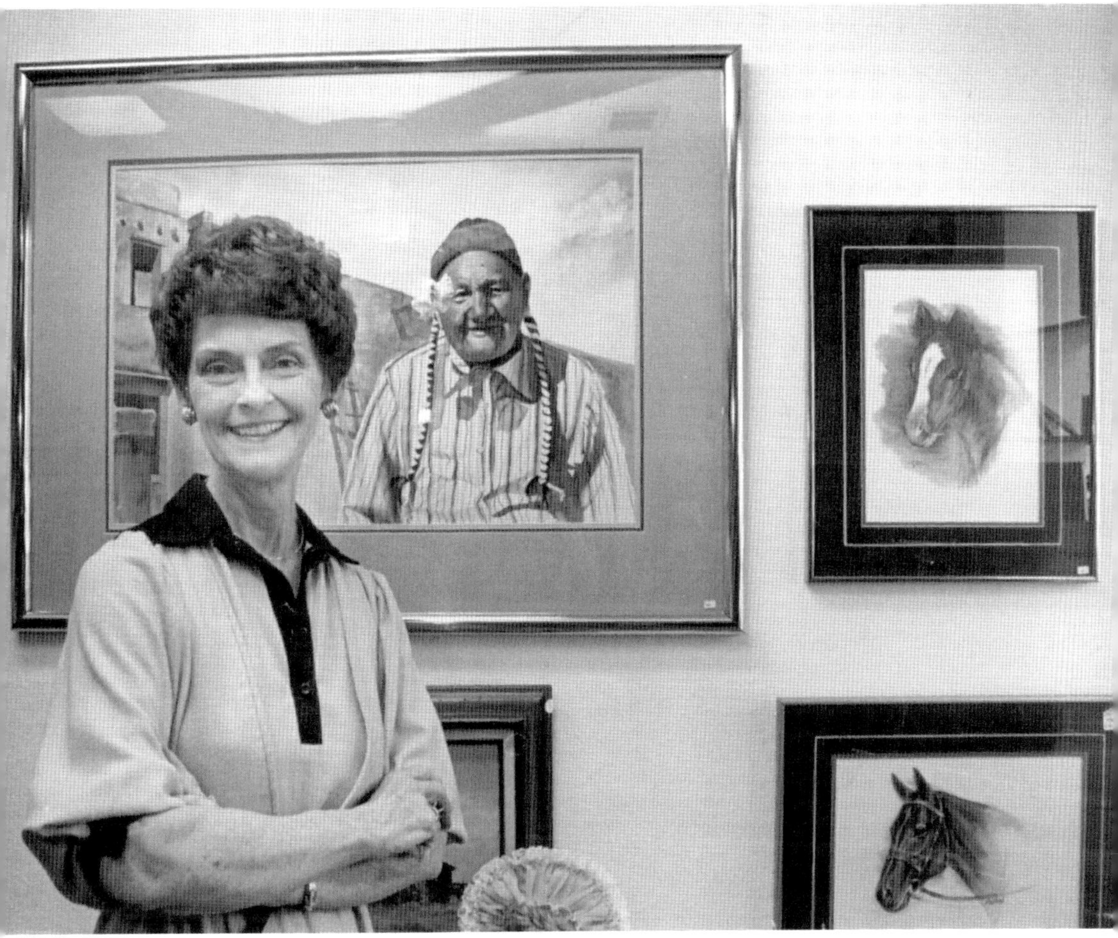

Artist of the Community

Martha F. Robbins (1925–1995), artist and community advocate, is best known nationally for her commissioned portraits in oil, pastel, and watercolor, and locally for her watercolors of community buildings and scenes. Art lovers have her paintings in private and corporate collections nationally and internationally. Robbins completed 39 watercolors and pen-and-ink drawings for *Portraits of Denton*, a book authored by Gayle Strange and Adelene Martin. Denton honored Robbins with the Community Arts Recognition Award in 1990. (Courtesy of DRC.)

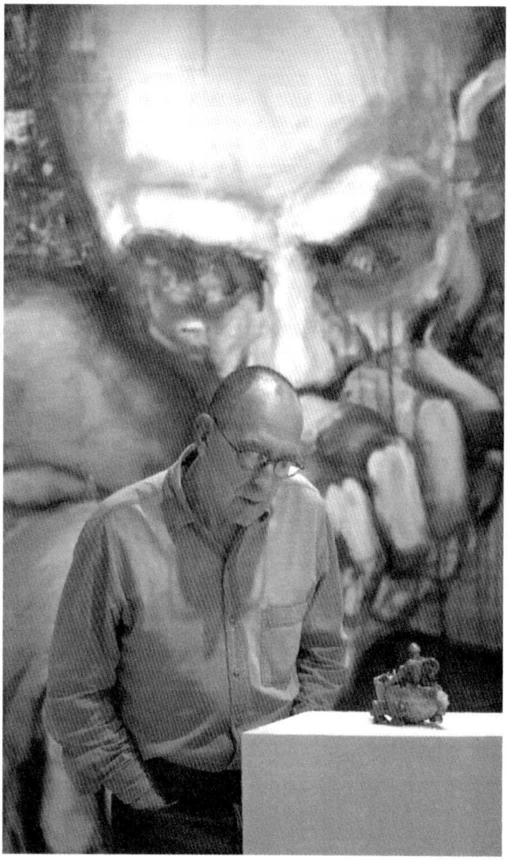

Favorite Professor

Robert William "Bill" McCarter, retired UNT regents professor of art, served as chairman for the Division of Art Education and Art History, codirector and cofounder of the North Texas Institute for Educators on the Visual Arts, coordinator of art education, and coordinator of the 2-D Design curriculum for the freshman core. McCarter received the Council Teaching Award and UNT Favorite Professor Award. In 2009, the university also awarded him with honorary alumnus status. (Courtesy of DRC.)

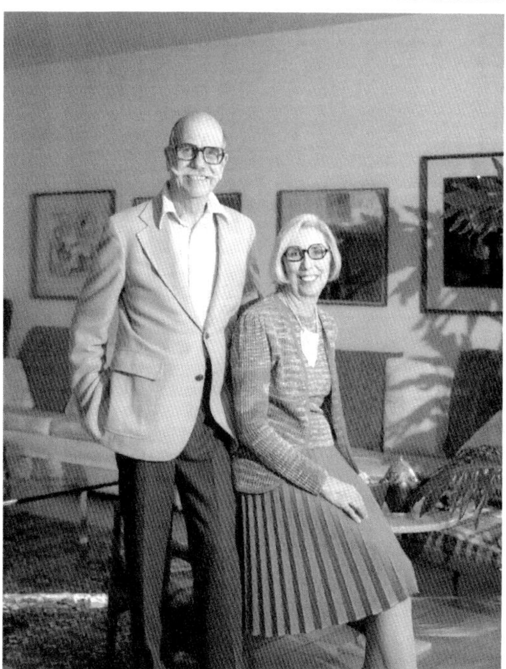

Devoted to the Arts

Ray Gough was a noted interior designer and UNT professor. Georgia Gough, also a UNT professor, served for 12 years on the Greater Denton Arts Council board and launched its annual fine craft competition, Materials: Hard & Soft. The arts council renamed its East Gallery in the Center for Visual Arts the Ray and Georgia Gough Gallery, a tribute to the Denton couple known for their artistic talents and contributions to the city's cultural scene. The Goughs were recognized in 2004 with the university's Green Glory Award for exceptional service to the university. (Courtesy of Monte B Photography.)

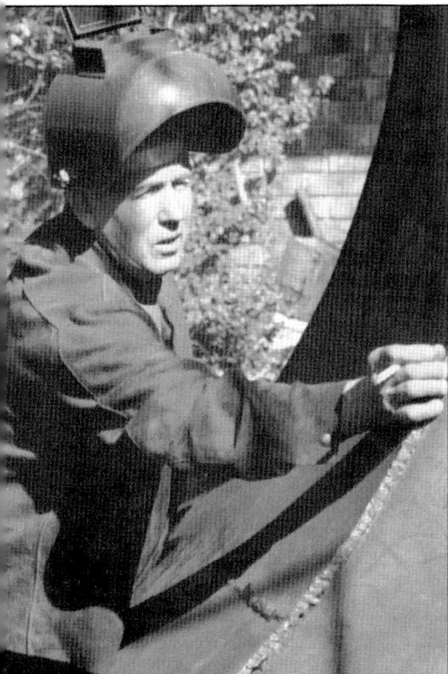

Man of Steel

John Brough Miller (1933–2010) served a year on the Dallas Museum of Fine Arts School faculty before joining the faculty of Texas Woman's University as professor of ceramics and sculpture, a position he held for 28 years. Miller described his sculptures, measuring from nine to thirty feet, as "existence in space" and "displacements." He took great pride and joy in giving personality and worth to steel which has little monetary value. These monumental sculptures were all created just outside his garage in his hometown of Argyle. His work can be seen in many public and private collections, including the Denton Fire Department Station 1, the Center for Visual Arts, Selwyn School, Texas Woman's University, Dallas Public Library, numerous art museums, airports, and universities. Miller's steel sculptures weigh between 1,000 and 4,000 pounds. *Elliptical Composition*, Miller's 3,800-pound, eight-foot, seven-inch sculpture (below) anchors the Greater Denton Arts Council parking lot. (Courtesy of TWU.)

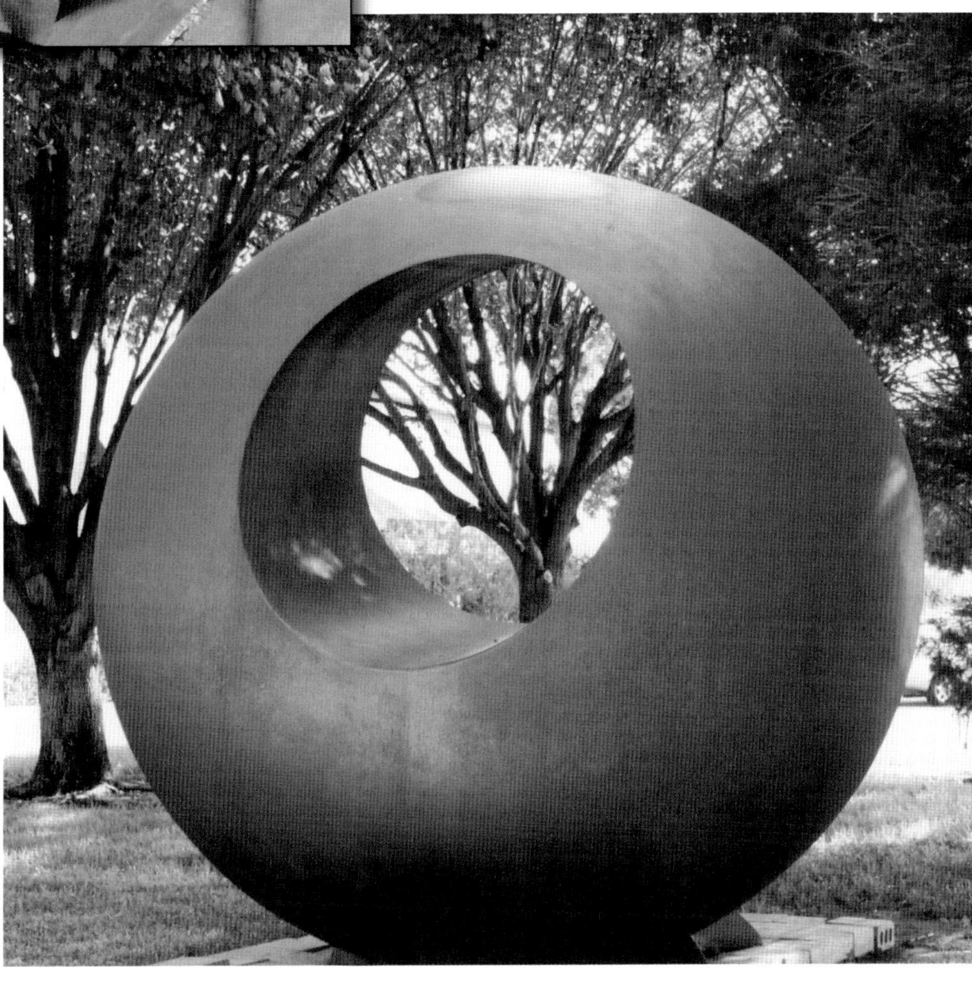

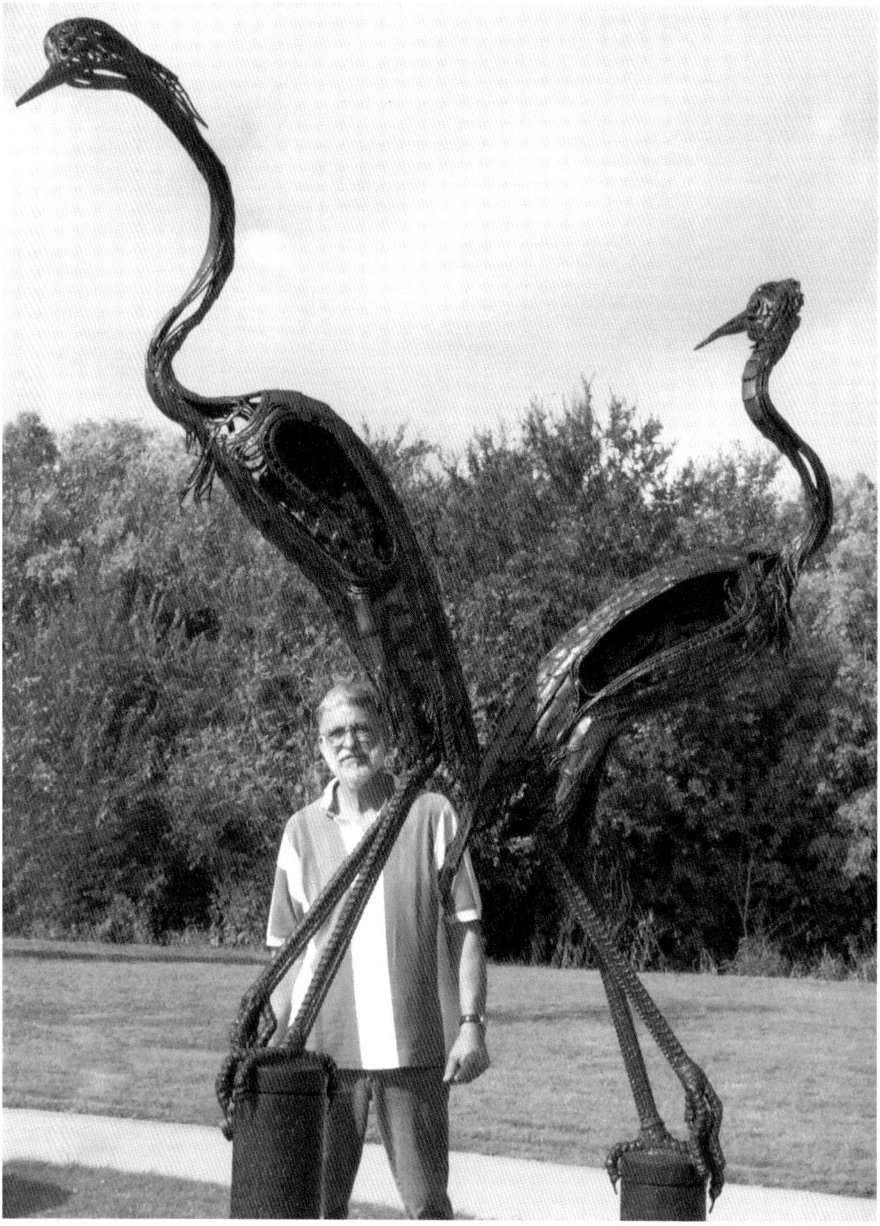

Public Artist

Artist George Cadell, who attended North Texas State to study bronzing, is inspired by Southwest Native American culture and wildlife. He welds steel and bronze sculptures for private buyers. However, it is his public art in Denton County and Oklahoma City for which he is most proud. For the past 30 years, he has crafted works for Texas's public landmarks, finding public art "gratifying as it provides the opportunity to communicate with people who may not be able to afford them." *Above All Integrity* sits in front of City Hall East. His work has earned him the Community Arts Recognition Award, which, incidentally, he casts for the annual award. A retired art teacher, Cadell taught at Denton High School for 26 years. The artist is shown here with his work *Harmony*, depicting a pair of herons who are right at home in South Lakes Park. (Courtesy of City of Denton.)

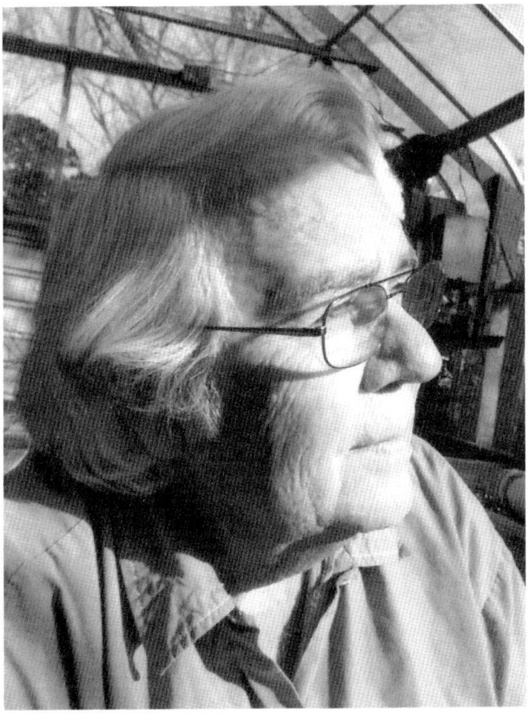

Showing his Mettle
Michael Eugene "Mike" Cunningham taught at North Texas State from 1968 to 1978 and then again from 1994 to 2004. His commissions and collections include the Anatole Hotel, Dallas; Waco's Baylor University; City of Grapevine visitors center; Cistercian Chapel, Dallas; the All War Memorial, Denton (below); and the stonework for the Denton Firefighters Memorial. Cunningham designed the Community Arts Recognition Award statue cast in bronze by George Cadell. The All War Memorial, located on the Denton courthouse lawn, honors citizens of Denton County who served in time of war. (Left, courtesy of Mike Cunningham; below, courtesy of Al Key.)

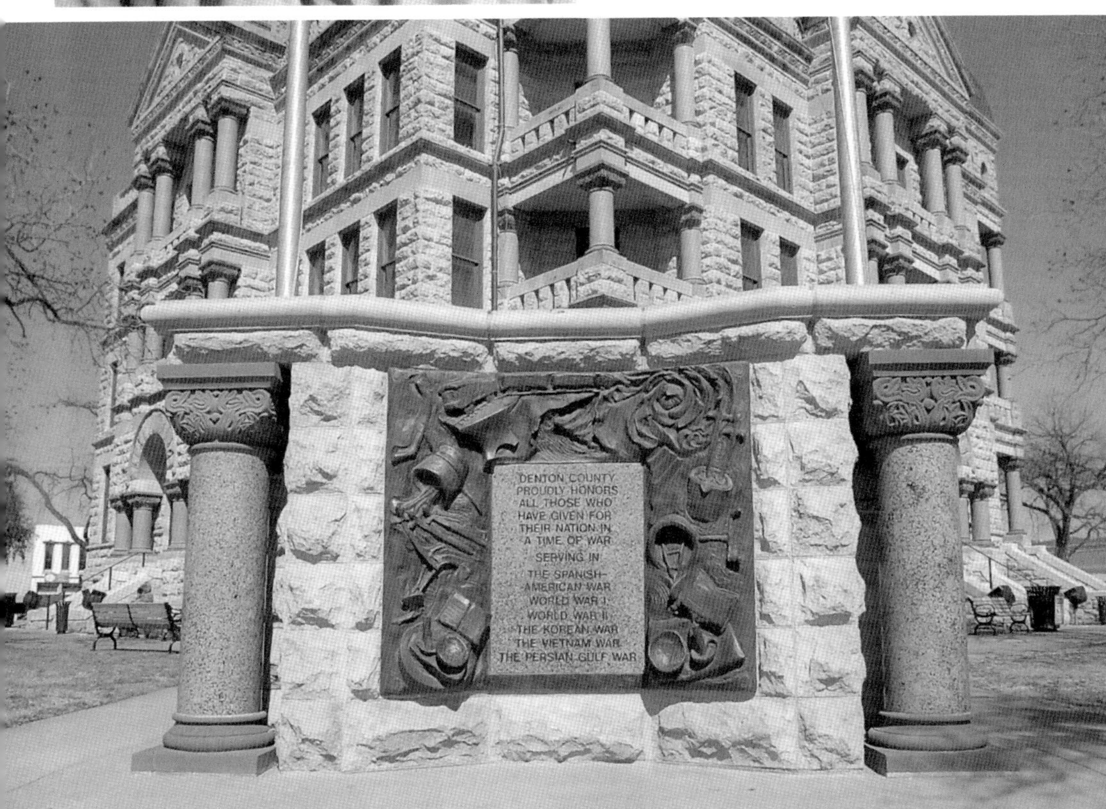

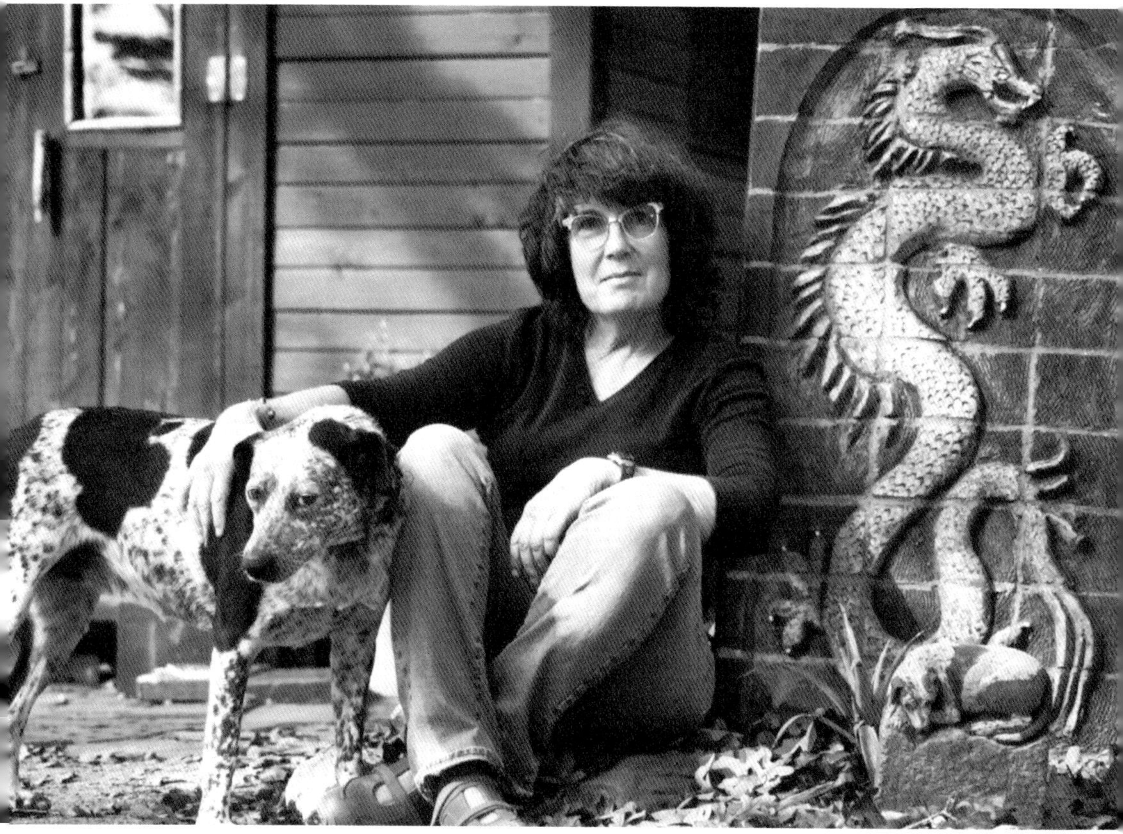

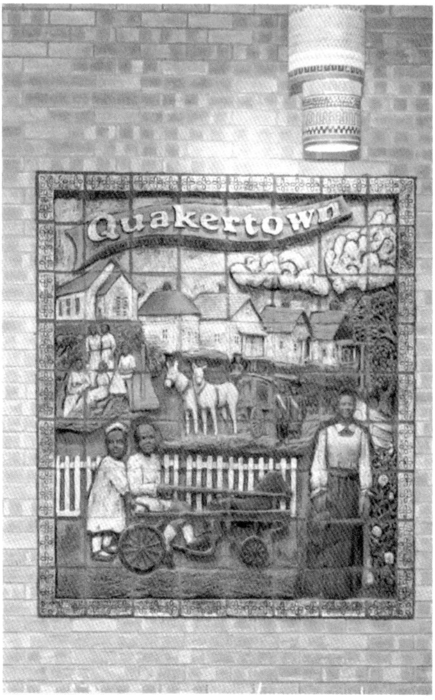

Of Clay and Brick

Paula Blincoe Collins (above) began her work by carving a brick sculpture for an office building in Oklahoma City using Acme bricks. Conoco Oil requested a 10-foot-by-84-foot bas-relief, glazed-brick mural carved from Denton's Acme Brick for its headquarters in Oklahoma. She has created two 20-foot-tall sculptures for St. Thomas Aquinas Church in Sugar Land, the *Resurrection* and the *Holy Family*, and a 30-foot-by-6-foot mural for the soccer venue at the 1996 Olympics. Collins became a pilot and bought her own airplane to simplify getting in and out of job sites. Her list of clients includes Fortune 500 companies across the country. Her 2008 brick sculpture *Historic Quakertown* (left), in the Denton Civic Center entrance, was the first public art commissioned by the City of Denton. (Above, courtesy of DRC; left, courtesy of the City of Denton.)

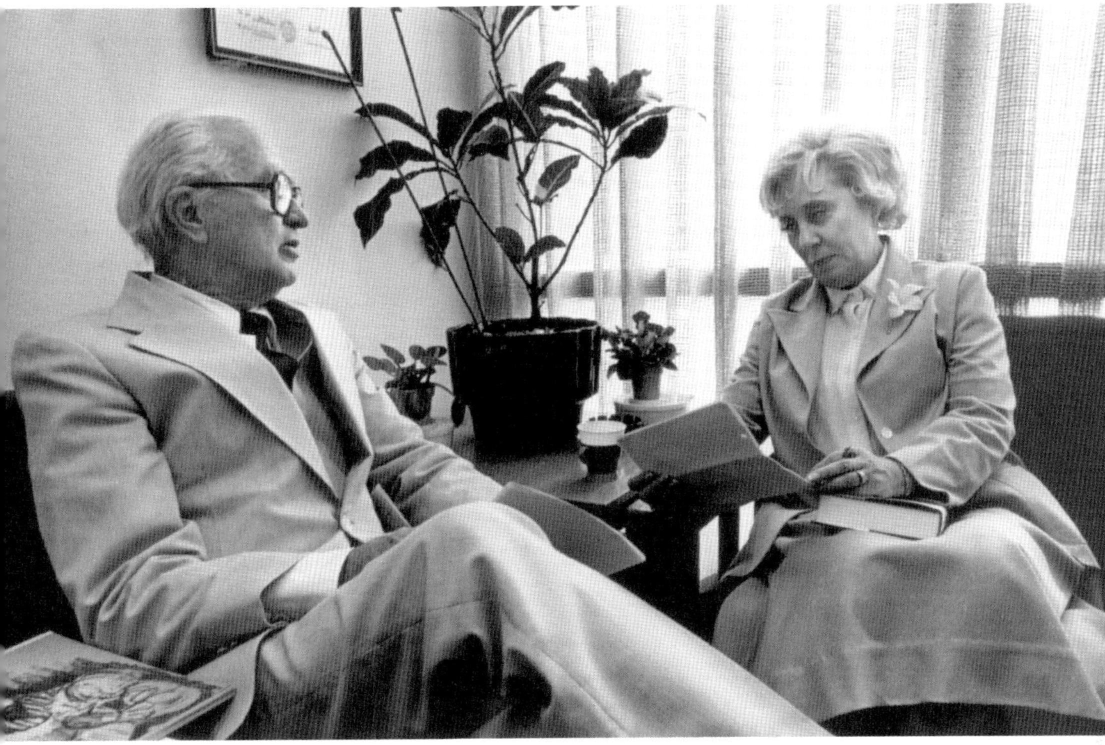

Public and Private Architect

Otha Neil "O'Neil" Ford (1905–1982) graduated from Denton High School, then studied machine drafting and architectural drawing at North Texas State for two years before completing his education through a correspondence school. Ford designed several homes and six civic structures in Denton, including the pool bathhouse, city hall, civic center, library, airport terminal, and the Little Chapel-in-the-Woods, using native brick, wood, and stone as his primary medium. Buildings constructed in his Texas Vernacular style of architecture seem to meld into their natural settings. Ford is shown chatting with Joella Orr, former Denton Public Library director. (Courtesy of DRC.)

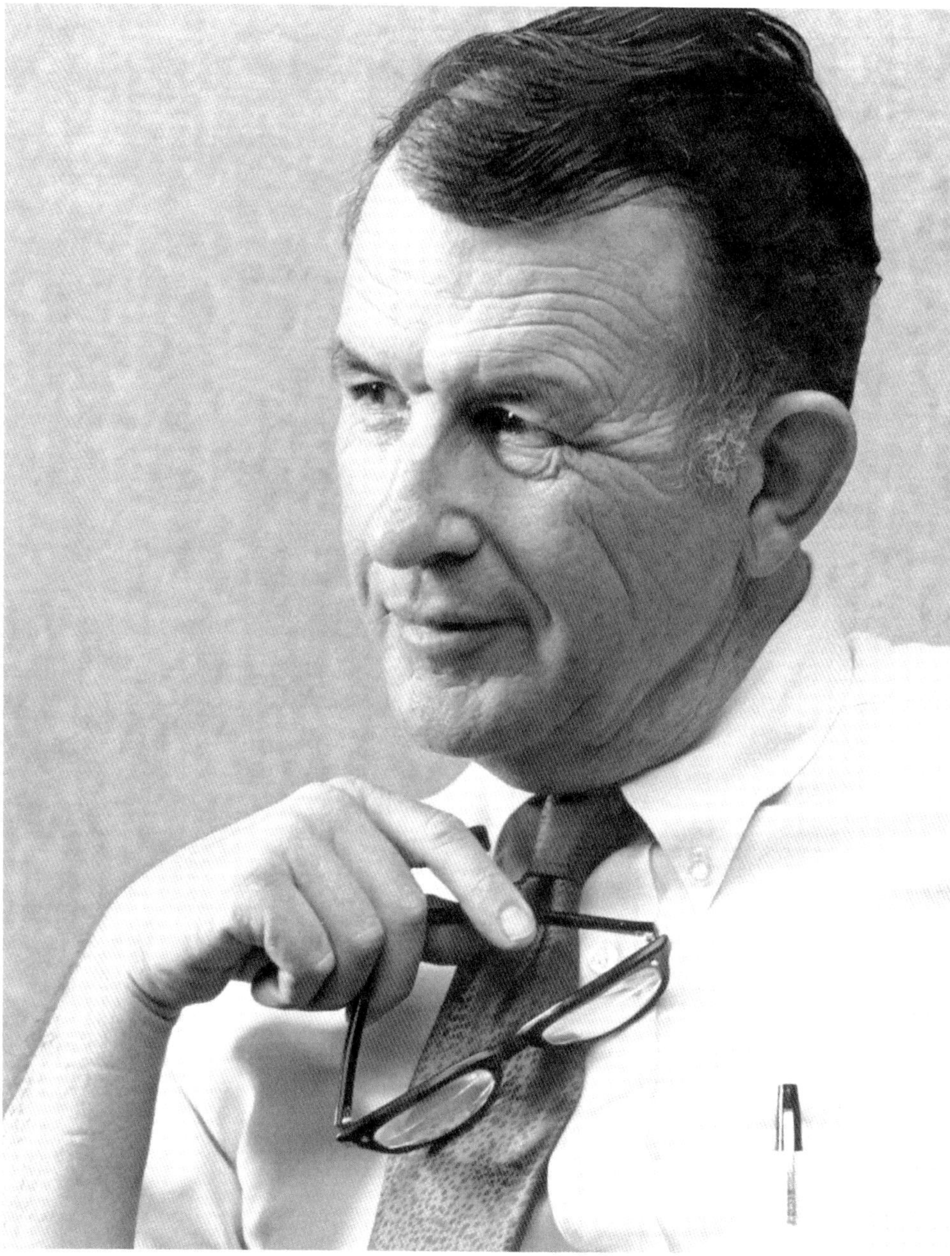

Protégé of O'Neil Ford

William Roland Laney III (1918–2002), a protégé of O'Neil Ford and Arch Swank, played a key role in the design and development of numerous projects throughout the city. His principal works were the Denton Civic Center, Civic Center Pool, North Texas Savings and Loan, the Davis Office Building, the Stockard Professional Building, the Varsity Shop, Denton Independent School District Administration Building, the new Denton Senior High School, Denton County National Bank, Trinity Presbyterian Church and Pearl Street Church of Christ educational wings, First Presbyterian Church fellowship hall, and several residences. He tirelessly served on dozens of city and community boards, but his legacy is in his landmark structures. (Courtesy of Georgia Laney Christensen.)

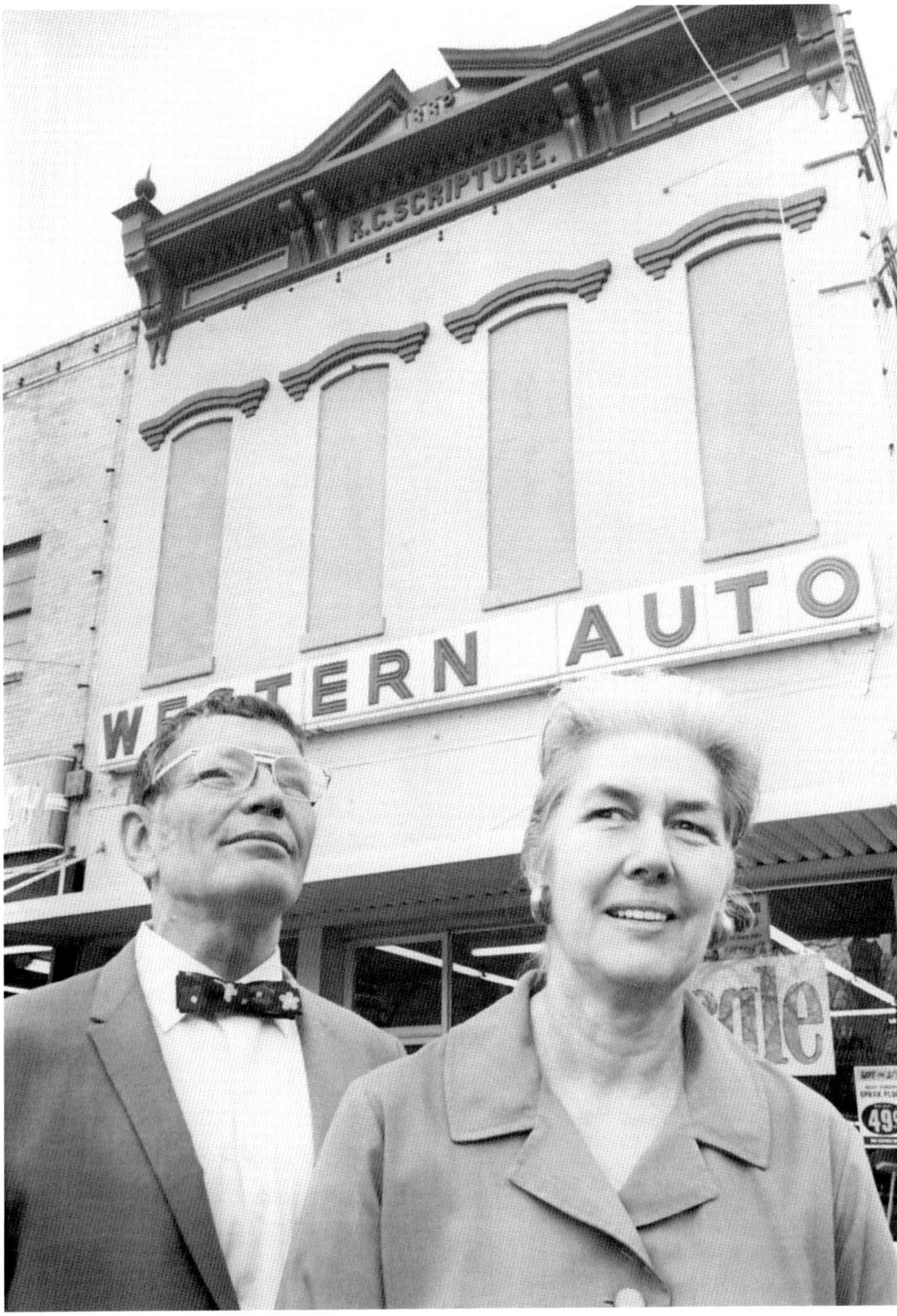

Architectural Partnership

Tom Polk Miller (1914–2000) and Mary Isabel Mount Miller (1916–2007) were partners in Mount-Miller Architects, a local architectural firm that designed dozens of homes and commercial buildings in Denton and supervised the restoration of the Scripture Building, the Southern Hotel into senior housing, and the Evers house. The Mount-Miller architectural firm designed the Denton Unitarian Universalist Fellowship. (Courtesy of DRC.)

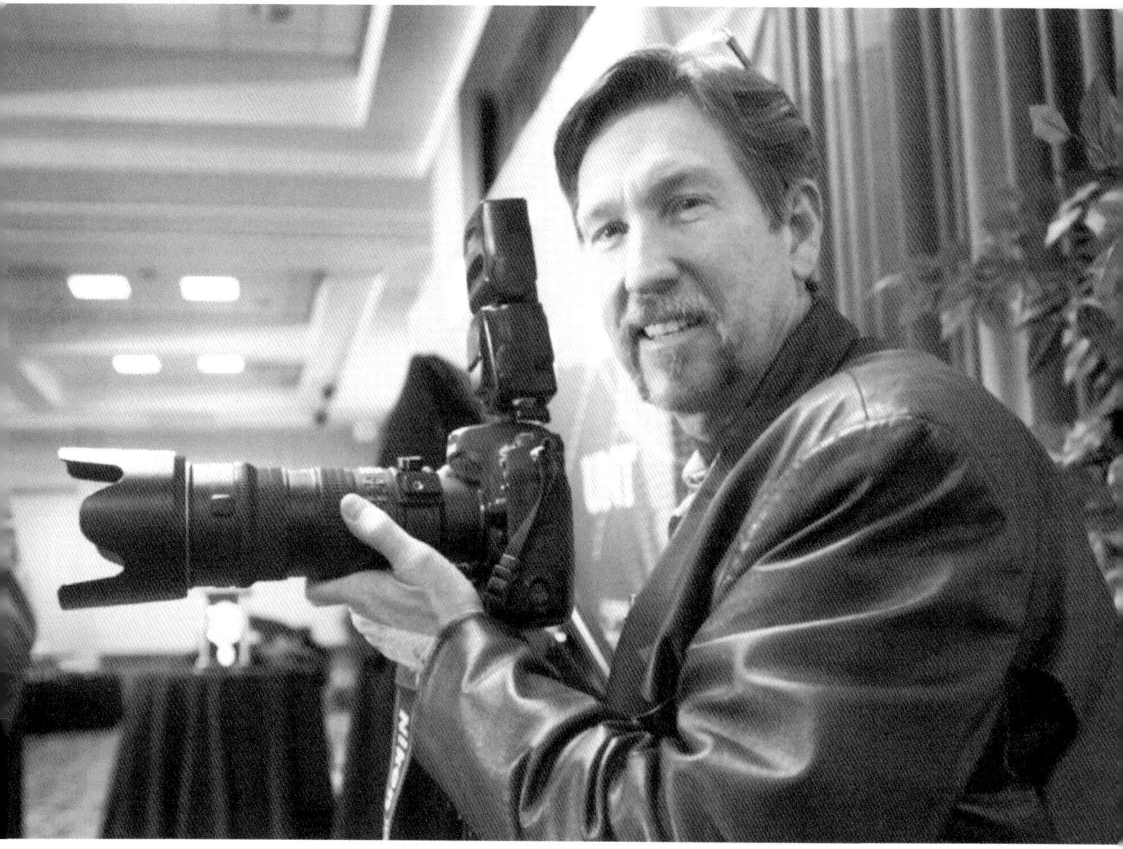

Key Moments

Photojournalist Al Key delights readers of the *Denton Record-Chronicle* with his magical view of their community. Key's photographs unlock his character and personality, while the power and beauty of nature leaves the observer to wonder how he caught those split-second moments on film. His extraordinary photographs also reveal his interests and provide insight into this talented man: a master of patience with a keen sense to catch seemingly spontaneous but carefully crafted images. Al Key has won the Texas Associated Press Managing Editors photojournalism award more than 25 times, a dozen National Press Photographer's Association awards, and twice has been given the Headliner's Foundation Charles E. Green Journalism Award for Photographer of the Year. He presses the shutter, and his viewers are completely immersed in a key moment. A stunning example of Key's art is the photograph at right, which he calls "Reflectricity." (Above, courtesy of Junebug Clark; at right, courtesy of AK.)

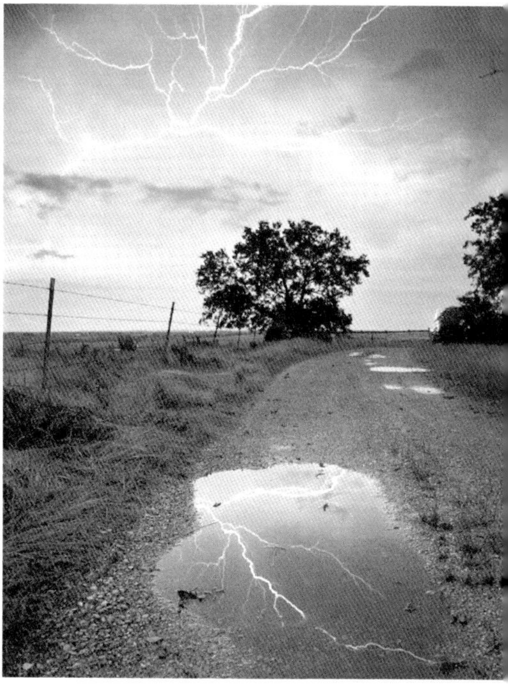

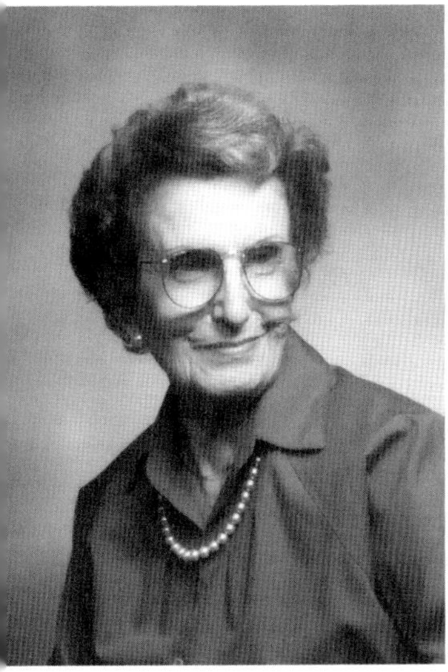

Head Lingerie Designer

Lura Mae Burton Kendrick (1910–2005), who received bachelor's and master's degrees from Texas Woman's University, taught at the university for eight years until 1940. She became vice president and head lingerie designer of Russell-Newman Manufacturing, a position she held for 30 years. Kendrick's interests in the community, particularly the Altrusa Club, Jane Marshall School, Flow Memorial Hospital, Handweavers Club, and the Arts Guild earned her the 1983 Community Arts Recognition Award. Her artistic and design abilities in "various and sundry art forms" led Texas Woman's University to name her distinguished alumna. (Courtesy of Jack Kendrick.)

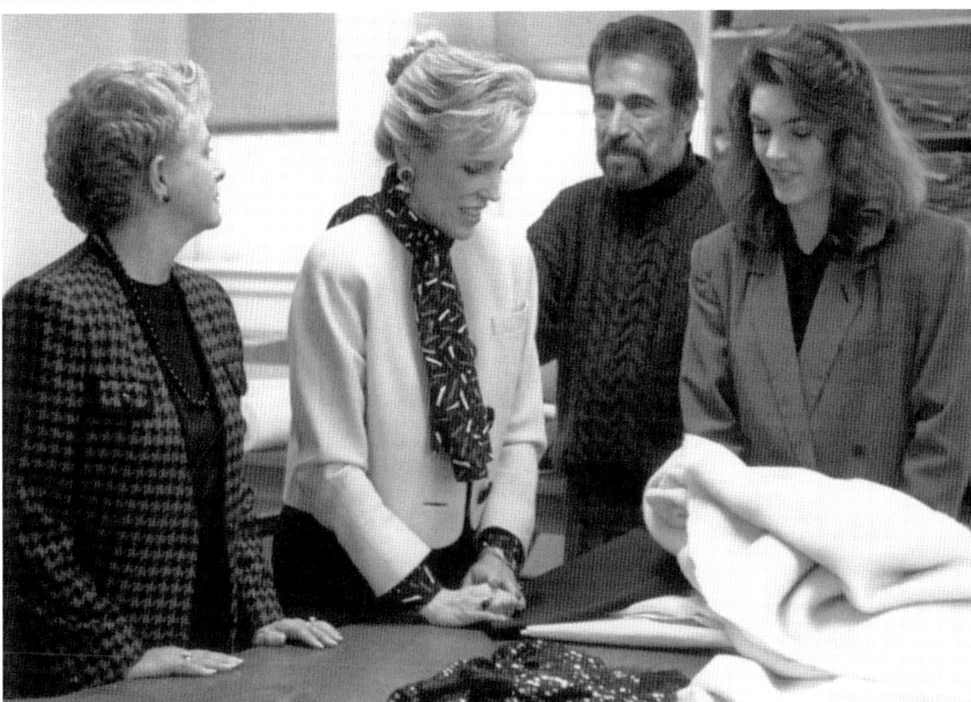

King of the Drop-Dead Dress

Leslie "Les" Wilk (1931–1995) was best known for his formal wear, especially the gowns he designed for Miss Texas and Miss America Pageant contestants. Wilk was appointed director of TWU's Southwest Institute of Design in 1981. The Woman's Collection at the university contains the 1990 inauguration outfits for Texas governor Ann Richards and the wife of Lt. Gov. Bob Bullock. Wilk's work in the Texas fashion industry was important, but his most valuable contribution was as an excellent teacher of fashion students. Wilk is shown here with, from left to right, former TWU president Shirley Chater, Jan Bullock, and student seamstress Shannon-Marie McDonnell. They are looking at the winter-white wool suit made for Governor Richards. (Courtesy of TWU.)

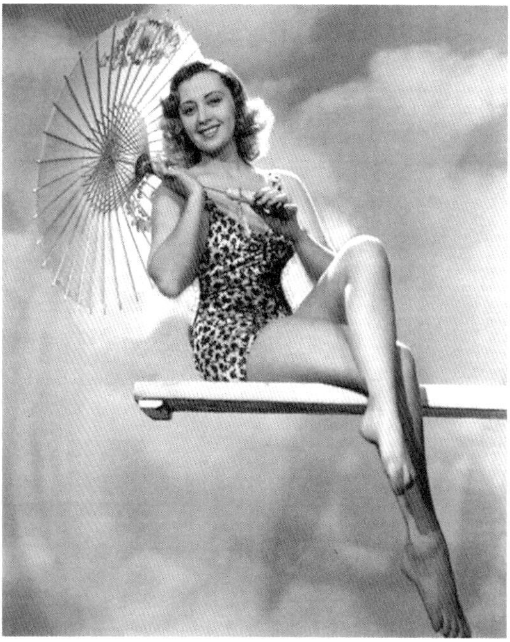

A Rose by Another Name

Rose Joan Blondell (1906–1979) won the Miss Dallas pageant and placed fourth for Miss America under the name Rosebud Blondell. In 1927, she attended North Texas State and performed in the Kiwanis Minstrel Shows and school drama club productions. A Warner Bros. contract led to appearances in television productions and more than 100 movies, two of which were released shortly before her death from leukemia: *Grease* and the remake of *The Champ*. (Courtesy of author.)

America's Oomph-Girl

Clara Lou "Ann" Sheridan (1915–1967) was born in Denton, attended North Texas State, and performed in the Saturday Night Stage Shows and Kiwanis Minstrel Shows. A Hollywood contract resulted from her winning a Paramount beauty contest. Bit parts occupied her career until she changed her name to Ann Sheridan and moved to Warner Bros. There, she was named America's "Oomph-Girl" and she began her 33 years of stardom. She shared the screen with Humphrey Bogart, Errol Flynn, James Cagney, Ronald Reagan, Jimmy Stewart, and Cary Grant. Sheridan starred with James Cagney (left) and Pat O'Brien (right) in the 1940 movie *Torrid Zone*, in which Cagney ad-libbed, "you and that 14-carat oomph." (Courtesy of author.)

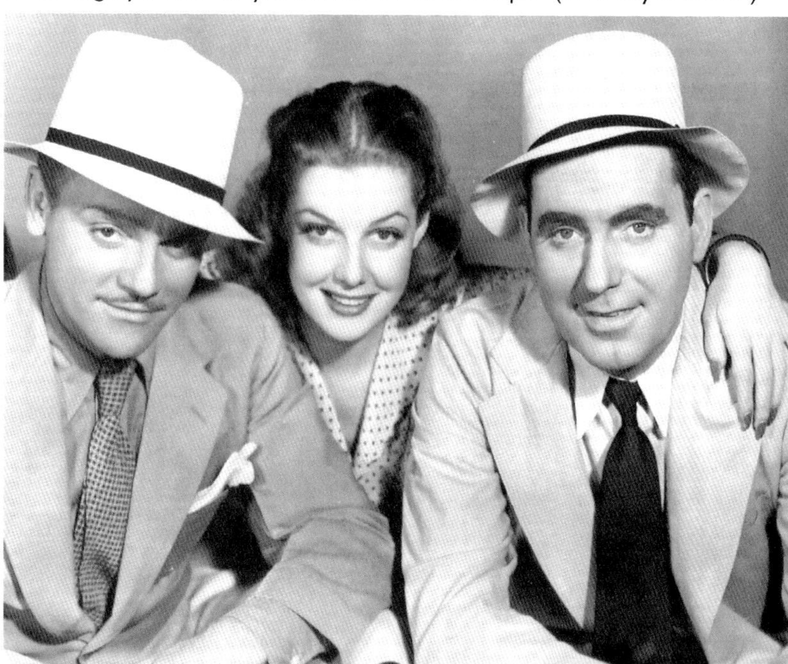

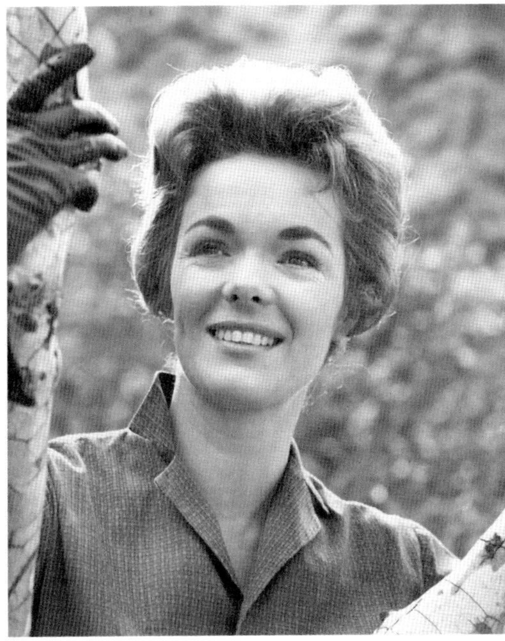

The Great and Magnificent
Nancy Gates, born in Denton in 1926, contracted with RKO at the age of 15. She performed in Denton's Kiwanis Minstrel Shows. Her 1942 film career started with *The Great Gildersleeve* and *The Magnificent Ambersons*. In 1943, she received heroine roles in B-movie Westerns and sci-fi films. Gates appeared in 34 films and serials and 55 television shows, including *Maverick*, *Perry Mason*, *Wagon Train*, *The Mod Squad*, *The Twilight Zone*, *Alfred Hitchcock Presents*, and *Dick Powell's Zane Grey Theatre*. (Courtesy of author.)

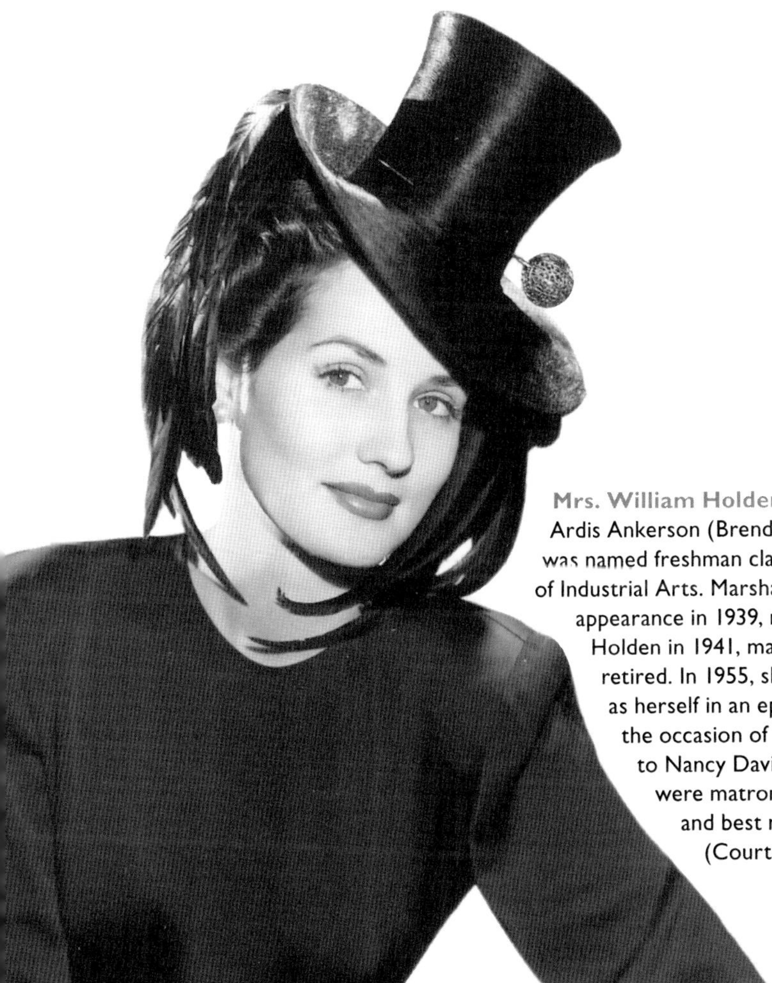

Mrs. William Holden
Ardis Ankerson (Brenda Marshall) (1915–1992) was named freshman class beauty at the College of Industrial Arts. Marshall made her first film appearance in 1939, married actor William Holden in 1941, made five more films, then retired. In 1955, she made an appearance as herself in an episode of *I Love Lucy*. On the occasion of Ronald Reagan's marriage to Nancy Davis in 1952, the sole guests were matron of honor Brenda Marshall and best man William Holden. (Courtesy of author.)

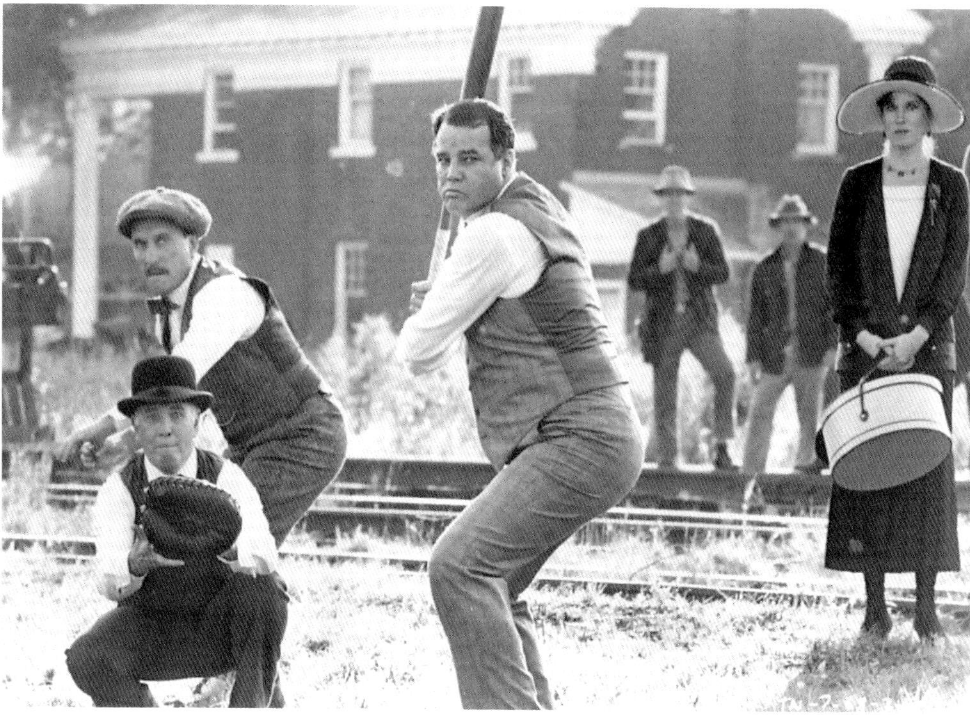

North Texan Walks Tall

Joe Don Baker graduated from North Texas State in 1958 and earned the university's Distinguished Alumnus Award in 1994. His acting credits include more than 45 movies, such as *Walking Tall*, *Cool Hand Luke*, and five James Bond films. His versatile character portrayals landed him such roles as an incorruptible Southern sheriff, a tough police detective, a sadistic mafia hit man, an eccentric intelligence operative, an inquisitive police chief, a Bond villain, a megalomaniacal general, a redneck father, and an aging good ol' boy. Baker, shown in this photograph at bat, played the "Whammer," a role modeled after baseball legend Babe Ruth, in the movie *The Natural*. (Courtesy of DRC.)

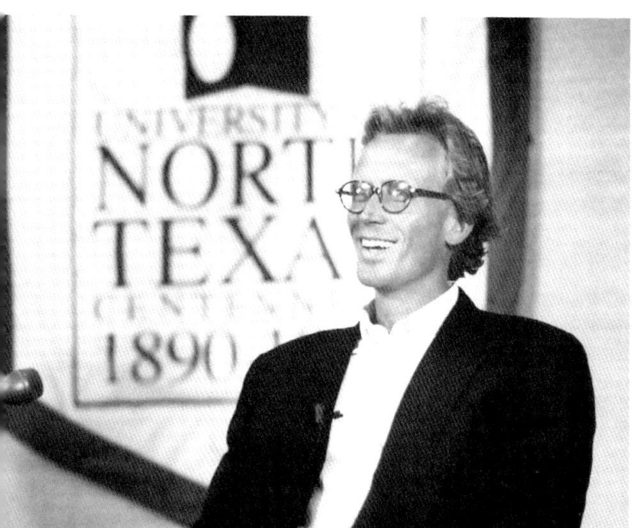

Science Fiction Star

While Peter Weller was enrolled at North Texas State University, he played trumpet in one of the campus bands. He graduated with a bachelor of arts degree in theater in 1969 and began his acting career after graduating from the American Academy of Dramatic Arts. He had roles in more than 50 television series and films, including *Robocop*, *Robocop 2*, and *Star Trek: Enterprise*. He was honored in 2013 with a UNT Distinguished Alumnus Award and was chosen for a 2014 Emerald Eagle Honors for his lifetime contribution to the American landscape. (Courtesy of DRC.)

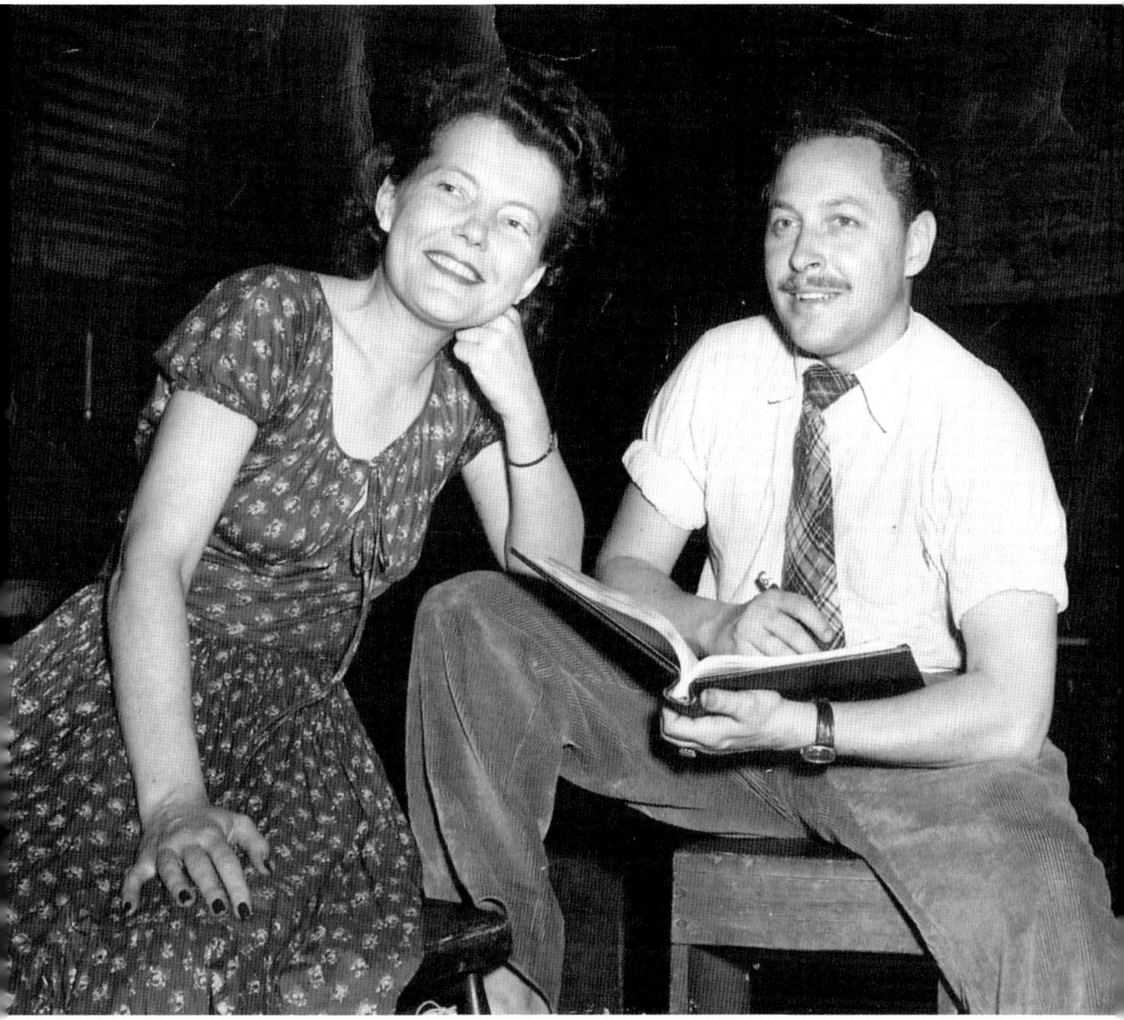

The Texas Tornado

Margaret Virginia "Margo" Jones (1912–1955) received bachelor's and master's degrees from the College of Industrial Arts. Jones's innovative concept of theater-in-the-round and her dynamic directing style earned her the nickname "The Texas Tornado." In 1955, she directed the world premiere of the play *Inherit the Wind* by Jerome Lawrence and Robert Edwin Lee. She also introduced the works of playwrights Tennessee Williams, William Saroyan, and William Inge. The Margo Jones Performance Hall on the TWU campus is named in her honor. Jones staged the first production of Tennessee Williams's 1948 play *Summer and Smoke*. She is shown here with Williams during rehearsal. (Courtesy of DRC.)

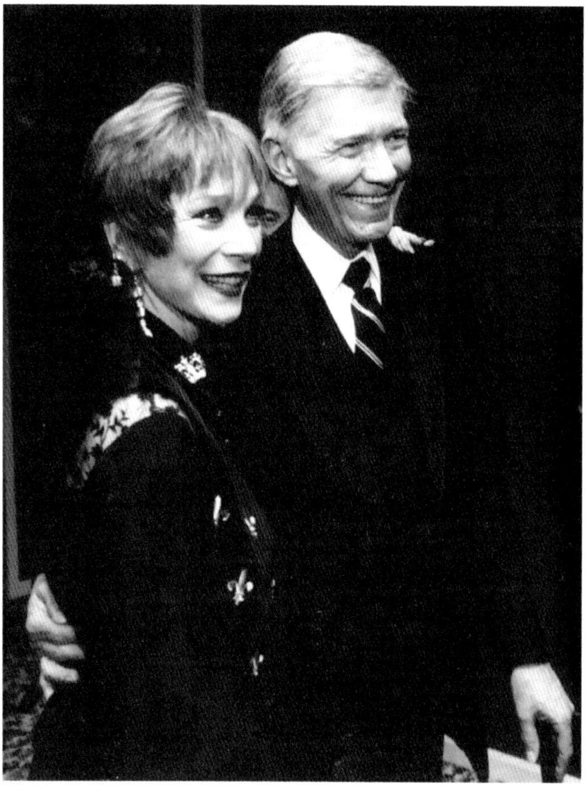

A Star on and off the Stage

Thomas Loyd "Tom" Hughes (1932–1994), producer of the Dallas Summer Musicals since 1961, staged memorable productions such as *Peter Pan* starring Sandy Duncan, *Calamity Jane* with Carol Burnett, and *Hello, Dolly!* starring Carol Channing. He graduated from North Texas State and was a recipient of an honorary doctorate and the Distinguished Alumnus Award from the school. He returned to the North Texas campus each spring to direct and act in a production benefiting drama students. The Gaylord-Hughes Scholarship has awarded more than 150 dance and drama students with full scholarships. Hughes is shown here with actress Shirley MacLaine. (Courtesy of DRC.)

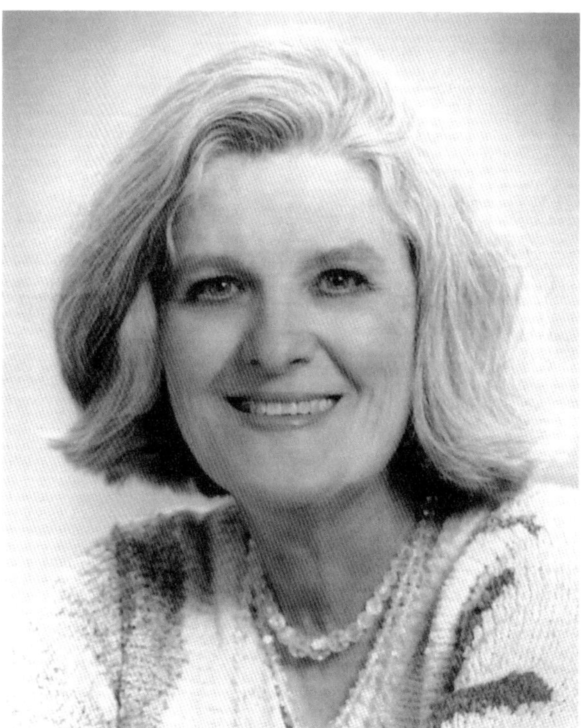

A Very Funny Lady

Rose-Mary Rumbley's unique presentation style has her audiences hooting, hollering, and rolling in the aisles. She does impeccable research on a topic and puts the Rumbley twist on the subject. This fourth-generation Dallasite received her doctorate in communications from North Texas State and, every year, she returns for a Denton Woman's Club fundraiser. The tireless Rumbley has written six books, teaches a theater course, and has appeared in movies. Rumbley married percussionist Jack Rumbley, a One O'Clock Lab Band member, whom she met while they were students at North Texas. (Courtesy of DRC.)

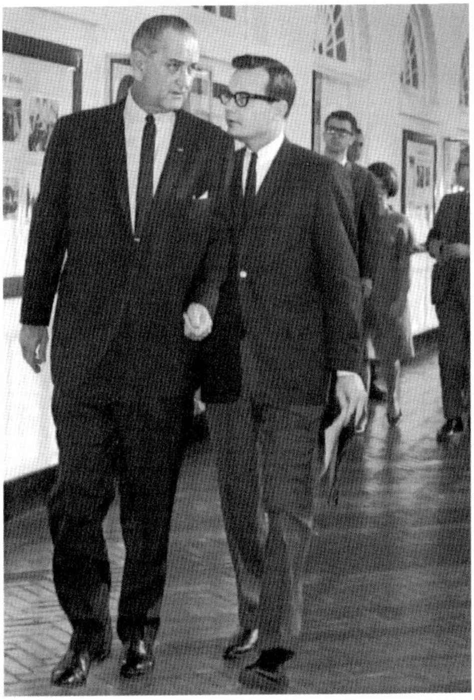

Public Journalist

Going by the name Marshall Bill Moyers (in deference to his hometown of Marshall, Texas), Billy Don Moyers worked as a reporter at KDNT while attending North Texas State. He was studying journalism in 1954 when Sen. Lyndon Baines Johnson offered him an internship in Austin. Moyers was deputy director of the Peace Corps under Pres. John Kennedy, and he served from 1965 to 1967 as White House press secretary under President Johnson. He returned to news reporting thereafter, working in on-air positions at NBC, CBS, and PBS. He most recently hosted *Bill Moyers Journal* on PBS. Moyers retired from broadcasting in 2010. (Courtesy of DRC.)

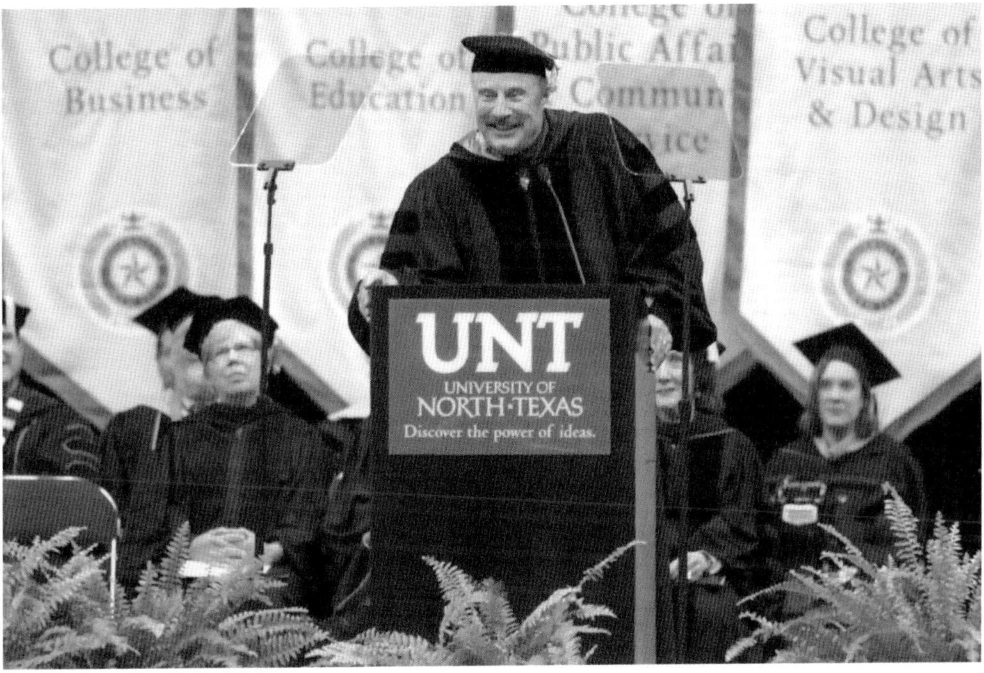

Dr. Phil

Phillip Calvin McGraw earned a PhD in clinical psychology from North Texas State in 1979. After a successful private practice, he joined *The Oprah Winfrey Show* as guest psychologist. His popularity with viewers and his unconventional approach to psychology has resulted in 14 years as host of *Dr. Phil*, an internationally syndicated CBS television show. (Courtesy of DRC.)

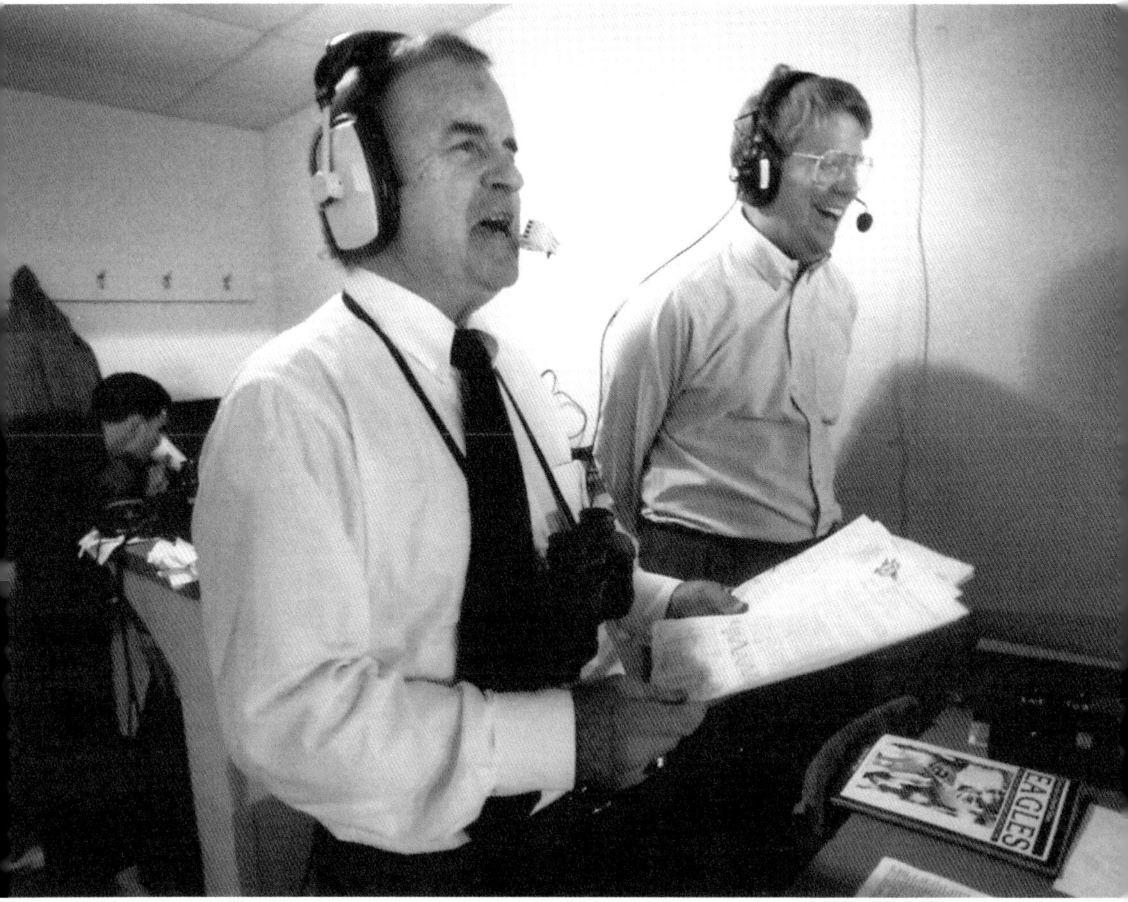

Voice of the Mean Green

Broadcasting legend William A. "Bill" Mercer was the play-by-play voice of University of North Texas Mean Green football and basketball from 1959 to 1994. When hired, Mercer was working for KRLD-TV in Dallas. Mercer was the announcer in 1959 at North Texas when Abner Haynes and Leon King broke the color barrier in Texas football. During his time at UNT, Mercer called games involving Kevin Adkisson, who later became one of the legendary Von Erich brothers in professional wrestling. In addition, Mercer was the voice of the Dallas Cowboys, the Texas Rangers, and the Von Erich–run World Class Championship Wrestling. Mercer also taught broadcasting courses at the university for more than three decades. The university named the press box at Apogee Stadium in Mercer's honor. Mercer (left) is shown here in the Fouts Field press box with fellow play-by-play announcer George Dunham. (Courtesy of DRC.)

CHAPTER FIVE

Superstars of Education

The mind is not a vessel that needs filling, but wood that needs igniting.

—Plutarch

Denton has emphasized the importance of education from the earliest subscription schools in 1858, public elementary and high schools in the 1860s, the establishment of an African American school as early as 1876 and its independent school district in 1881, the organization in 1890 of its first college, and the addition of its second college in 1903. The African American Fred Douglas[s] and Fred Moore schools had dedicated, highly qualified principals and teachers. The Denton Independent School District was integrated in 1969.

In 1890, the Denton city council accepted a donation of 10 acres for the site of a Normal College building. Construction of the first campus building began in January 1891 and was completed that summer. During its 125-year history, the University of North Texas (UNT) underwent seven name changes, reflecting the institution's growth: Texas Normal College and Teacher Institute (TNC) (1890), North Texas Normal College (NTNC) (1894), North Texas State Normal College (NTSNC) (1901), North Texas State Teachers College (NTSTC) (1923), North Texas State College (NTSC) (1949), North Texas State University (NTSU) (1961), and the University of North Texas (UNT) (1988).

A charter was granted for a second college in Denton in 1901, with the first classes held in 1903. Texas Woman's University (TWU) has undergone five name changes during its existence, reflecting a transition from an all-women's industrial college to a coed university. The names of the school were as follows: Texas Industrial Institute and College for the Education of the White Girls of the State of Texas in Arts and Sciences (1901), Girls Industrial College of Texas (GIC) (1903), College of Industrial Arts (CIA) (1905), Texas State College for Women (TSCW) (1934), and Texas Woman's University (TWU) (1957).

The educators and administrators who worked tirelessly to achieve excellence for students attending Denton's pubic schools and universities make up a roster of intelligence, discipline, and fortitude. Fred Moore and Alice Moore Alexander strived to bring quality education to African American children. Public-school teachers, such as Ema Ruth Russell and A.O. Calhoun, prepared students for life. Administrators, such as Drs. Mary Evelyn Blagg Huey and Alfred F. Hurley, grew enrollments and scholarships at their universities while assuring high-quality education. The public schools and universities have ignited the minds of internationally renowned musicians, writers, business owners, scientists, educators, and two Miss Americas.

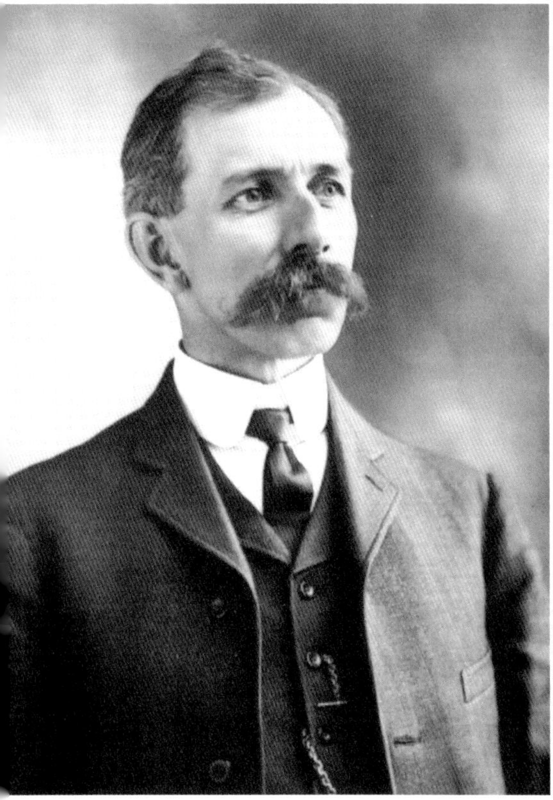

First President of Texas Woman's University

Cree Telford Work (1867–1949), first president of the Girls Industrial College (1903–1910), expressed his philosophy that the college would give "culture of the highest order, scholarship of the most efficient kind, and domestic and industrial training of the most modern and practical type . . . training women who will be competent, intelligent and refined, well-fitted for self-support." Work's philosophy continues to guide the institution to this day. (Courtesy of TWU.)

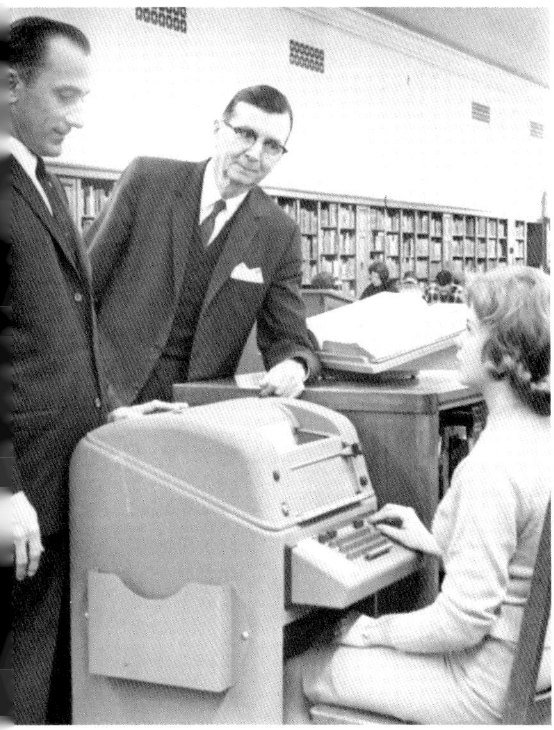

Passion for Higher Education

Although Joshua Chilton was the first president of Texas Normal College, James Carl "J.C." Matthews (1901–1996) led the way in the 1950s to the school becoming financially viable and attaining its status as a research institution. His 47-year career at North Texas spanned from his days as a student (class of 1925), to instructor and director of the Demonstration School, professor of education, director of student teaching, dean of education, and then vice president. In 1951, Matthews (center) was named the university's eighth president and served for 16 years. His legacy includes implementing the first doctoral education program in 1951, overseeing desegregation in the 1950s, and presiding during the change from North Texas State College to North Texas State University. Matthews instilled a passion for achieving higher education in three generations of his family—3 children, 10 grandchildren, and 16 great-grandchildren. Numerous other extended family members also attended the university. (Courtesy of UNT.)

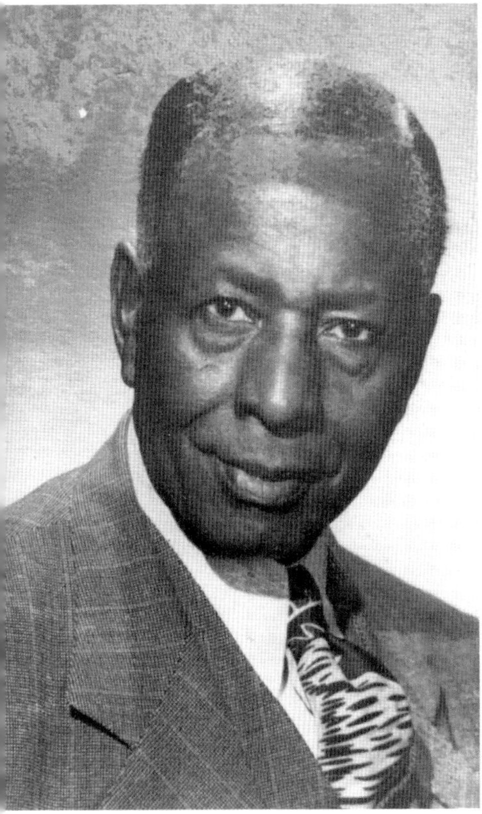

African American Educational Leader

Denton-born Fred Douglas Moore (1875–1953) was adopted by his stepfather after his father abandoned his mother before Fred's birth. He graduated from Prairie View State Normal and became an educational leader for nearly 40 years. He was the city's first African American principal. Before becoming principal of Fred Douglas[s] School, he operated a barbershop. When the school was named for him, Moore exclaimed, "I am happier than the president of the United States." Fred Moore Park and Fred Moore School are named in his honor. (Courtesy of DRC.)

Following in Her Father's Footsteps

Alice Moore Alexander (1907–2007) followed the path of her father, Fred Moore, and became a beloved schoolteacher at Fred Douglas[s] School. She graduated from Texas College, Tyler, and obtained a master's degree from Texas Southern University, Houston. "Miss Alice" taught kindergarten and first grade in the Denton school district for 45 years. She was active in the county historical commission and with her church until she passed away at age 100. (Courtesy of DRC.)

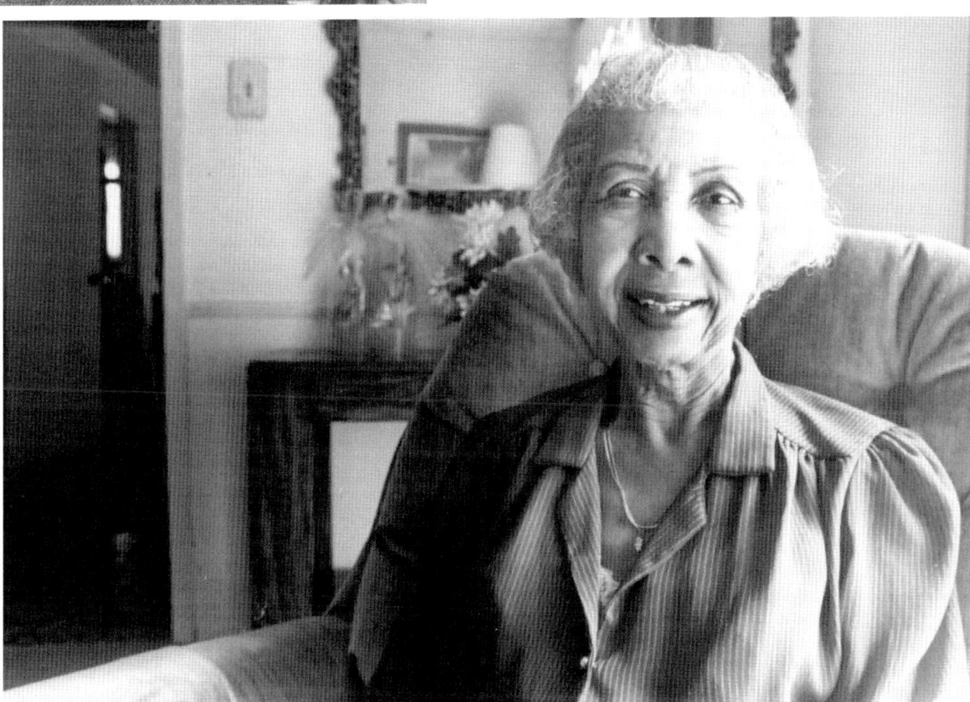

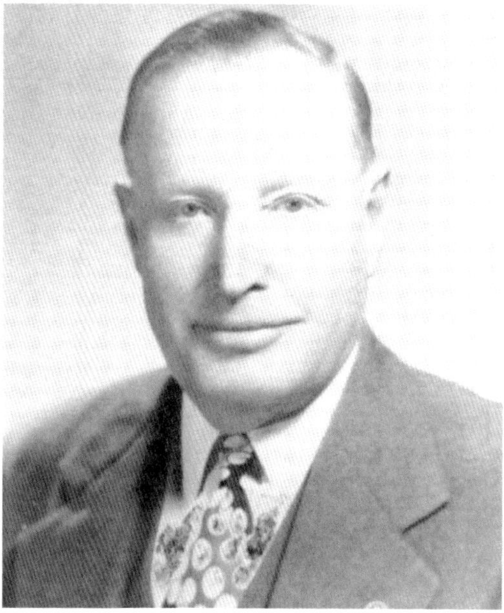

"Prof" Calhoun

A middle school is named after Amos O'Neil "A.O." Calhoun (1891–1973). Situated on Congress Street in Denton, the building opened in 1924 as a high school and was renamed Calhoun Junior High School in honor of "Prof" Calhoun, principal for 33 years until he retired at the end of the 1956–1957 school year. It became Calhoun Middle School in 1992 and remains so today. There is agreement in the community that the red brick building on Congress is a grand old school, named after a grand administrator. Former students of the school describe their beloved "Prof" as "a level-headed man who was always there for the students and teachers" and "a fair man who was not afraid to make a judgment." (Courtesy of DRC.)

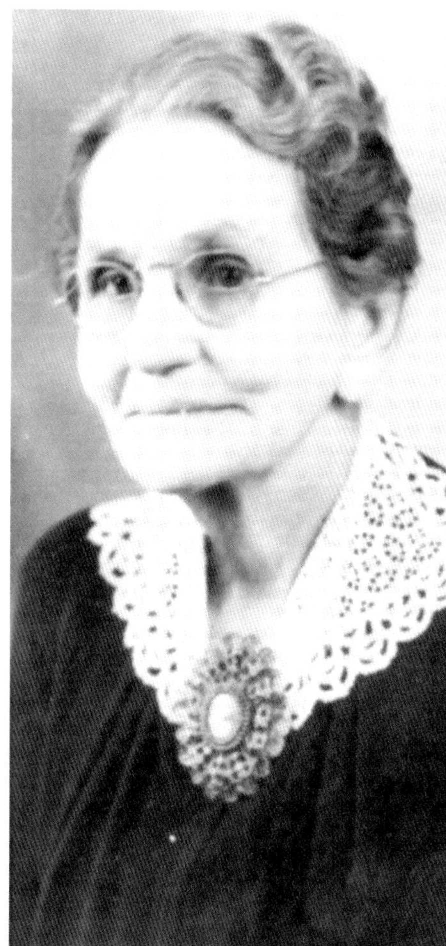

Preserving and Teaching Self-Sufficiency

Edna Westbrook Trigg (1868–1946) was a pioneer leader of Texas women in rural club work. The US Agricultural Department asked Trigg in 1911 to supervise Texas's first Girls' Tomato Club. After legislation was enacted establishing the Agricultural Extension Service at land grant colleges, Trigg became the first county home demonstration agent in Texas in 1916. Stationed in Denton, she also served on staff of the College of Industrial Arts, overseeing courses in home demonstration. Under her direction, Denton County became one of the top Texas counties in canned-food production. Trigg organized girls' clubs throughout the county and worked to increase scholarship funding for rural girls. (Courtesy of DCOHC.)

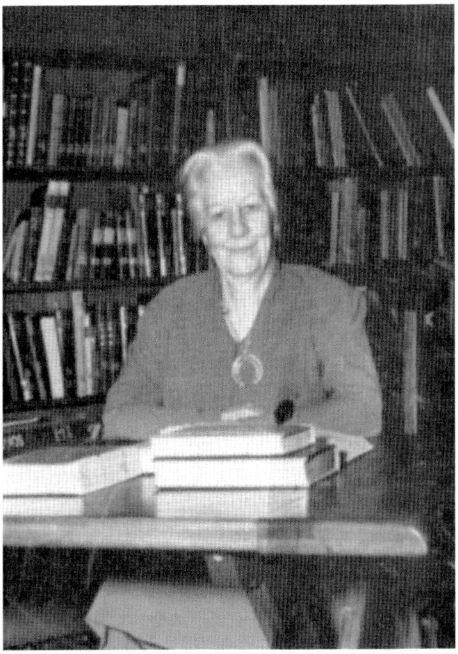

Mary Marshall Arts
Mary Marshall (1878–1959) began her career at College of Industrial Arts in 1916 as associate professor of art. She was promoted to chairman of the art department in 1930, having just moved into her new home at 1819 Bell Avenue. The home was the first design by O'Neil Ford, whom Marshall had met when he was a student at Denton High School. In 1943, five years before she retired, Marshall became aware of the great need for professional occupational therapists brought about by the ravages of World War II. She developed a course in that therapy at the university, which is recognized today as the largest occupational therapy school in the United States. (Courtesy of TWU.)

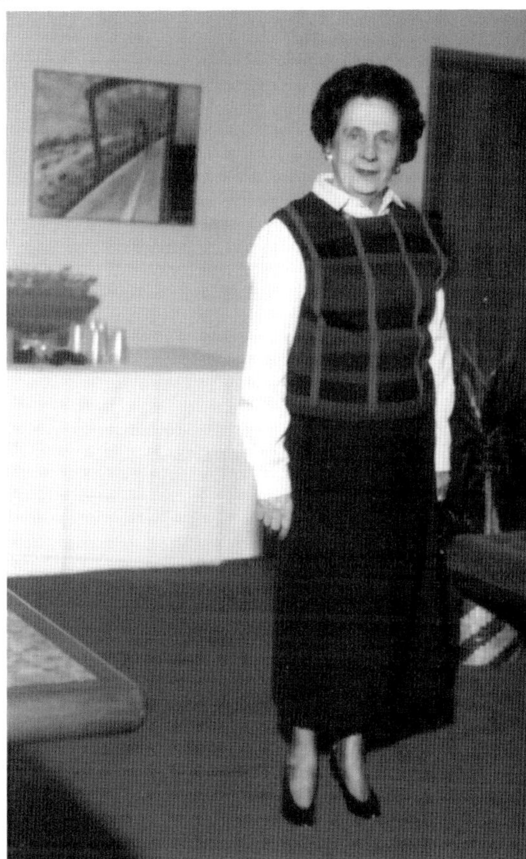

Gracious and Generous and Good Scout
Gertrude Gibson (1910–2004), nicknamed "Miss TWU," worked at Texas Woman's University for 53 years until her 1987 retirement. She worked in the offices of the dean of women, admissions, registrar, and development. She signed her notes and messages "GG," which her friends variously defined as Good and Generous, Gregarious and Garrulous, Genteel and Glamorous, Gracious Giver, and Go-Getter. Gibson purchased the Marshall house. Upon her death, she donated her home to the university as a guesthouse for visitors. Gibson was given the Good Scout Award by the Boys Scouts of America. (Courtesy of TWU.)

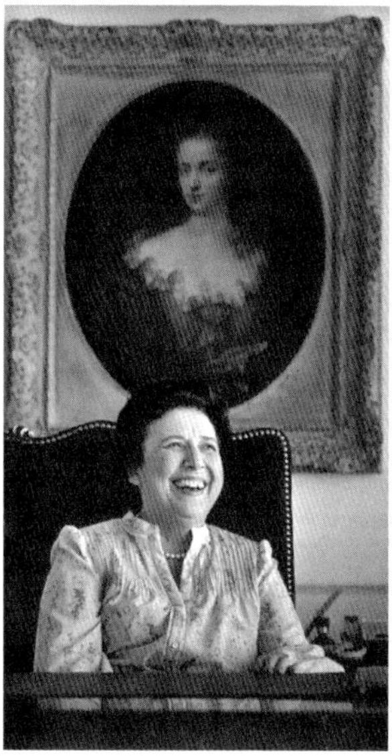

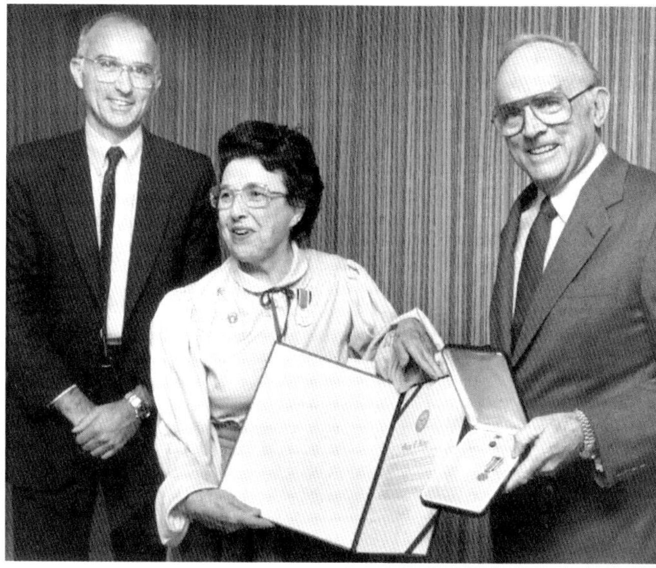

Portrait of a "First Lady"

Mary Evelyn Blagg Huey governed as the first woman and only alumna president of Texas Woman's University from 1977 until 1986 after serving as dean of the graduate school and a professor of government. The Governor's Commission for Women inaugurated the Texas Women's Hall of Fame in 1984, and Huey, Lady Bird Johnson, and Barbara Jordan were three of the first twelve women recognized. Retired from presidential duties, Huey edited *Traditions* for the university's centennial in 2001. The same year, she received the Lifetime Achievement Award from the Alumnae Association. Her connection to the Texas Women's Hall of Fame reappeared in 2003, when the university opened its State Hall of Fame Museum, honoring 114 women. The new library Huey had fought so hard for during her presidency bears her name. Huey's community honors include the Otis Fowler Award and lifetime board membership for United Way of Denton County.

Active as a member of the Nature Conservancy, Huey was a Texas director for 10 years. She has lifetime membership in the Native Plant Society of Texas, of which she is a founding member. A ruling elder of the First Presbyterian Church, Huey became a missionary to the Good Shepherd Hospital in Kananga, Zaire. An honorary colonel in the US Army herself, Huey headed the committee to build the All War Memorial, a tribute to Denton County war veterans. As chair of the Defense Advisory Committee on Women in the Service from 1983 until 1986, she was awarded the Secretary of Defense Medal for Outstanding Public Service. In the right photograph, she is shown with assistant secretary of defense Lawrence Korb (left) and deputy secretary of defense Paul Thayer. In 2003, Dr. Huey received the Mildred and Taylor Hawk Award, which recognizes recipients' extraordinary contributions in preservation of Denton County's history. In her case, it highlighted her active years as Denton County Historical Commission chairman. Her spectacular accomplishments included the reorganization and refurbishing of the Courthouse-on-the-Square Museum. (Courtesy of DRC.)

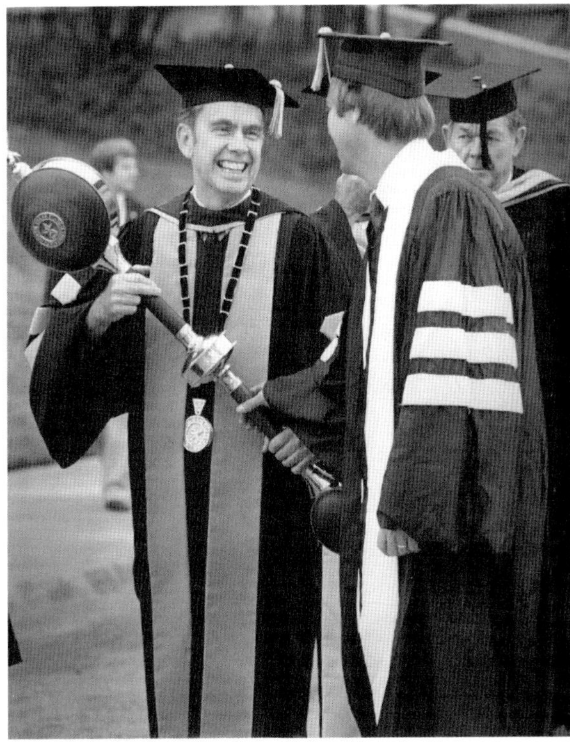

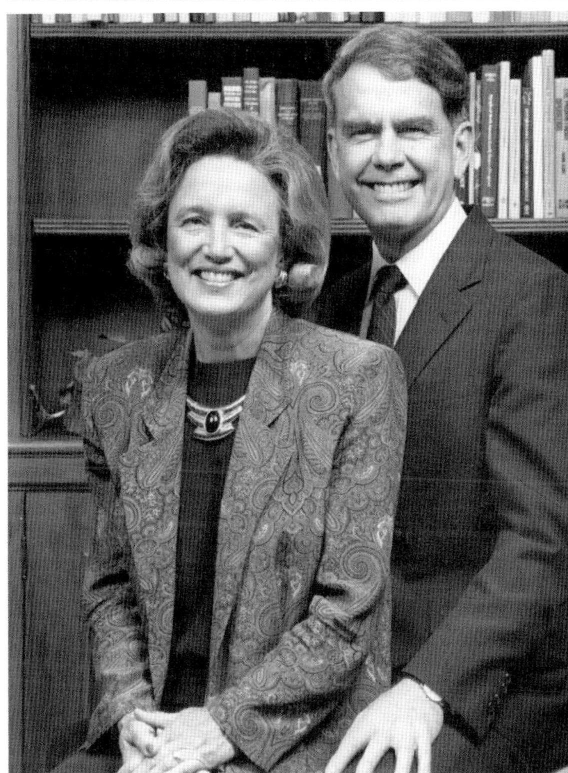

Unsung Hero of Higher Education

Alfred F. Hurley (1928–2013) had a distinguished 30-year military career and was a professor at the Air Force Academy before coming to the University of North Texas in 1980 as professor of history and vice president for administrative affairs. He was appointed president and system chancellor of the university and health science center in 1982, serving for 18 years, the longest-serving president to date. Hurley is credited with rebranding the university into a top-tier public research institution, significant enrollment increases, and substantial growth in construction, research funding, and the endowment fund. Under his governance, the university's standing as an academic institution was elevated through the creation of the Texas Academy of Mathematics and Science, a residential, research-oriented program for gifted high school students to attend college while finishing high school. Hurley gave his wife, Johanna, credit for his successful leadership, and the university recognized their efforts in 2002, when the administration building was renamed the Alfred F. and Johanna H. Hurley Administration Building. The couple is seen in the below photograph. The *Dallas Morning News* highlighted Hurley as an "unsung hero of higher education," noting that his chief legacy "was his willingness to take risks to expand higher education." In the above photograph, Hurley (left) holds the university mace. Visible in the background is Walt Parker, vice president for external affairs. (Both, courtesy of DRC.)

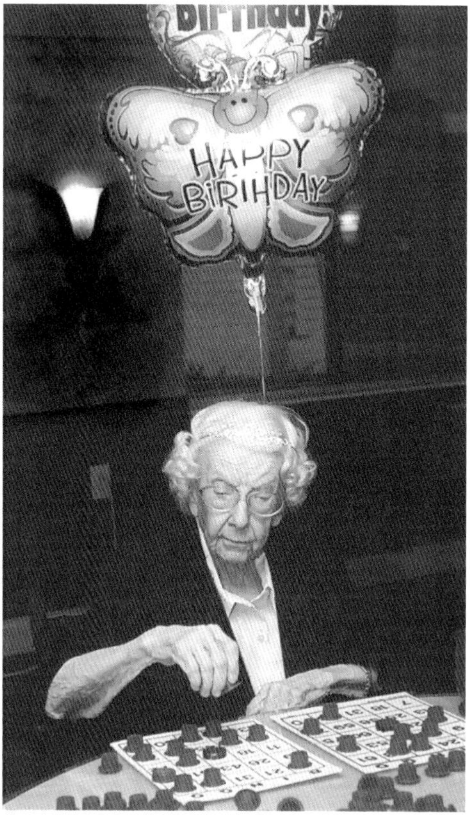

Force of Nature for the Arts
Ema Ruth Russell (1908–2012) directed high school choral programs that won state competitions in her hometown of Denton for 15 years. After retirement, Russell devoted more than 40 years as an active leader of the arts. She was founding member of the Denton Community Chorus and the Greater Denton Arts Council, as well as cofounder of the Arts Guild. Since its inception, the guild has raised more than $1 million for the arts. In 1981, Russell won the Community Arts Recognition Award. She was recognized again in 1985, when the Center for Visual Arts' rehearsal hall was named in her honor. (Courtesy of DRC.)

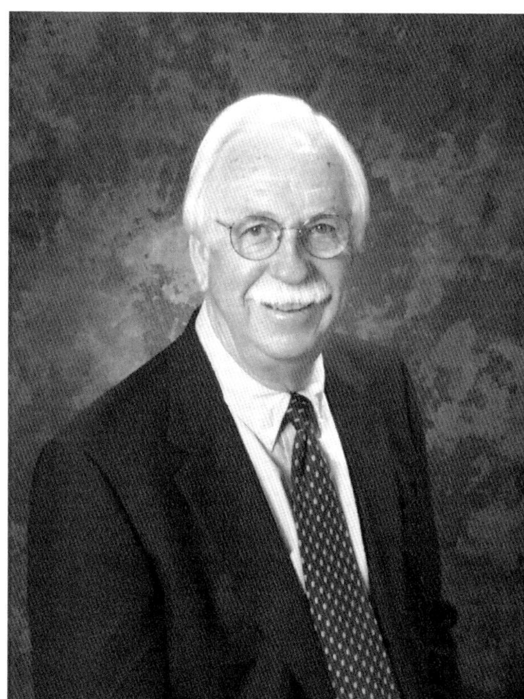

Art Educator Extraordinaire
D. Jack Davis began his career at North Texas State as professor of art in 1971. During his 33-year tenure, he served as Department of Art chairman, associate vice president for academic affairs, vice provost, and dean of the College of Visual Arts before stepping down in 2004. Following retirement, he functioned as the director of the North Texas Institute for Educators on the Visual Arts, which helps train art teachers. He was awarded the Greater Denton Arts Council's Community Arts Recognition Award for arts education and the National Art Educator of the Year Award. (Courtesy of UNT.)

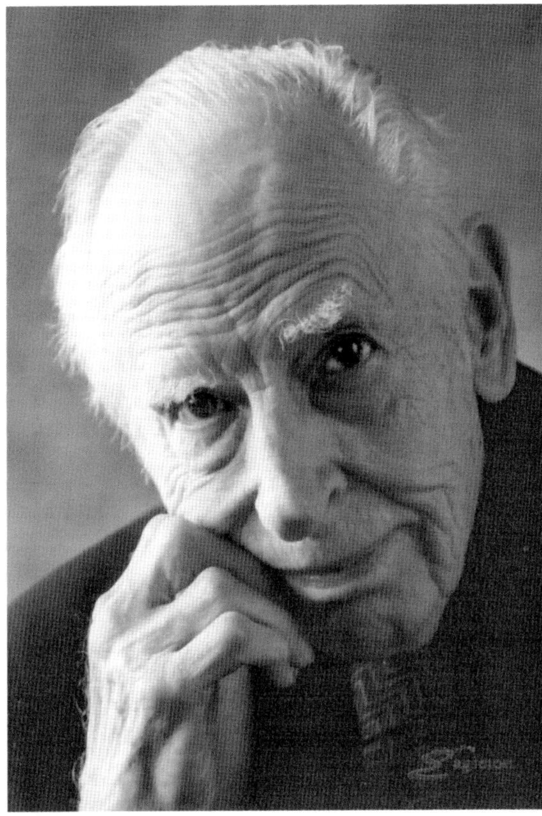

Outstanding Music Theorist
Robert W. Ottman (1914–2005) earned a doctorate from North Texas State in 1956 and became an internationally renowned music theorist. His 12 textbooks are used worldwide. During his 35-year North Texas appointment, he served as professor of music theory, chairman of the theory department, and conductor of the Madrigal Singers. He and his wife, Shirley, donated a French baroque-style organ for the university's main auditorium. He was awarded the 2004 President's Citation for extraordinary service to the university. (Courtesy of Walter Eagleton.)

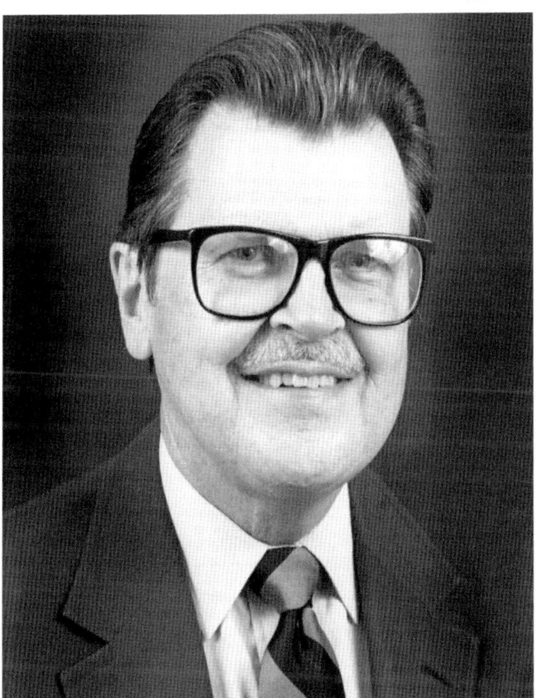

Teacher, Translator, and Collaborative Artist
Harold Heiberg (1922–2013), professor of music at the University of North Texas for 33 years, was a gentleman of the utmost dignity and artistic distinction. As a teacher, collaborative artist, and accompanist, his impact upon hundreds of North Texas students and faculty colleagues was immeasurable. Heiberg has translated more than 250 choral and operatic works in English versions from German, Italian, and French. (Courtesy of UNT.)

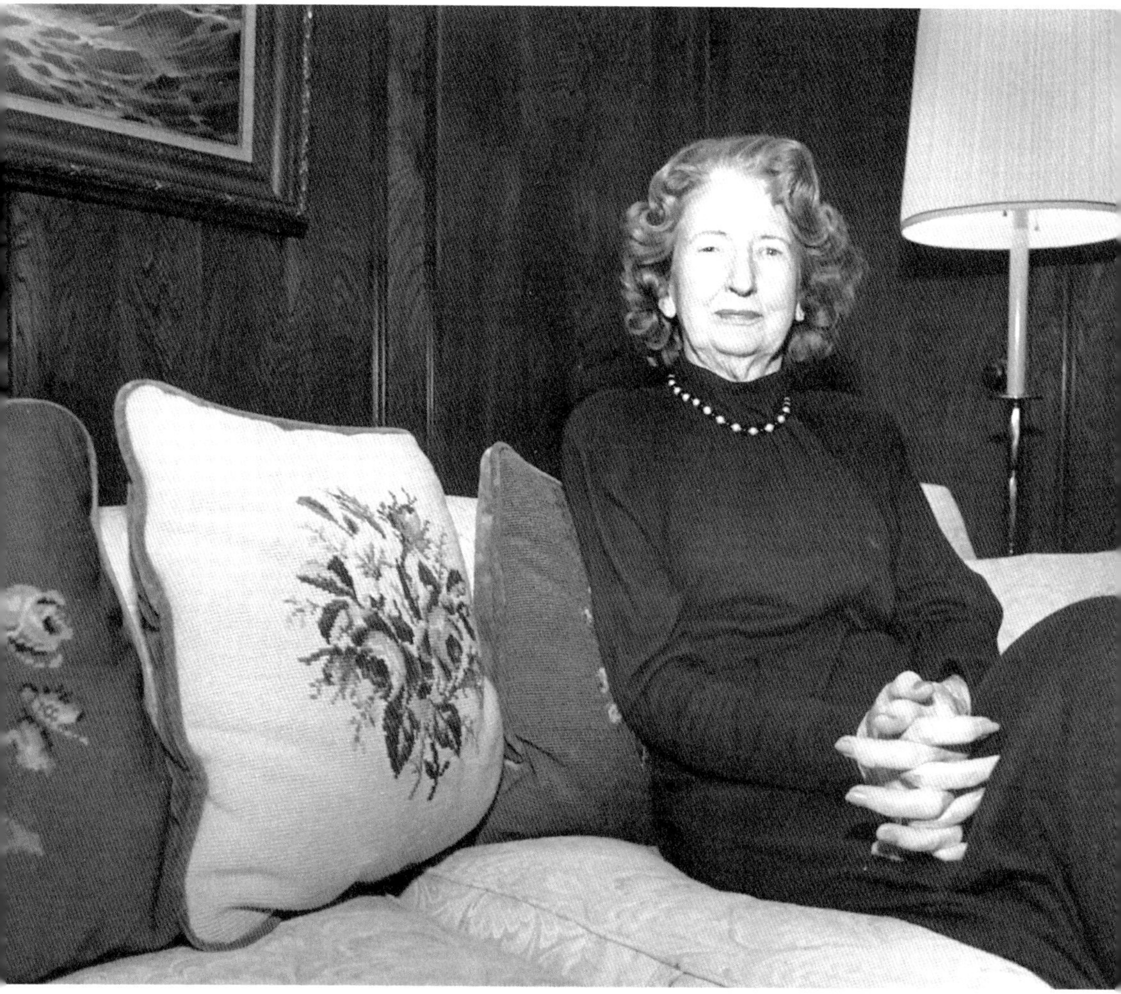

No Bamboozling Big Red

Imogene Bentley Dickey Mohat (1909–2000) taught in the Paris public schools and served as dean of Paris Junior College before coming to North Texas State Teachers College in 1943. Mohat garnered the respect, admiration, and fear of her girls during her 24-year career as dean of women at North Texas until she returned to teaching English full time. Colleagues, students, and the city honored Mohat during her long and distinguished career. She was beloved, brilliant, and could not be bamboozled by the stories of the students who snuck in late from dates. She also was affectionately called "Big Red," due to her statuesque posture and flaming red hair. (Courtesy of DRC.)

CHAPTER SIX

Superstars of Athletics

If you believe in yourself, have dedication and pride and never quit, you'll be a winner. The price of victory is high, but so are the rewards.

—Paul "Bear" Bryant

Friday Night Lights, a book later turned into a movie and a popular television program, portrays the mania of high school football in Texas. However, many Denton athletes managed to go beyond the hype to become young men and women not only of athletic ability, but also possessing finely honed business and leadership skills after the crowd "no longer roared."

The goal of the athletic ideal is a "healthy mind and a healthy body." From earliest times, it was believed that there was a link between the development of the mind, body, and spirit. This included the idea that a well-educated person would be instructed in all three areas.

Denton's high schools and universities produced many athletes who moved on to professional careers, some with international recognition. Integration of North Texas State in the 1950s led to opportunities for several students to become professional football players, such as Abner Haynes, Leon King, and Joe Greene. The courage and sense of fairness that was exhibited by coaches, such as Odus Mitchell and Fred McCain, led to North Texas State being one of the first schools to break the interracial barrier in college sports. Mitchell and Hayden Fry took the North Texas Mean Green to new heights.

Championship high school coaches, such as Curtis Collins, instilled in young athletes many character-building traits that would serve them well later in life. Among the lessons these young people were taught were the following: give it everything you have, prepare in body and mind, stay on task and get the job done, work with others to complete a goal, and manage time so as to have a well-balanced life of work, family, and friends.

Winning golf teams produced PGA golf champions, an award-winning gymnastics program claimed an Olympic gold medal winner, and a family of brothers created a wrestling dynasty.

Athletics do indeed teach much beyond winning on the field. This chapter highlights some of the amateur and professional players, as well as their teachers, who have brought honor and victory to their hometown.

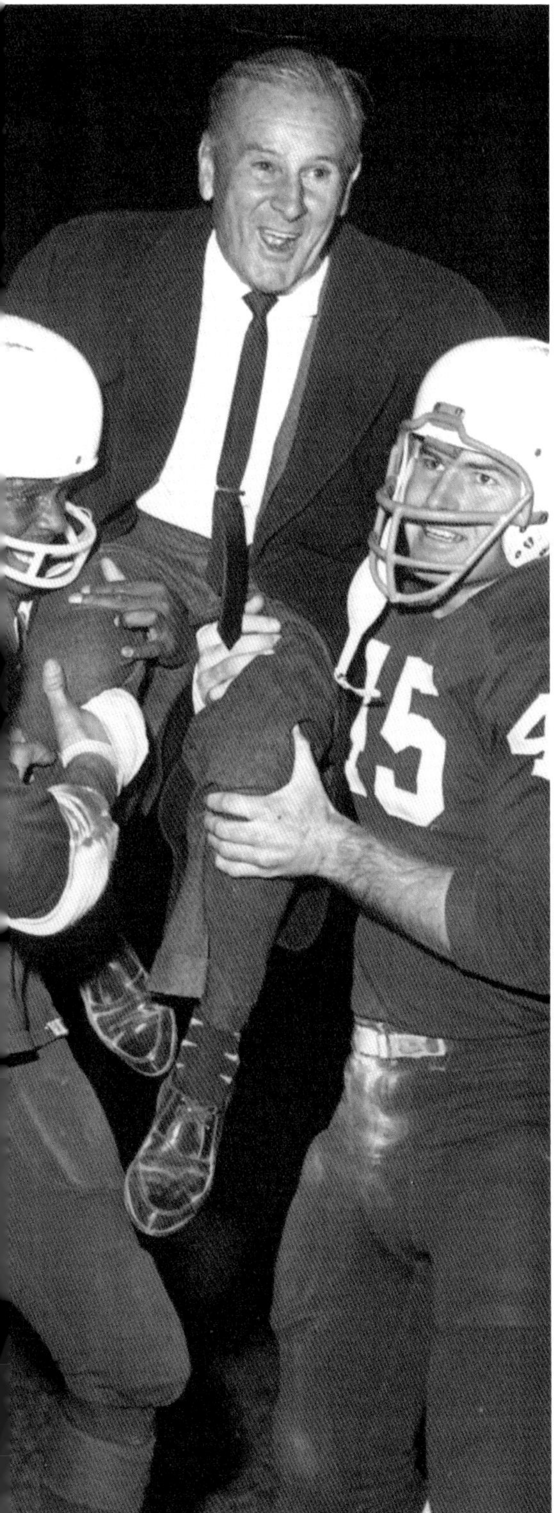

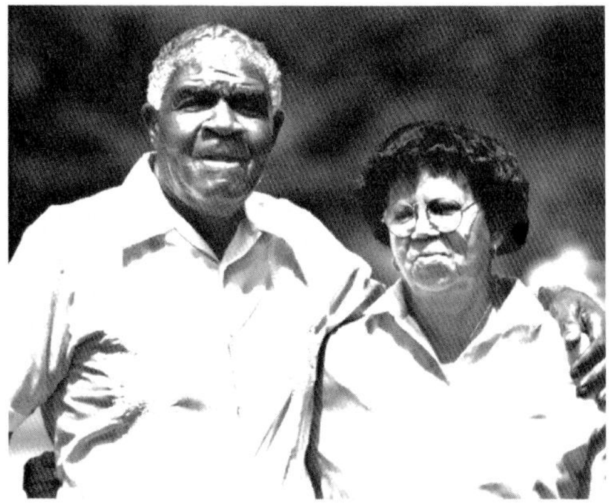

Legendary Coach (ABOVE)
Curtis H. Collins Sr. (1920–1996) is a legend because of the impact he made on so many lives as a coach and administrator. Collins came to Denton in 1954 as the football, basketball, and track coach for the Fred Moore High School Dragons. His teams won seven district titles and went to four state playoffs. In 1967, Collins helped integrate Fred Moore High School with Denton High. He continued coaching and was dean of students at Denton High until his 1986 retirement. The new DISD athletic facility was named the C.H. Collins Athletic Complex in his honor. Shown here with his wife, Esta, Collins exhibited integrity, honesty, ambition, character, and leadership to his students and family. (Courtesy of DCOHC.)

Winning Coach 42 Years (LEFT)
James Odus Mitchell (1899–1989) was a successful coach both at the high school and collegiate levels, amassing a 289-129-17 record during his 42-year coaching career. Mitchell was head football coach at North Texas State College from 1946 until 1966, compiling a record of 122-85-9. From 1946 to 1952, the Mean Green enjoyed seven consecutive winning seasons, a school record. Mitchell's teams played in three bowl games and earned 10 conference championships. He was named National Coach of the Year in 1966, and in 1986, he was inducted into the Texas Sports Hall of Fame. (Courtesy of UNT.)

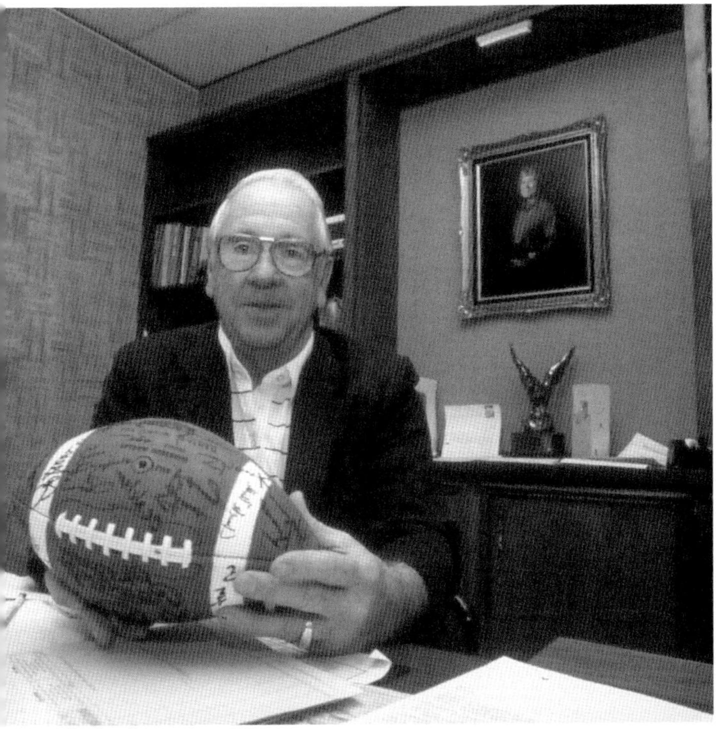

Breaking the Barrier
Fred Noel McCain (1923–2013) was a major force in the development of the North Texas State athletic program. McCain was quarterback of the teams that went to the Optimist Bowl, the Salad Bowl, and had a record 10-win season. He joined Odus Mitchell's staff as assistant football coach, helping break the color barrier by recruiting Abner Haynes and Leon King to the program in 1956. During his 37-year career, McCain served as director of athletics twice and was inducted into the university's 1987 Athletic Hall of Fame. (Courtesy of DRC.)

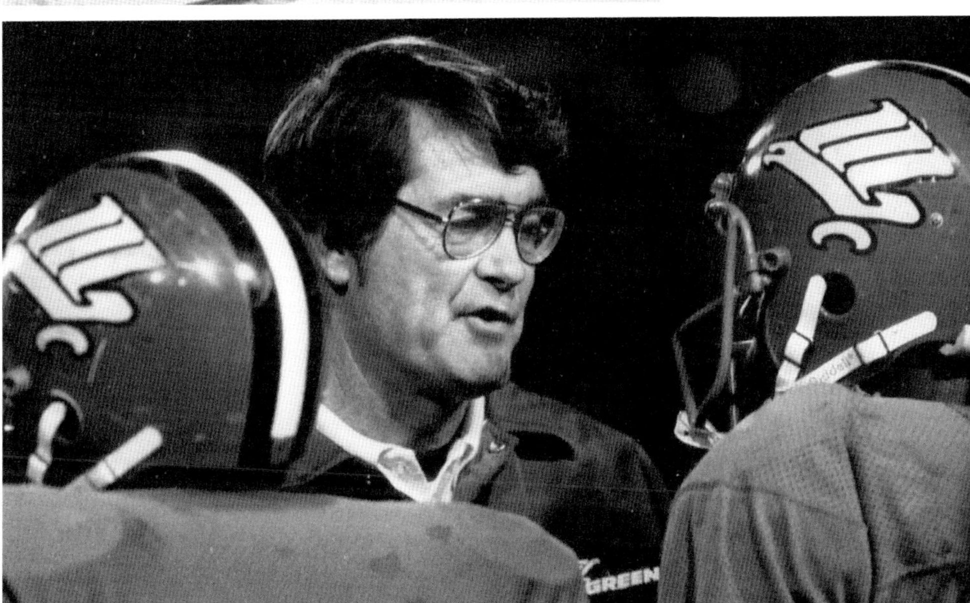

Coach
John Hayden Fry turned around North Texas State's failing football program, compiling a 40-23-3 record over six seasons. Fry left in 1978 to become the University of Iowa's head coach. The title character of the television show *Coach*, starring Craig T. Nelson as "Hayden Fox," was loosely based on Hayden Fry. One of Fry's assistant coaches at Iowa, Dan McCarney, is now the head coach at the University of North Texas. (Courtesy of DRC.)

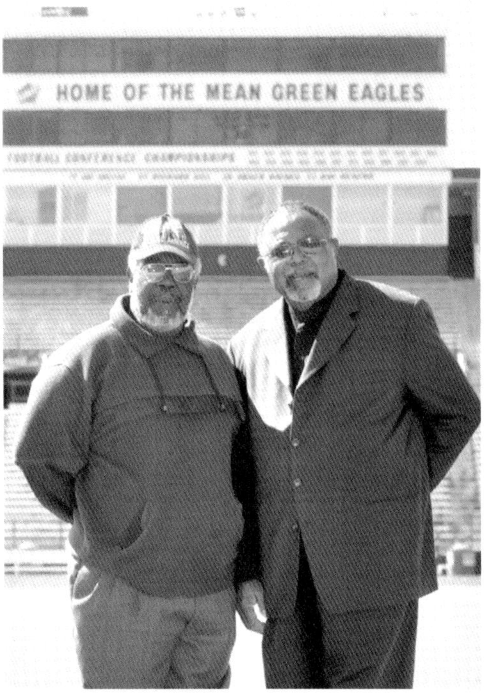

Hero of Football
Abner Haynes and Leon A. King became the first African American students in Texas to break the color barrier for intercollegiate sports at North Texas State in 1956. Haynes went on to play with the Dallas Texans, Kansas City Chiefs, Denver Broncos, Miami Dolphins, and New York Jets. He is one of a few athletes who played high school, college, and professional football in North Texas. His program Heroes of Football connects former professional players with their communities. Haynes (left) teamed up again with King at the home of the Mean Green Eagles at Fouts Field. (Courtesy of DRC.)

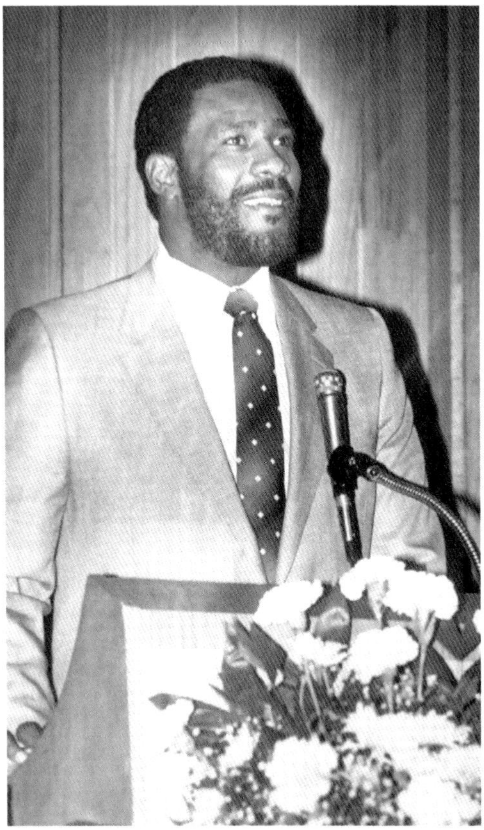

"Mean Joe" Greene
Charles Edward "Mean Joe" Greene played varsity football at North Texas State University from 1966 until 1968 and was selected as a College Consensus All-American, the only university alumnus to win that honor. He led the Pittsburgh Steelers' Steel Curtain defense that resulted in four Super Bowl titles. In 1983, Greene was appointed to the North Texas board of regents, making him the first African American to serve as a regent of any Texas state university. In 1987, Greene was inducted into the Pro Football Hall of Fame. Despite his national prominence, Greene remains close to his alma mater. He was selected 2013 Emerald Eagle Honoree. (Courtesy of DCOHC.)

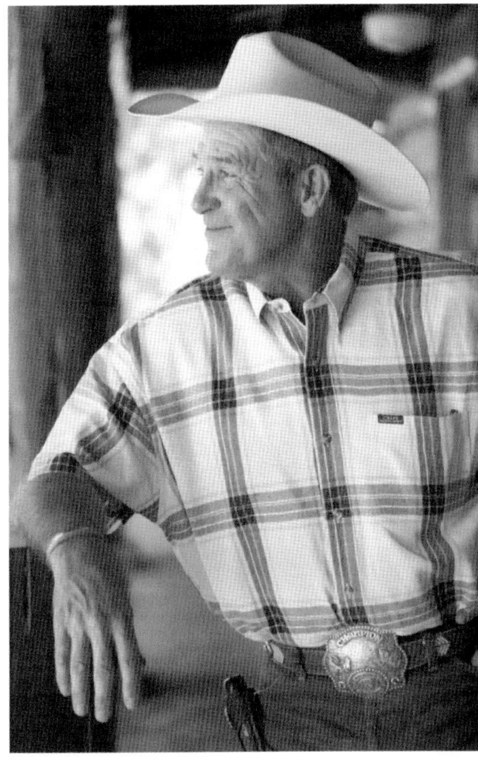

Once a Cowboy, Always a Cowboy
Denton-born Walter Benton "Walt" Garrison debuted with the Dallas Cowboys in 1966 and played until 1974. He finished his career with 3,886 yards rushing and 1,794 yards receiving and a Super Bowl win in 1972. A real cowboy, Garrison spent time on the professional rodeo circuit in the off-seasons. It was a rodeo accident that ended his professional football career. The title of his biography, *Once a Cowboy*, refers to his college career with the Oklahoma State Cowboys, his career with the Dallas Cowboys, and his life as a rodeo cowboy. He is an inductee in the Texas Cowboy Hall of Fame and the Texas Sports Hall of Fame. Garrison now runs his ranch in Denton County and has created a line of Western food products. (Courtesy of DRC.)

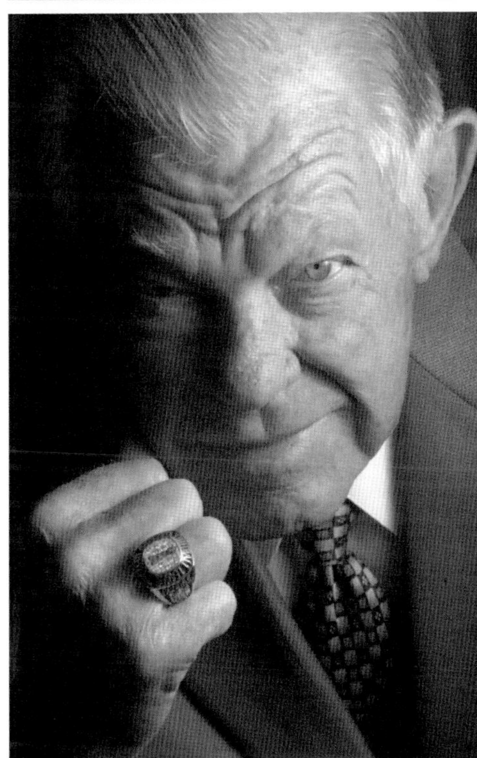

Life of Politics and Football
Walter Earl Parker (1917–2010) coached football at Denton High School and served five consecutive terms in the Texas House of Representatives beginning in 1969. He then functioned as vice president for government affairs, helping the University of North Texas secure funding from the Texas Legislature for 25 years. Parker worked for 42 years as an AFL/NFL official, refereeing more than 300 football games. He is shown here with his NFL ring. (Courtesy of DRC.)

Olympic Gold

Louise Dorothy Ritter, 1982 graduate of Texas Woman's University, won a major upset at the 1988 Olympic Games in Seoul, Korea, upsetting the reigning world champion and world record holder in the high jump. She equaled her own barely seven-week-old American record of six feet, eight inches to win gold. Ritter had trained with US Olympic coach Dr. Bert Lyle at Texas Woman's University and had represented the United States seven times before her golden success. She was selected to the Texas Women's Hall of Fame in 1988. (Courtesy of DRC.)

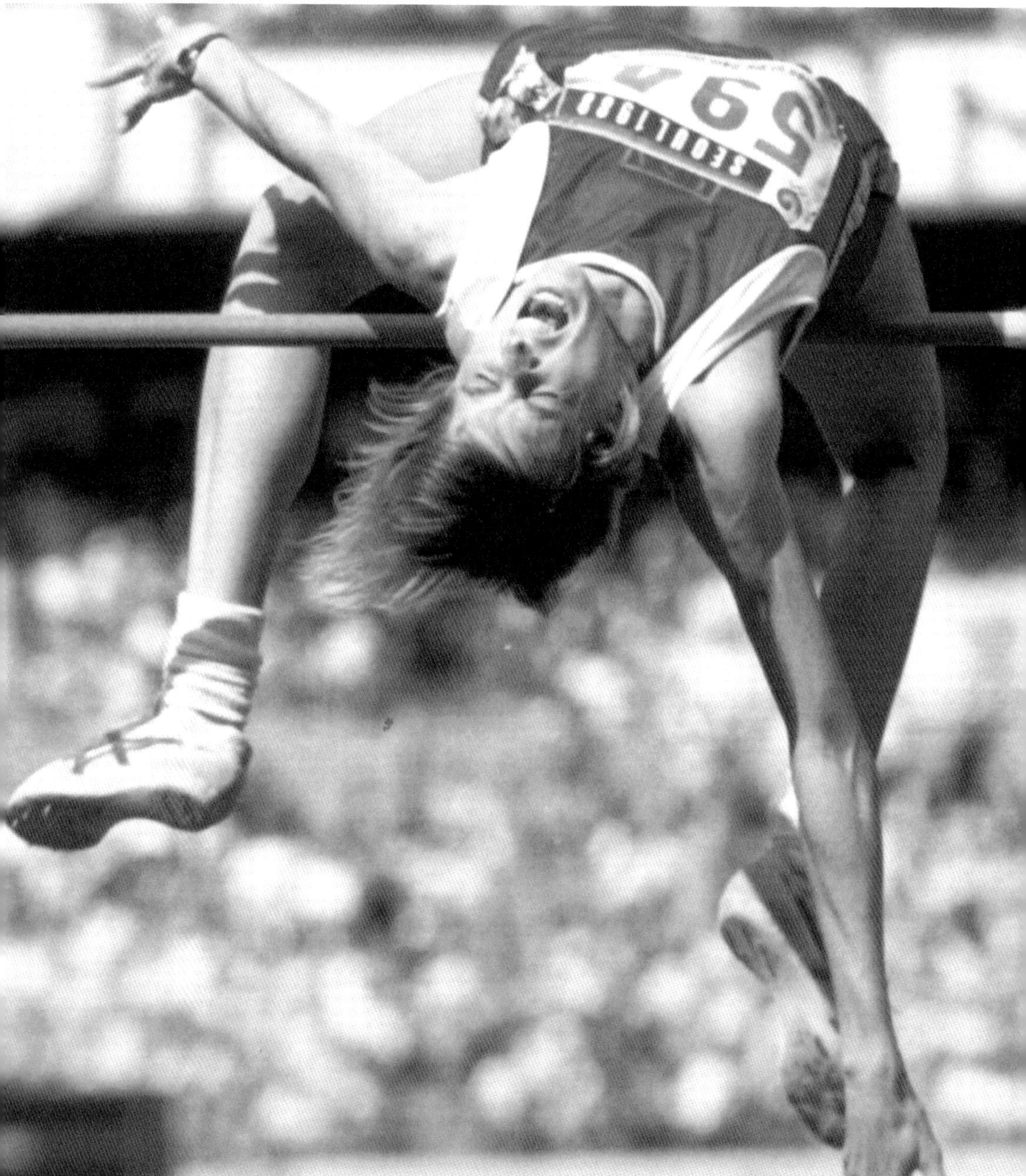

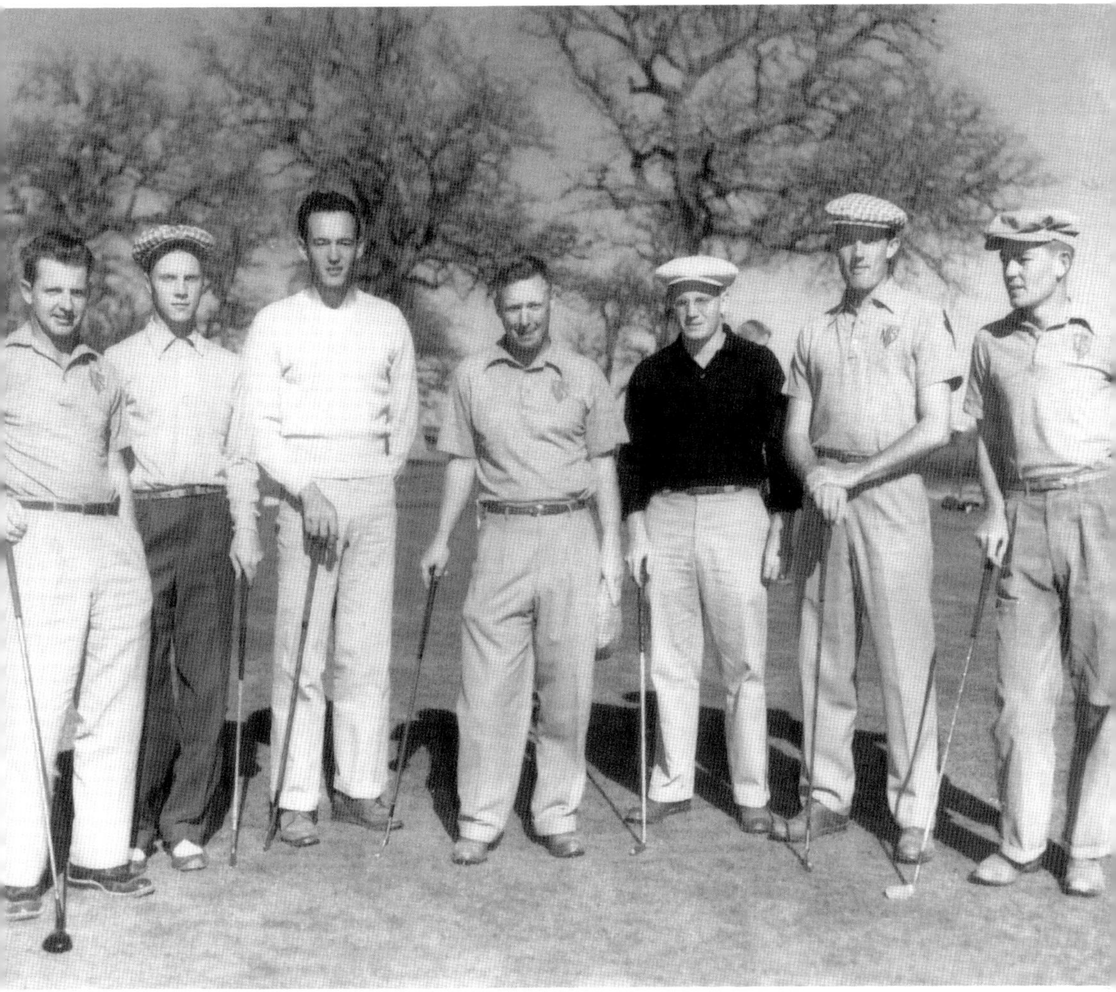

Four by Fore

Don January played golf at North Texas State under coach Fred Cobb from 1949 to 1952, when the college won four consecutive NCAA Division I Championships. January won 10 PGA Tour titles and 22 Senior PGA Tour events in his professional career. One of his teammates at North Texas was Billy Maxwell, who won seven PGA Tour events. The 1951 and 1952 NCAA champion team and its coach are shown here. From left to right are Joe Conrad, unidentified, Marion Hiskey, Billy Maxwell, Fred Cobb, Don January, and Buster Reed. (Courtesy of DCVB.)

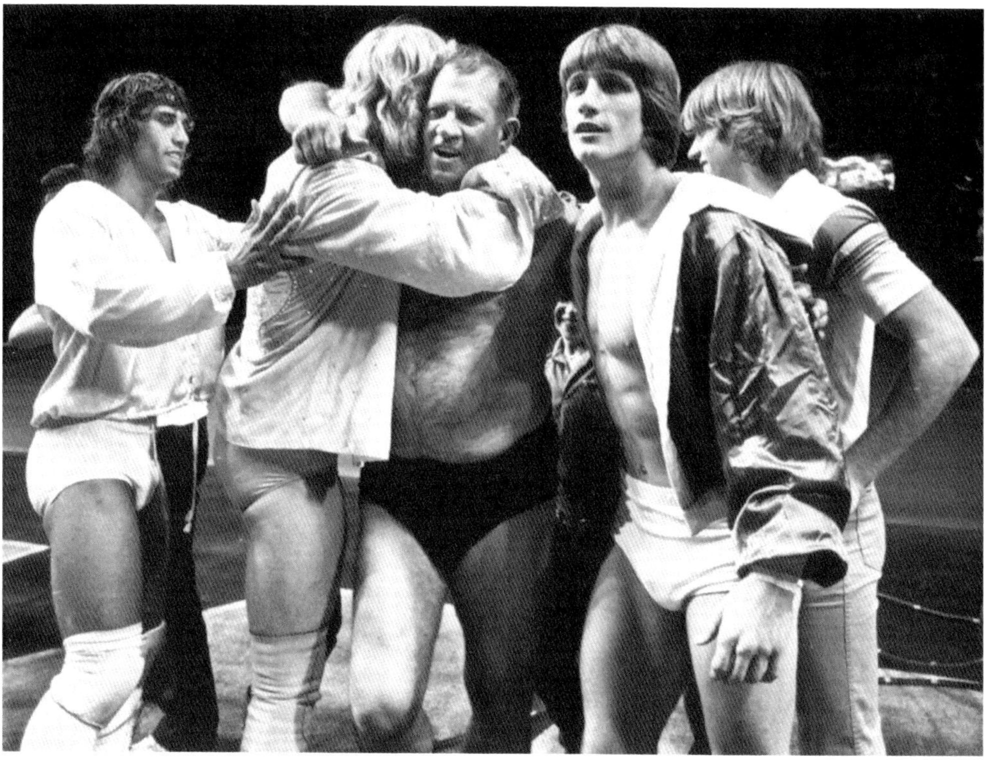

Wrestling Dynasty

David and Kevin (Adkisson) Von Erich were student athletes at North Texas State University before joining their father as world-class wrestlers. Professional wrestler "Iron Claw" Jack Barton Adkisson (1929–1997), aka, Fritz Von Erich, had five sons who participated in World Class Championship Wrestling. In the above photograph are, from left to right, Kerry (1960–1993), David (1958–1984), Fritz, Kevin, and Chris (1969–1991). Mike (1964–1987) is shown in the photograph at right. Tragic deaths shortened the lives of five of Von Erich's six sons. Jack Jr., Von Erich's first-born son, died at age six of accidental electrocution. Kevin, the last of the brothers, runs the family business, while his two sons, Ross and Marshall, have continued the legacy and entered the wrestling arena. (Courtesy of DRC.)

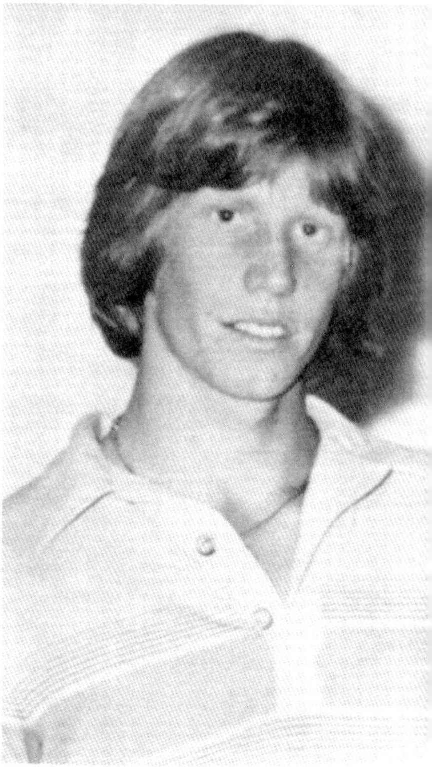

CHAPTER SEVEN

Superstars of Space, Medicine, Technology, and Innovation

Equipped with his five senses, man explores the universe around him and calls the adventure Science.

—Edwin Hubble

Pioneers in the fields of space exploration and research, medical development, Internet technology, and other scientific advances have always found a nurturing home in Denton.

The American Association for the Advancement of Science's study, *Science for All Americans*, points out that a good science education helps students "develop the understandings and habits of mind they need to become compassionate human beings able to think for themselves and to face life head on. It should equip them also to participate thoughtfully with fellow citizens in building and protecting a society that is open, decent, and vital."

The city's intellectual and can-do attitude developed and encouraged professors whose interests were in formulating healthy foods for astronauts, which subsequently found practical uses on Earth; a doctor who devoted his life to taking care of women's health, which led to the creation of an agency that takes care of terminally ill patients and their caregivers; space voyagers whose research in the outer atmosphere and on terra firma led to medical breakthroughs; scientists and engineers whose interests lie in the effects of space flight on humans and whose inventions and methodologies contributed to their fields of research; a visionary in the field of digital capture systems; and everyday citizens who astronomically set a land-speed record.

The environment of two universities that fostered outside-the-box thinking and provided like-minded colleagues stimulated these men and women. Entrepreneurs find a business atmosphere that is conducive to success and university courses of study that embolden their curiosity and inventiveness.

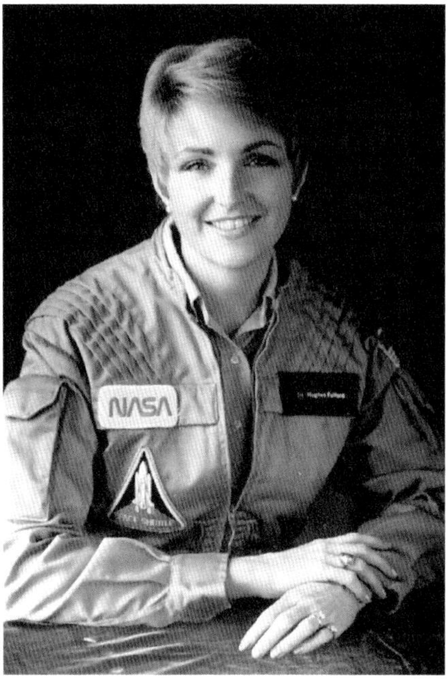

Pioneer Civilian Scientist in Space

Millie Hughes-Fulford, a 1972 Texas Woman's University graduate, was among the first women civilian scientists in space when, in 1991, she flew aboard the Spacelab *Life Sciences 1*, the first Spacelab mission dedicated to biomedical studies. The nine-day mission flew more than 3.2 million miles in 146 orbits, during which Hughes-Fulford studied the physiological changes that occur during space flight and investigated the body's gravitational changes. Hughes-Fulford continued her research as a biochemist directing cellular research at the Veteran's Affairs Medical Center and professor at the University of California Medical Center in San Francisco, where she continues her study of the effects of spaceflight on astronauts. She was honored with TWU's Woman of Achievement Award. (Courtesy of DRC.)

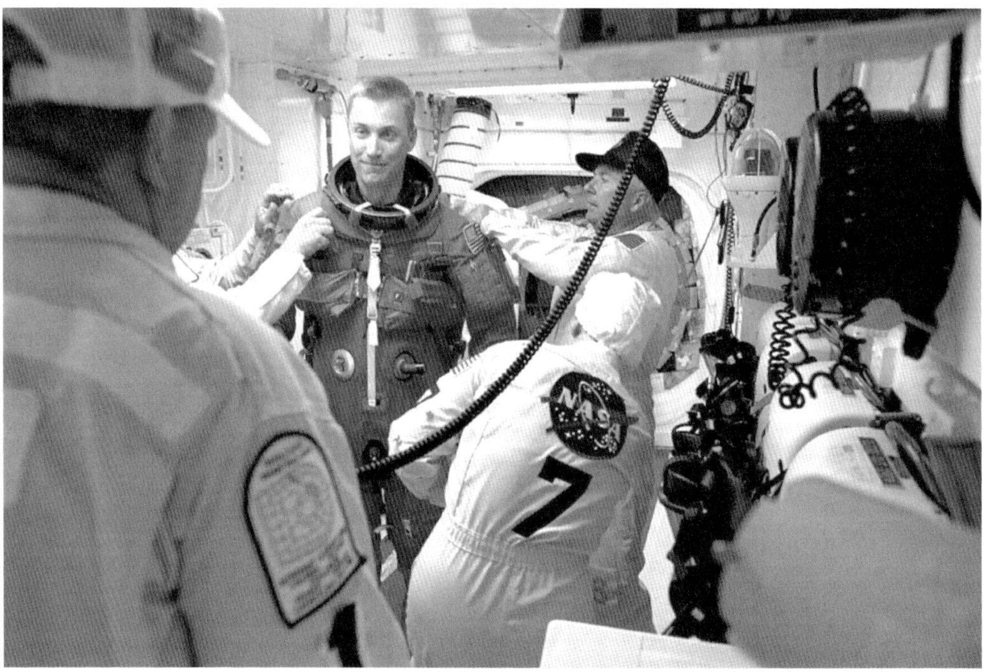

Space Shuttle *Columbia*

James Anthony Pawelczyk, a University of North Texas doctoral graduate, was a payload specialist aboard the 16-day STS-90 Space Shuttle *Columbia* flight in 1998. The seven-person crew served as experimental subjects and operators focusing on the effects of microgravity on the brain and nervous system. STS-90 orbited the Earth 256 times, covered 6.3 million miles, and logged more than 381 hours in space. Pawelczyk was awarded the NASA Space Flight Medal. He is currently a physiologist at Penn State University. (Courtesy of DRC.)

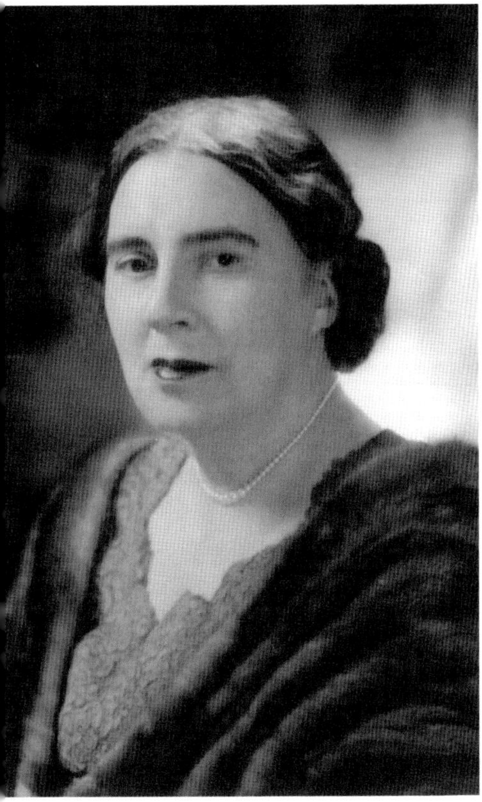

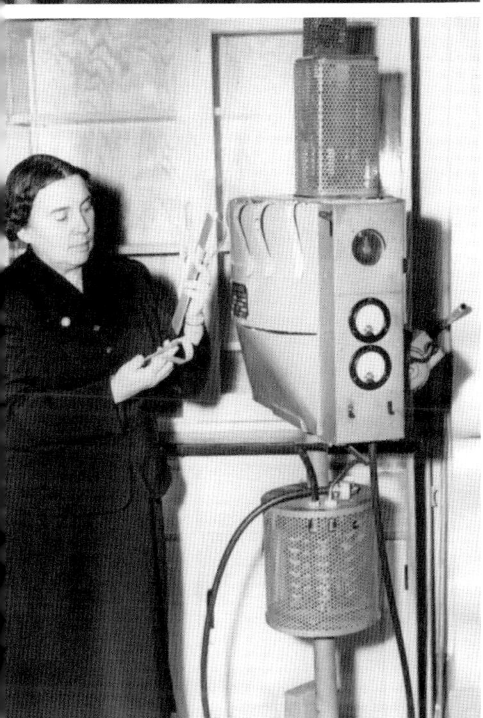

Distinguished Research Career

Pauline Gracia Beery Mack (1891–1974) enjoyed a distinguished 54-year career at Penn State University and Texas Woman's University in the field of research and development. Her research on nutrition in children led to exploration in connection to nutrition, bone density, and calcium loss during manned space flights. She devised the first method and designed the first equipment to quantitatively measure bone density from X-rays. She contributed to knowledge regarding school lunches to supplement nutritional deficits, undetected heart ailments in seemingly healthy young athletes, cholesterol concerns, fireproofing fabrics, and improving textile industry standards, to name a few. Mack won the Silver Snoopy Award for her contributions to manned space flight. The methodologies she developed became widely used, and her contribution to science is undeniable. (Courtesy of TWU.)

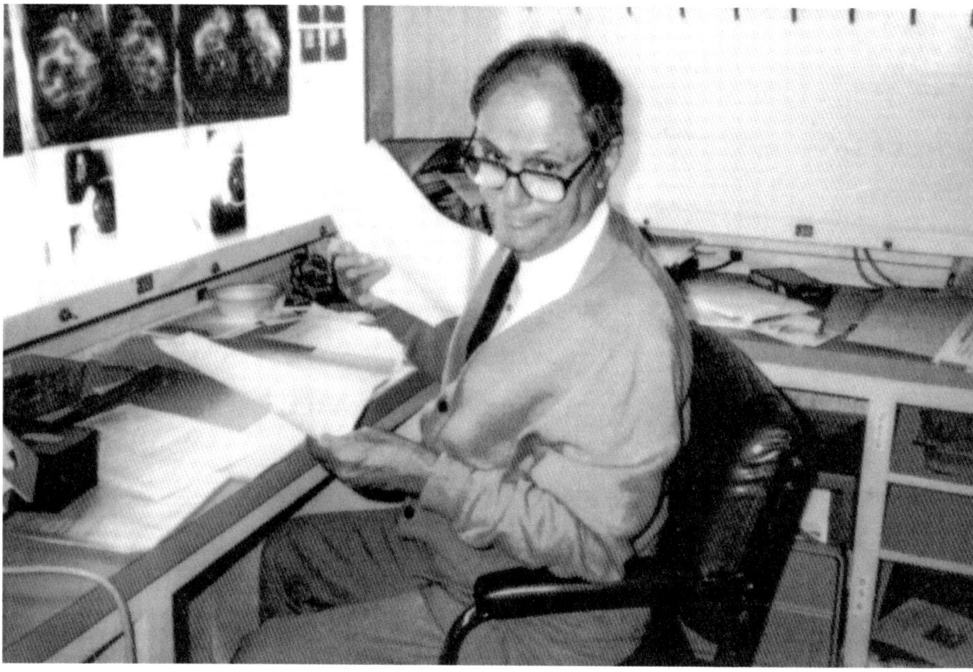

Renaissance Man

Robert Minturn Lockwood III (1922–2010) was a longtime, greatly respected radiologist who provided exceptional care for his patients for 52 years at Family Radiology Clinic. A devoted medical professional, his interests outside of that profession earned him respect as a renaissance man. He loved fossil-collecting, gardening, and bird-watching, and he wrote poetry and plays. A key to his legacy for the community is the work of caring professionals providing end-of-life services to patients and their family members and friends through a nonprofit home health care facility he established. Ann's Haven Hospice provides for patients regardless of condition or ability to pay. "Doc Lock" wrote a memorial for Charles Williams, his friend and the rector of St. Barnabas Church, an excerpt of which applies to him as well: "Now please live on in us your friends. We are now more connected because you cared about us." (Courtesy of Sandy Lockwood.)

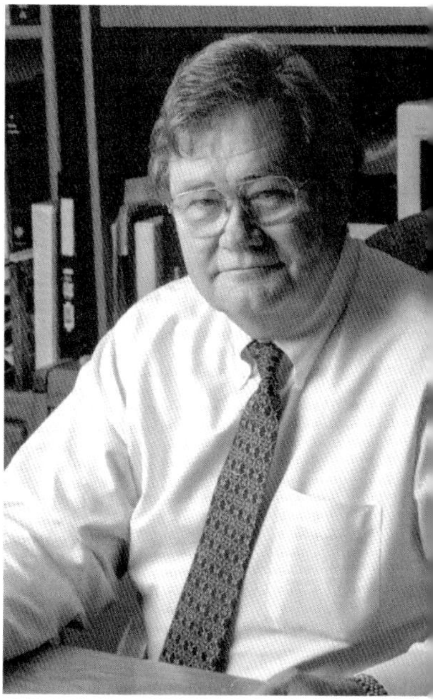

Fateful Day in Nation's History

Charles James "Jim" Carrico (1935–2002) was the first surgeon called upon to attend Pres. John F. Kennedy when he was brought to Parkland Hospital in Dallas after he had been shot. It was such a traumatic event for the second-year surgery resident that he did not speak about his experience for more than 30 years after that fateful day. Carrico had begun his journey to Parkland after graduating from Denton High School and North Texas State and attending medical school. He became a specialist in trauma surgery and, eventually, chair of two hospital surgical departments. UNT named him distinguished alumnus in 1991 for his notable medical career. (Courtesy of Sue Carrico.)

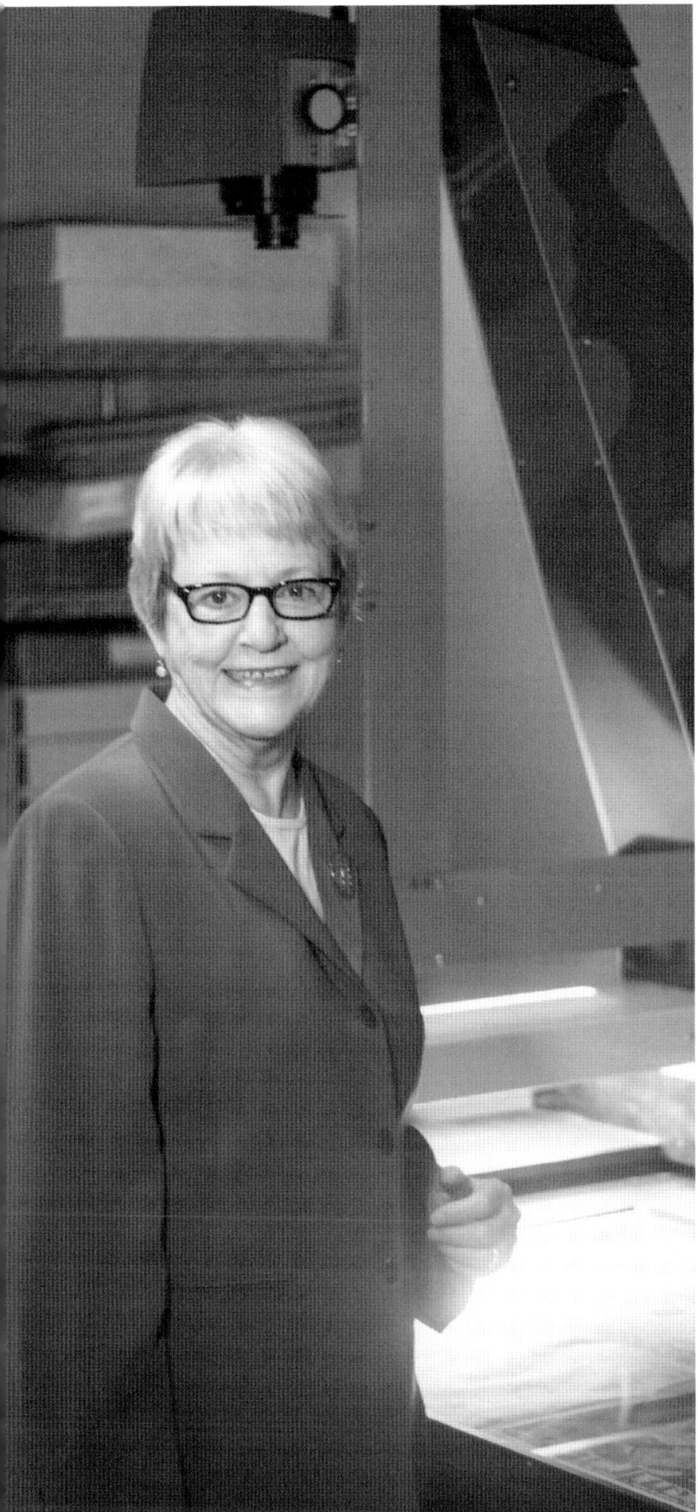

Technology and Digital Library Pioneer

Cathy Nelson Hartman is truly a visionary in the fields of technology and digital library science. Hartman started the Portal to Texas History from an idea she had in 1999 to provide a digital gateway to the history of Texas through archive imaging, archival storage of electronic files, digital preservation, and metadata development. Since its inception in 2002, more than 3.5 million items have been archived with the cooperation of 250 partners. Hartman started the Cyber Cemetery, a collaborative effort with the US Government Printing Office to provide permanent public access to the websites and publications of defunct US government agencies and commissions. Because of that project, the University of North Texas is the only university in the United States, besides West Point and the Naval Academy, to be an Affiliated Archives of the National Archives and Records Administration. Hartman is currently chairman of the steering committee for the International Internet Preservation Consortium, a global network of experts archiving the Web for future generations. Because of the innovation and vision of scholars and librarians like Cathy Hartman, future researchers will have access to primary resource information published on the World Wide Web that would otherwise be lost. (Courtesy of UNT.)

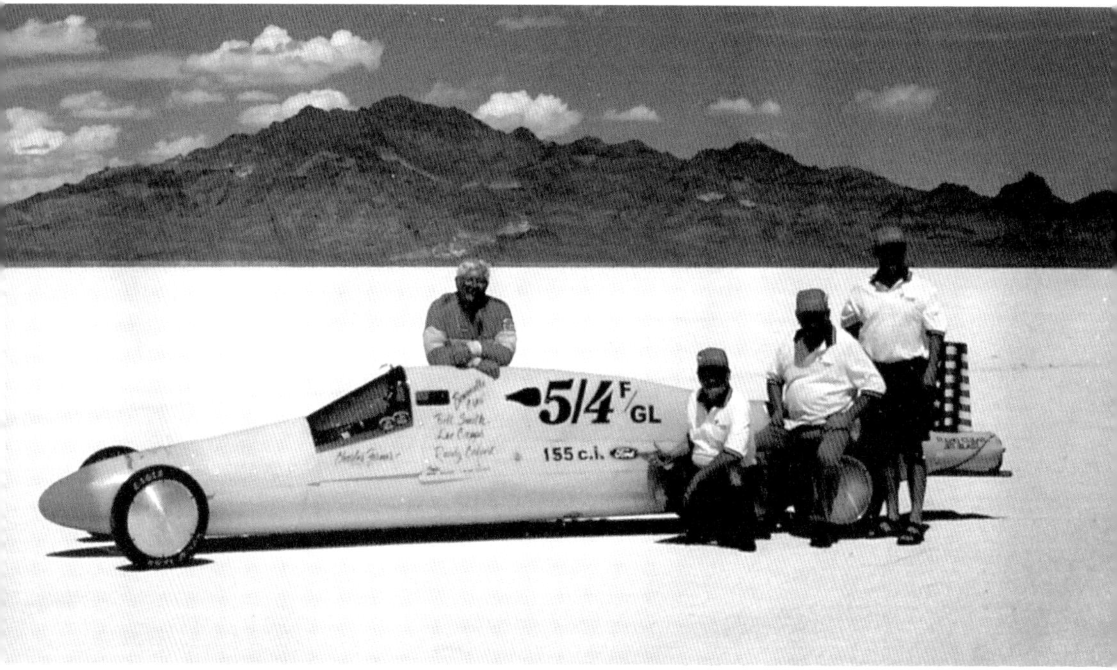

The Salt Flats Five

Shown here are, from left to right, Charles Farmer, Lee J. Capps, Bill Smith, and Randy Calvert. These Denton residents, along with Alan Calvert (not pictured), built a Class F/Gas Lakester classification car that set a new world land-speed record of 198.225 miles per hour on August 19, 2004, at Utah's Bonneville Salt Flats. The modified Capps-built motor in their record-breaking car was a small four-cylinder motor from a Ford Pinto with 2,500 cubic centimeters of displacement compared to the 3,000-cc motor used by the previous record-holder. Smith said, "A lot of the cars we competed against had corporate sponsorships and cost between a quarter and a half million dollars. Our car cost $12,000." (Courtesy of Peggy Capps.)

CHAPTER EIGHT

Superstars as Community Spirits and Civic Heroes

Never doubt that a small group of thoughtful committed citizens can change the world; indeed, it's the only thing that ever has.

—Margaret Mead

Ronald Reagan was an outspoken advocate of community service in America. He once said that voluntary service is like a "spirit that flows like a deep and mighty river through the history of our Nation." That same selfless spirit flows through the city of Denton and courses through the veins of its citizens. Every community has individuals who give of themselves, not for selfish reasons, but for love of their town and its residents. Others grow up in the town and take those traits with them into the world. Denton overflows with such individuals. Lovers of theater and the arts, two Miss Americas, historical preservationists, fundraisers, and community activists have all sprouted from the soil and soul of Denton. And these Superstars have not gone unrecognized by the world or their community.

The Greater Denton Arts Council gives the Community Arts Recognition Award (CARA) in honor of those who have significantly enhanced the cultural life and status of Denton through outstanding achievement in the field of fine arts or for service to the arts in the community. These recipients have enhanced the cultural life and status of Denton through longstanding and widespread support of the arts and arts organizations.

The Otis Fowler Award is the highest and most prestigious honor presented by the Denton Chamber of Commerce. According to the criteria originally established in 1960, the award is bestowed upon a deserving individual "who by regular engagement in [his or her] business, profession, or calling . . . [has] made a marked contribution to the progress and welfare of the community."

The Governor's Commission for Women established the Texas Women's Hall of Fame to honor the state's most accomplished women. Inductees include first ladies, teachers, astronauts, and athletes. Texas residents submit nominations, and a bipartisan, independent panel of judges selects the recipients who will be inducted into the hall of fame at its biennial awards ceremony.

The University of North Texas and Texas Woman's University present awards honoring individuals who have served those universities in meritorious ways.

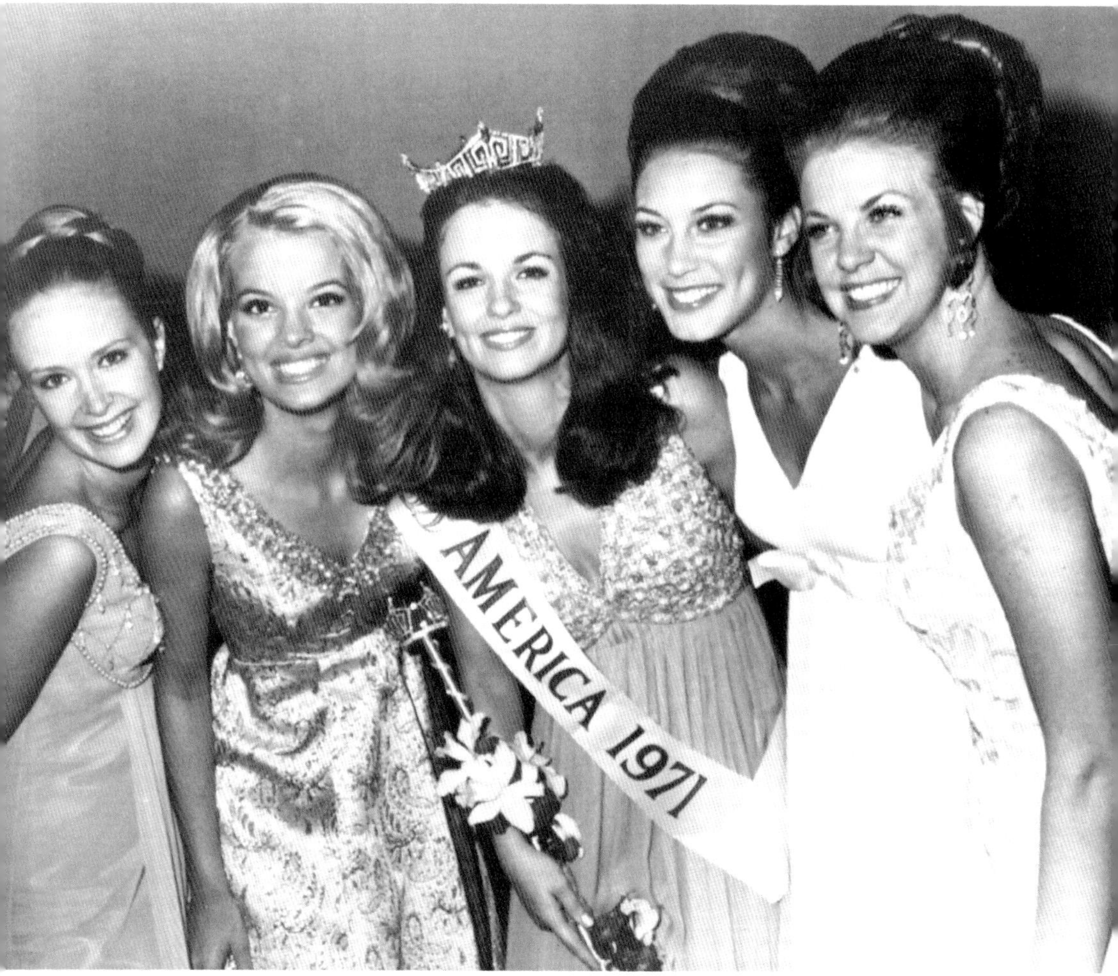

Miss America Never Says Never

Denton-born Phyllis George, Miss Texas 1970, attended three years at North Texas State until she won the title of Miss America in 1971. She was one of the first women to have a nationally prominent role in television sports coverage, joining CBS Sports to cohost *The NFL Today.* Additionally, George was a coanchor of the *CBS Morning News*. She had the opportunity to interview Pres. Bill Clinton on her show *A Phyllis George Special.* In 1998, she anchored a talk show called *Women's Day* on the cable network Pax. Her entrepreneurial business, Chicken by George, was so successful that Hormel Foods bought the company after just two years in operation. As first lady of Kentucky, George promoted her adopted state's arts and crafts. She has written five books, including an inspirational book entitled *Never Say Never: Ten Lessons to Turn You Can't Into Yes I Can.* In the book, George shares her tips for turning trials into triumphs. She was awarded the University of North Texas Emerald Eagle Honors in 2014. Here, Phyllis George (center) poses with her court, from left to right, Karen Johnson, Claudia Turner, Margaret Walker, and Christine McClamroch. (Courtesy of DCOHC.)

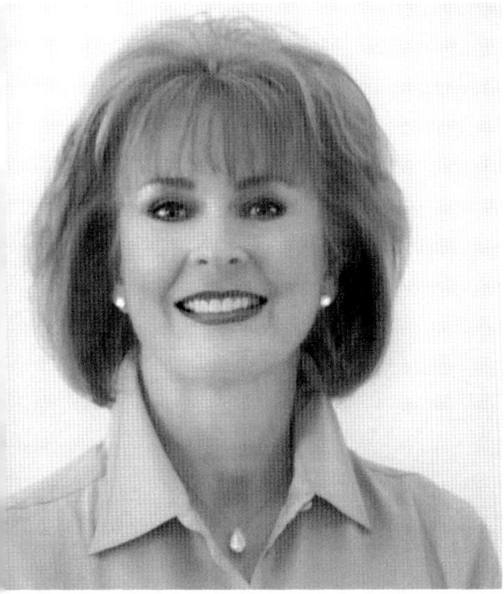

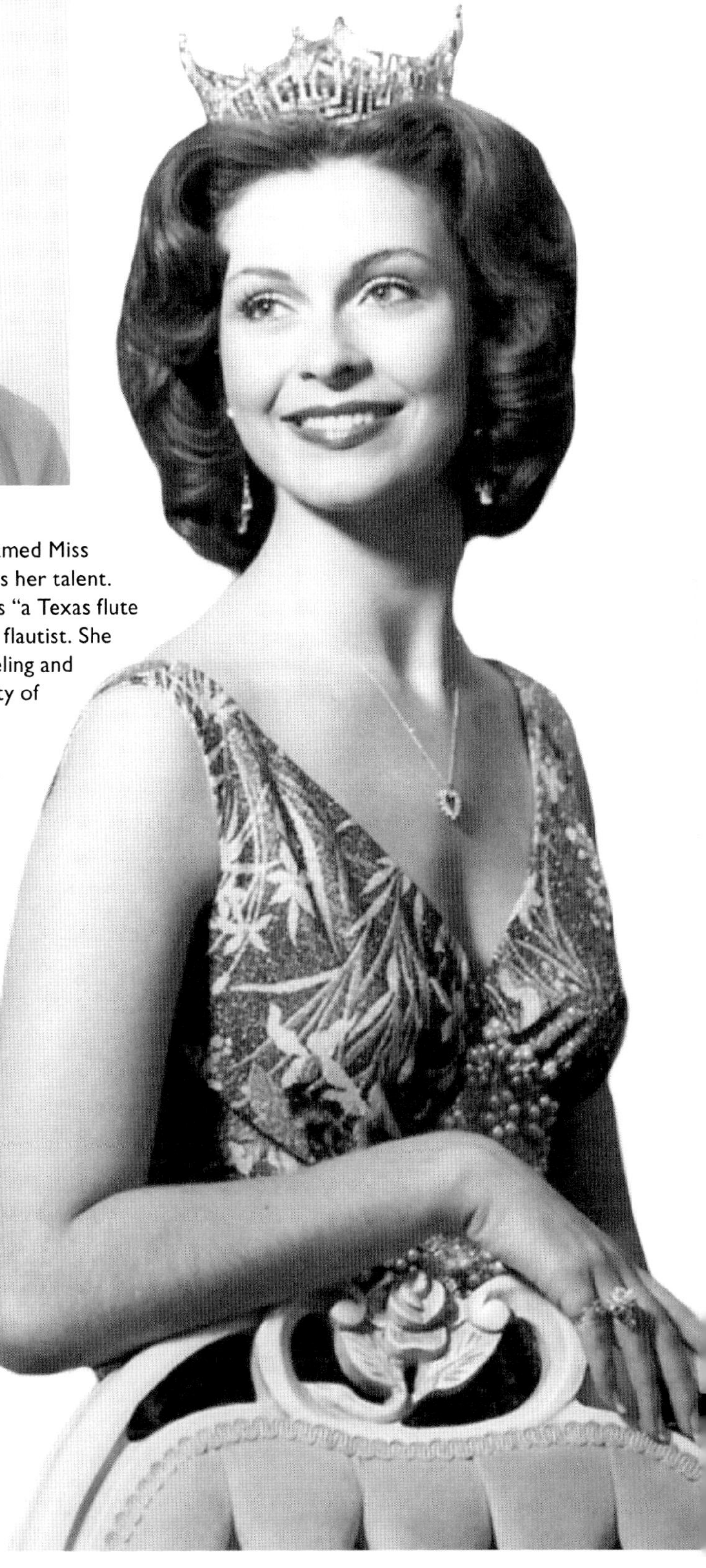

Beauty and Brains

Shirley Jean Cothran Barret was named Miss America in 1975, playing the flute as her talent. Years later, she described herself as "a Texas flute tooter," downplaying her skills as a flautist. She earned a master's degree in counseling and student services from the University of North Texas and a doctorate from Texas Woman's University in early childhood education. As a member of the Denton school board for four years, she once said, "Having gone from first grade through my PhD in Denton, I have a soft spot for Denton schools." She is a popular public speaker among Christian women's groups, bringing a message of hope and of getting through rough times. Barret is involved in numerous charity and Christian-related activities while reserving time for her husband and four children. (Above, courtesy of Shirley Barret; right, courtesy of Virginia Williams.)

Theatrical Lives

Frank Rawls Barrow (1922–2006) lived in Denton for 71 years. He was a successful businessman, a leader in his church, and mayor. In 1959, when Barrow was mayor, the couple hosted a reception for Lyndon and Lady Bird Johnson at the Pat Boone Inn just before LBJ announced his run for national office. Coincidentally, Betty Ann Barrow later played the part of an elderly nursing home resident that thinks she is Lady Bird Johnson in the Denton Community Theatre production of *Daughters of the Lone Star State*. After retirement, the Barrows went on the road with Donna Trammell's production *A Slice of Texas Toast*, raising more than $1 million for nonprofits. After Frank's death, Betty Ann continued with her theater work, winning a national award in 2007 for best costume design for the millinery work she did for the one-act play *Crowns*. One of the richest gifts the Barrows have given to the city was the Denton Community Theatre, helping found the theater and serving the organization for more than 30 years. The Barrows were recognized by Denton with the Community Arts Recognition Award. Their son, Mike Barrow, who studied theater at UNT, is now the managing director of the Denton Community Theatre. Indeed, the apple did not fall far from the tree. (Courtesy of DRC.)

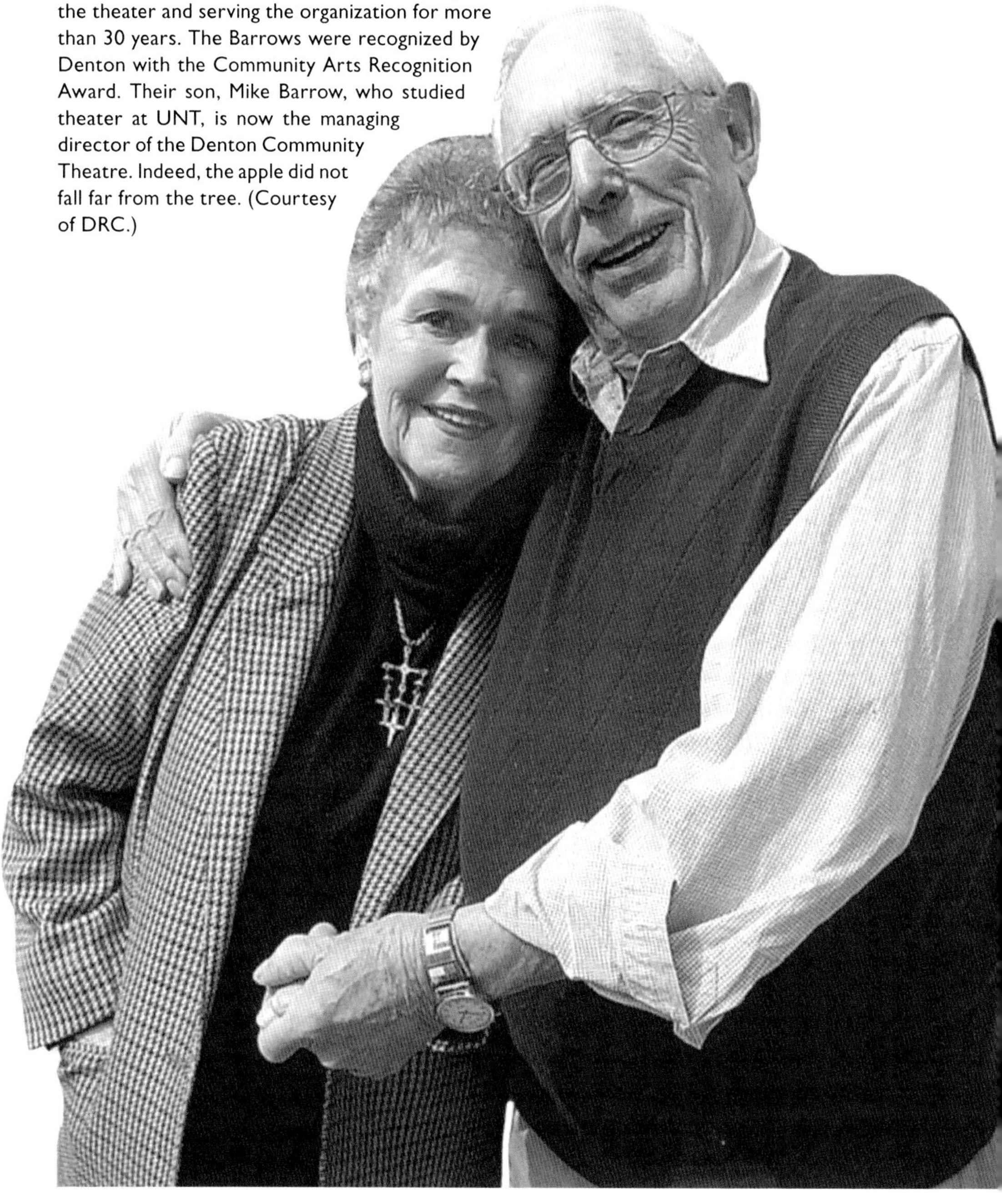

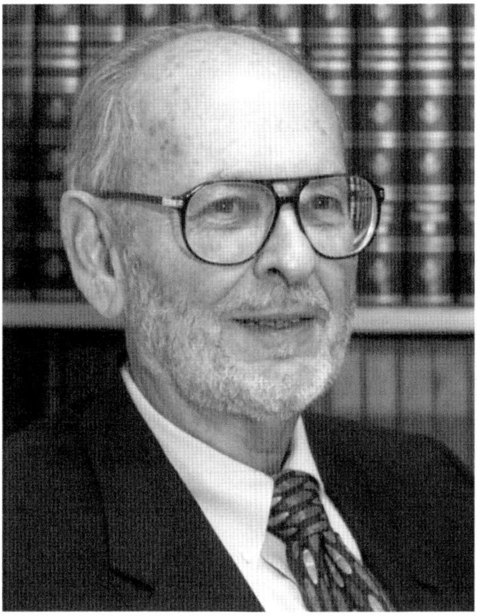

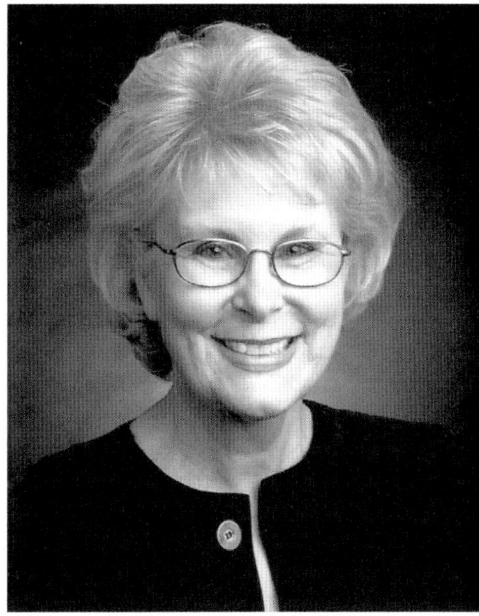

Couple Dedicated to Service
Horace Brock (above left) and Euline Brock (above right) have served selflessly on numerous community boards, including the arts council and community theater. Horace spearheaded the campaign to renovate the Campus Theatre, raising more than $1 million. A renowned accounting professor at University of North Texas, he wrote the oil and gas accounting textbooks used at universities worldwide. Euline, a history professor at Texas Woman's University, served Denton in public office for more than 20 years. During her tenure as a city council member and mayor, she supported the city's public art project and was a champion for community civil rights issues. In the photograph below, the Brocks are seated at right. Pictured with them from left to right are Lee J. Capps, Peggy Capps, and former UNT president Lane Rawlins. (Above left and above right, courtesy of DRC; below, courtesy of UNT.)

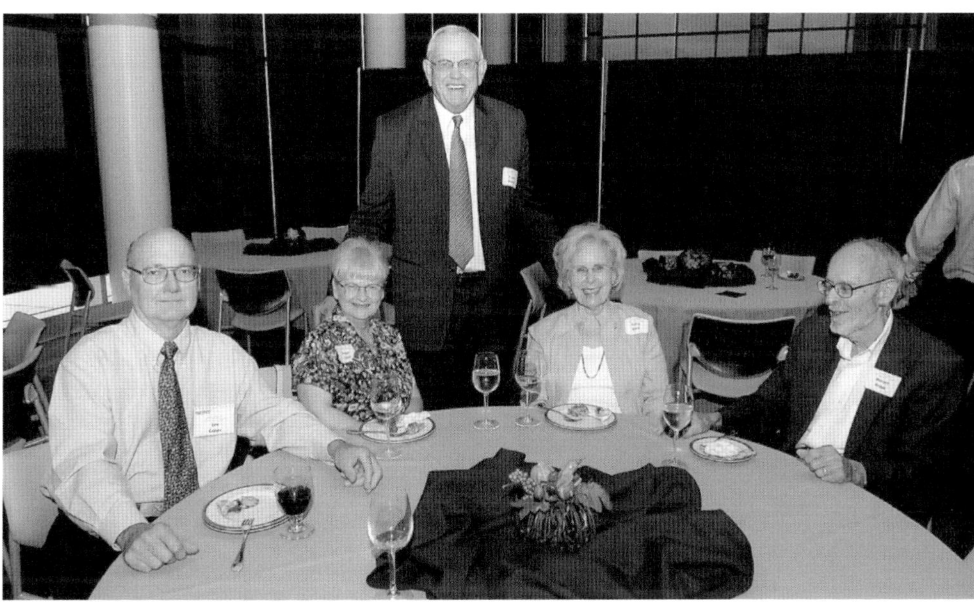

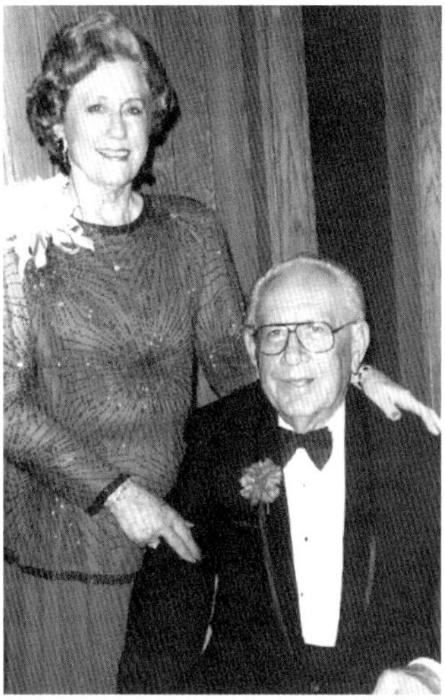

Catering to the Community

Maurine Floyd (1921–2001) operated M&M Catering with Martha Len Nelson for many years, cooking for nearly every charitable event held in Denton. Floyd was one of the founders of the Arts Guild and the Denton Benefit League. She and her husband, John B. "J.B." (1916–1993), held a charity ball to benefit local nonprofits in the early 1970s. This fundraiser became the Denton Benefit League Charity Ball. It has raised more than $4 million for local charities. J.B. Floyd was the owner of Schmitz-Floyd-Hamlett Funeral Home from 1955. His comforting personality lightened the burdens of the bereaved. The Floyds are shown here upon the occasion of receiving the Otis Fowler Award. (Courtesy of DRC.)

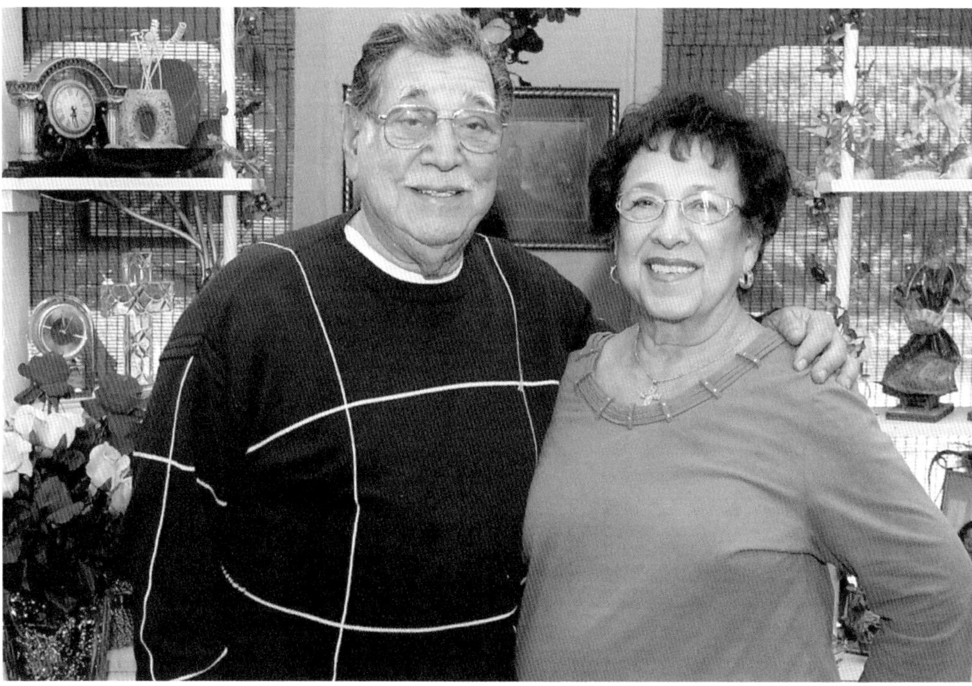

Popo and Lupe and the Pope

Emilio "Popo" and Guadalupe "Lupe" Gonzalez raised themselves from humble beginnings as cotton-field and migrant workers to owners of their own hair-styling salon. They also became community leaders, volunteers, and activists. Popo's activities included assisting Hispanic parishioners; establishing Familias Unidas and its incorporation with the Latino Urban League of American Citizens (LULAC); and working with the Catholic Jail ministry. Together, they worked hard on activities with Immaculate Conception Catholic Church in the city, the YMCA, Big Brothers and Big Sisters, Juvenile Board, Traffic Commission Board, Child Welfare Board, War on Drugs, Selective Service Board, Hope Board, Civil Service Commission, and Hispanics at Risk. Their exceptional service to the Catholic Church did not go unnoticed. In 2011, this longtime Denton couple was awarded the Benemerenti Medal for such service to the church by Pope Benedict XVI. (Courtesy of DRC.)

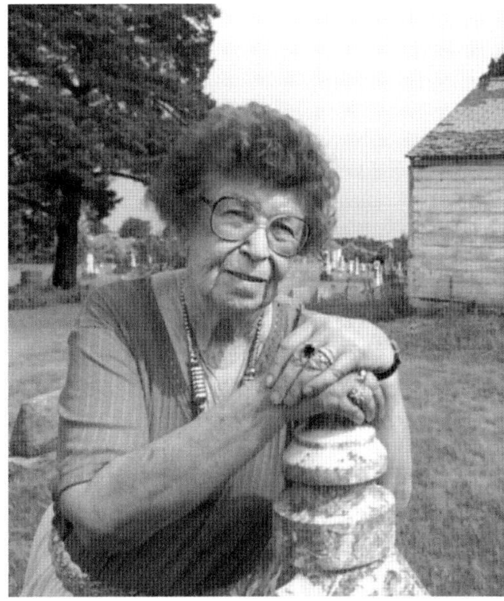

Passionate Preservationist

Being orphaned at three years old had a profound effect on the life of Mildred McCauley Hawk (1918–2004). She graduated from Denton High School and Texas State College for Women. In 1942, she attended War School to learn to drill and rivet. She went to work for General Dynamics Aircraft in Fort Worth as a "Rosie the Riveter," working on the flight lines, building airplanes for 31 years. Hawk was the mainstay behind preservation of the Denton County historical bridges. She donated the Bayless-Selby house to the county for a museum. Hawk suffered from a reading disability that later in life led her to establish the Hawkeye Reader Program. Upon her death, she left an endowment to assure that the third-grade reading contest would continue, and she funded a scholarship in reading at TWU. Mildred McCauley Hawk Elementary School was named in her honor. Hawk had a true "maverick" spirit. (Courtesy of DRC.)

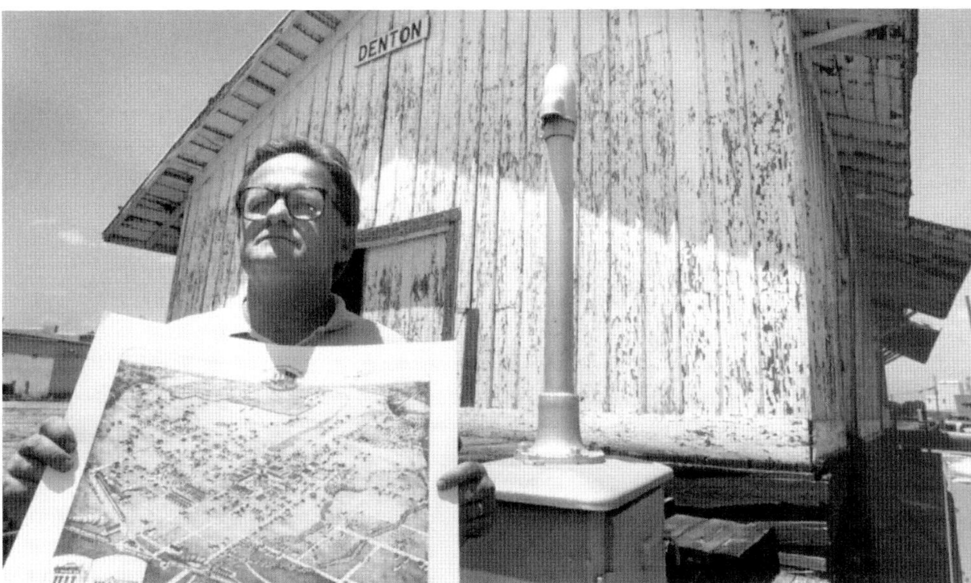

Community Activist and Agitator

Mike Cochran has aggravated, agitated, and exasperated most civic leaders with whom he has come into contact. This controversial community activist and historian has proven his mettle by choosing the path of greatest resistance. Among his efforts have been the following: protesting when TWU president Mary Evelyn Huey ordered pesky flocks of birds to be eradicated from campus; being escorted out of historical commission meetings for opposing procedural irregularities; defending his neighborhood from encroachment by inappropriate development; publicly objecting when Stonewall Jackson School was to be torn down; being the dissenting voice on city matters as a councilman; and campaigning for a name change to a public park. Every community needs a Mike Cochran. Cochran is shown here in front of the now-demolished train depot, holding an Augustus Koch 1883 bird's-eye map of Denton. (Courtesy of DCOHC.)

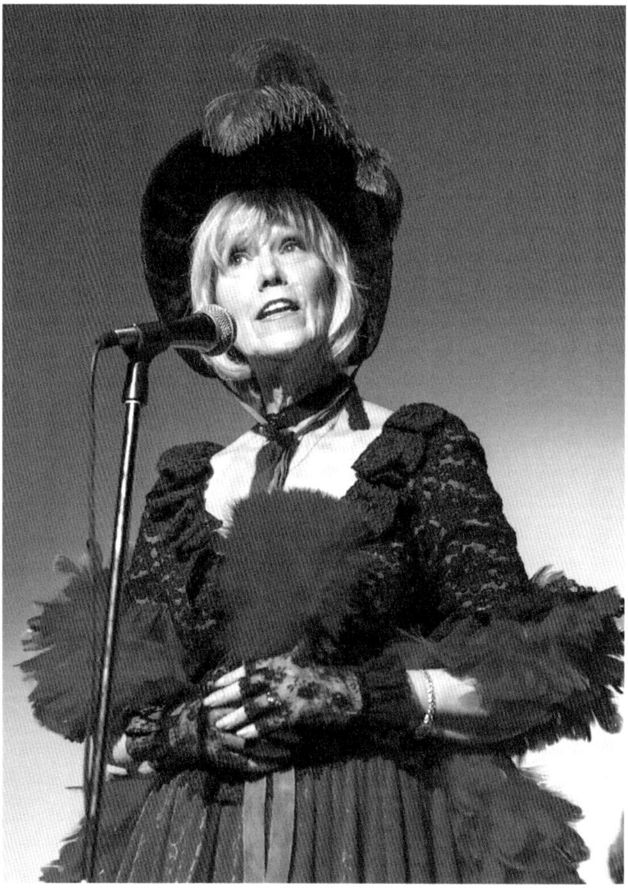

Life is a Parody, My Friend
Donna Trammell, a lyricist, parodist, playwright, and director, has more than 900 song lyrics and 50 full-length scripts to her credit. Her highly successful theatrical production company, specializing in large-cast fundraising productions designed for nonprofit organizations, has raised more than $2 million for charities across the Southwest. Among her major writing projects have been the University of North Texas Centennial celebration musical *Forever Green*; the Denton sesquicentennial musical *Square Roots*; and *Almost Angels*, the 150th birthday celebration at Denton's First United Methodist Church. Trammel's musical parody *Square Roots* celebrates the uniqueness of Denton. In it, she explained the nature of the city's streets. (Courtesy of Mikel Galicia.)

One-Way Trees
(melody of the song "Trees")

Oh, think how lovely it would be
A town where ev'ry street's a tree.
How quaint and lovely to explore
Chestnut, Walnut, and Sycamore;
To pass the summer days upon
Mulberry, Maple, and Pecan.
What better place for Denton folk
Than Hick'ry, Locust, Elm, and Oak
Oh, trees are made by God they say
But only fools make streets one-way!

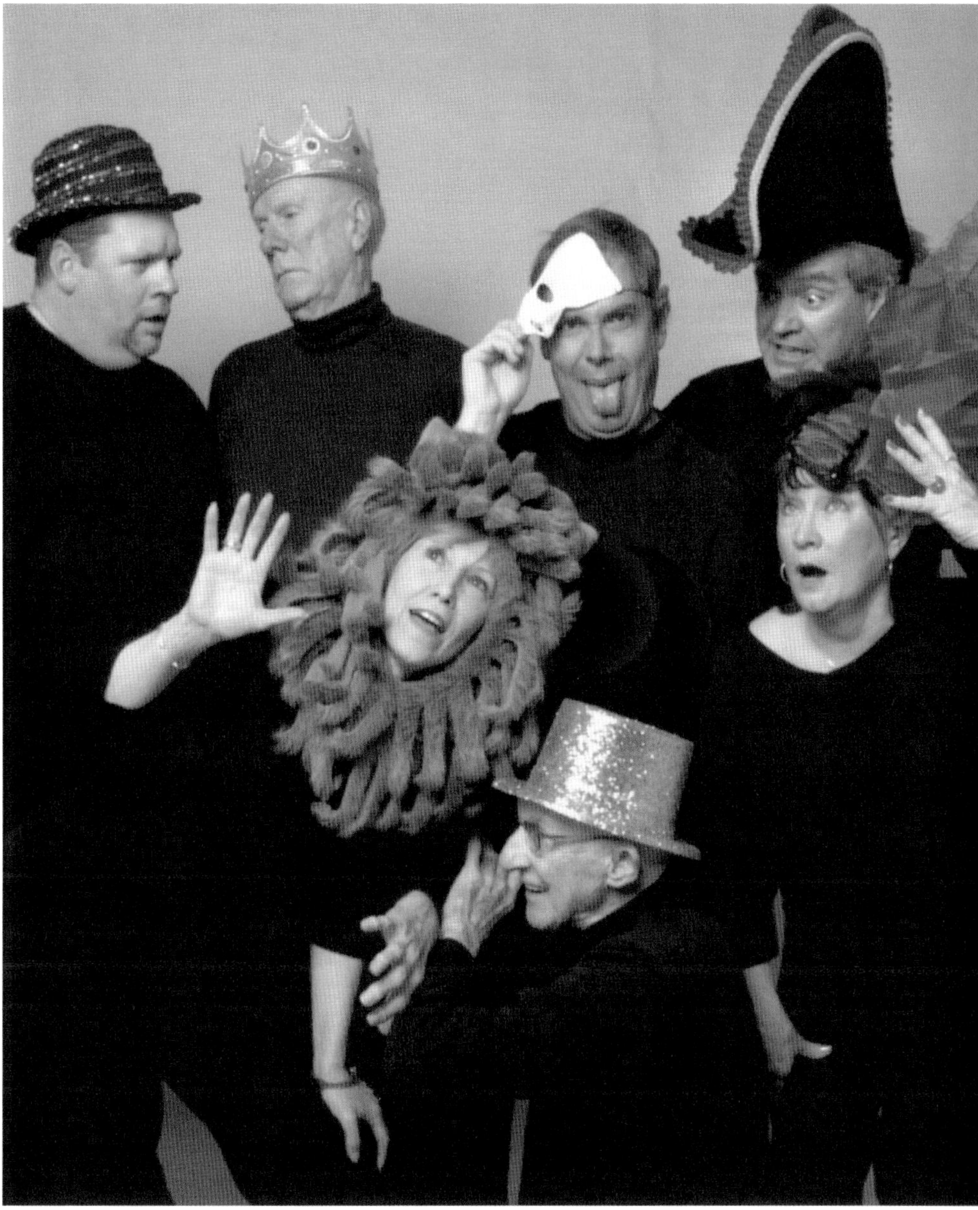

Phenomenal, Peerless, Passionate Parody Performers

The Trammell Group performs as an ensemble for charitable events each year, delighting audiences with Donna Trammell's unparalleled rhyming parodies and songs. This talented musical troupe includes, from left to right, (first row) Donna Trammell, Bob Rogers, and Kay Lamb; (second row) Scott Crew, Lindsay Keffer, John Evarts, and Buster Maloney. (Courtesy of DRC.)

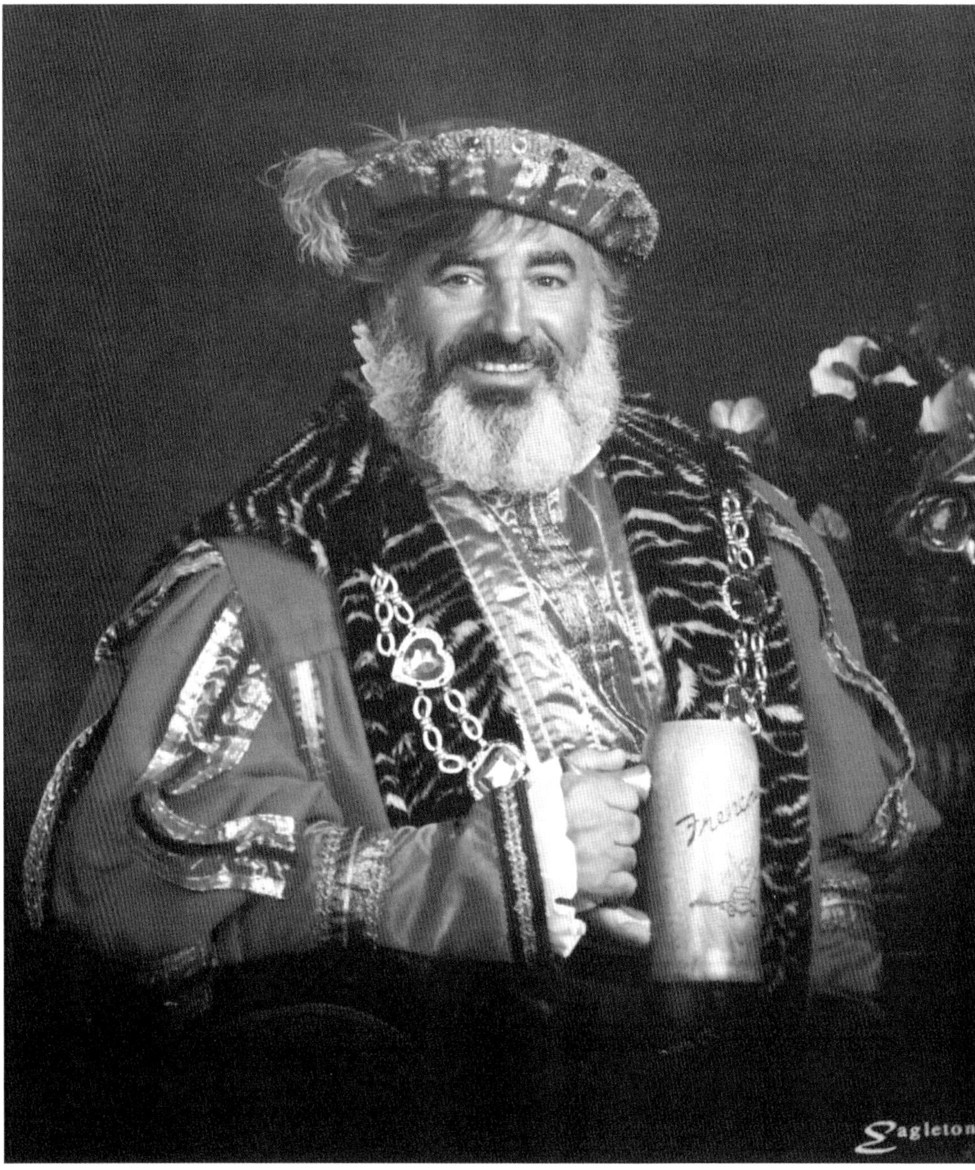

King of Orange
Andre "Frenchy" Rheault is one of Denton's most visible characters. His orange vans are parked all around town, advertising his lawn-care business as well as community events. Rheault is one of the few people in Denton who has an ice-cream flavor named after them. "Frenchy's Orange Sherbet" at Beth Marie's Old Fashioned Ice Cream is a favorite of lovers of orange. Rheault and his wife, Teri, were recipients of the Hearts and Heroes Award, given by Health Services of North Texas Hearts. The award honors outstanding citizens and organizations that are dedicated to leadership, philanthropy, and community service. Denton's own Texas Poet Laureate, Karla K. Morton, a fellow recipient of the award, wrote about the "King of Orange": there is "nobility in the man who works with his hands." He is able to down trees "in a single bound"; he literally "moves the earth." When he hears of a person or organization that needs help, or a need for a helping hand, his generosity is limitless. (Courtesy of Walter Eagleton.)

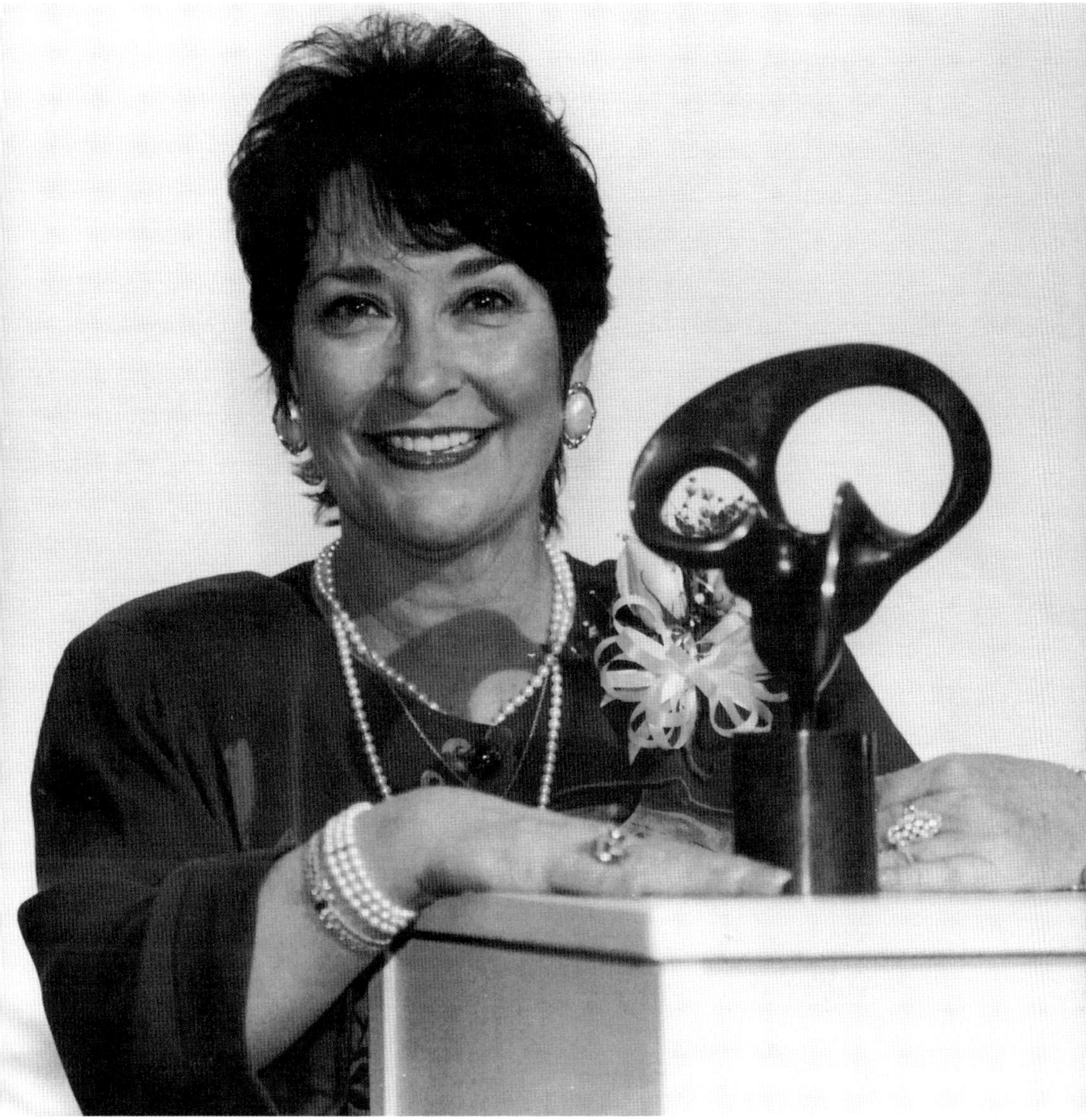

All for the Arts and Jazz

Carol Williamson Short serves as executive director of the Denton Festival Foundation, which conducts the annual Denton Arts and Jazz Festival. The event has raised more than $300,000 during the 34 years of its existence, benefiting continuing arts facilities, preservation projects, and public art. Short also was cofounder of the Arts Guild with Ema Ruth Russell and created, organized, and produced the first Auction for the Arts. It was this indefatigable woman who, as a board member of the Greater Denton Arts Council, helped convince the city to donate the building that is now the Patterson-Appleton Center for the Visual Arts. She won the Community Arts Recognition Award in 1998 and the Otis Fowler Award in 2007. Upon receiving the CARA, Short was described as organized, intelligent, talented, determined, and possessing phenomenal people skills. The Denton Festival Foundation, under Short's leadership, won the 2012 TWU Founder's Award. (Courtesy of DRC.)

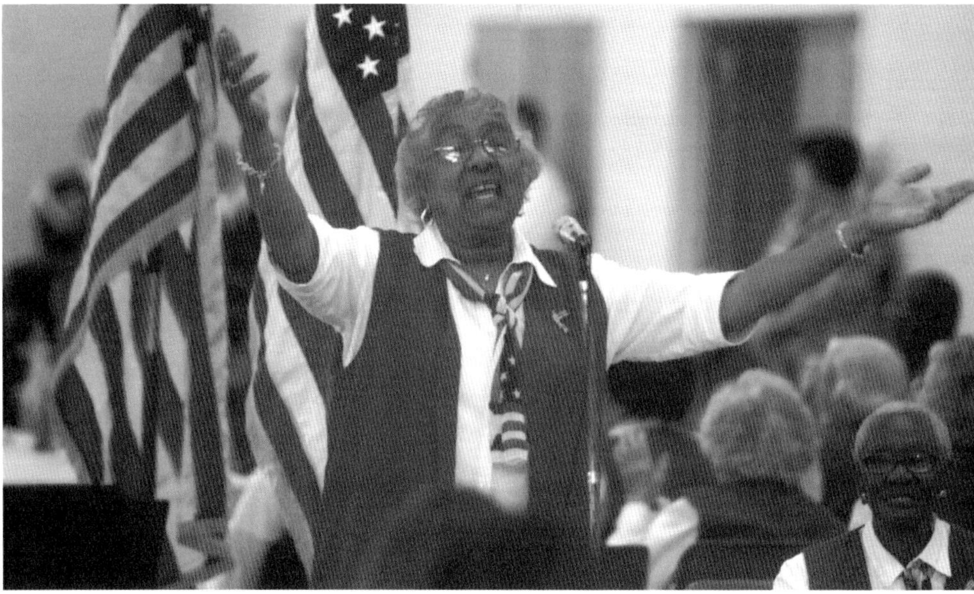

Fearless Leaders (ABOVE, RIGHT, AND OPPOSITE PAGE)

Alma Clark, Betty Kimble, Ruby Cole, Catherine Bell, and Charlye Heggins (1933–2013) have been, and are, active leaders in so many of Denton's organizations that it is difficult to name them all. As founding members of the Denton Christian Women's Inter-Racial Fellowship, they have fought to improve streets and sewage systems in the poorer part of Denton and to enable equal educational opportunities for all children. These ladies worked for the city/county elections department and were members and officers of the local NAACP. Alma Clark (this page, right), as custodial department supervisor at UNT, sent her three children to college. She served for many years on the Denton County Historical Commission and on the board of Denton's after-school program. Betty Kimble (this page, above), currently manager of the American Legion Senior Center in southeast Denton, also served on the Denton Christian Pre-School Board and won the 2008 Carol Riddlesperger Community Service Award. She and Ruby Cole are lifetime members of the Fred Moore Day Nursery School Board. Catherine Bell (opposite page, top right) was a teacher's aide for the school district, served as local NAACP president, and sat on numerous city boards. Cole (opposite page, top left) was instrumental in setting up community-oriented policing (COP) for southeast Denton; the city received the COP of the Year Award. She was chairman of Neighborhoods Improving Community Environments (NICE) and served on the city planning and zoning commission for six years. Charlye Heggins (opposite page, bottom) served for three terms on the Denton City Council. She advocated for a park honoring former city councilman Carl Gene Young, renaming of Civic Center Park to Quakertown Park, and naming the Loop 288 pedestrian bridge for Martin Luther King, among other efforts for her council district. These community leaders provided immeasurable service on the advisory board to create the Denton County African American Museum. They continue to make their voices heard for that unique cause. (Courtesy of DRC and Fred Moore Day Nursery School.)

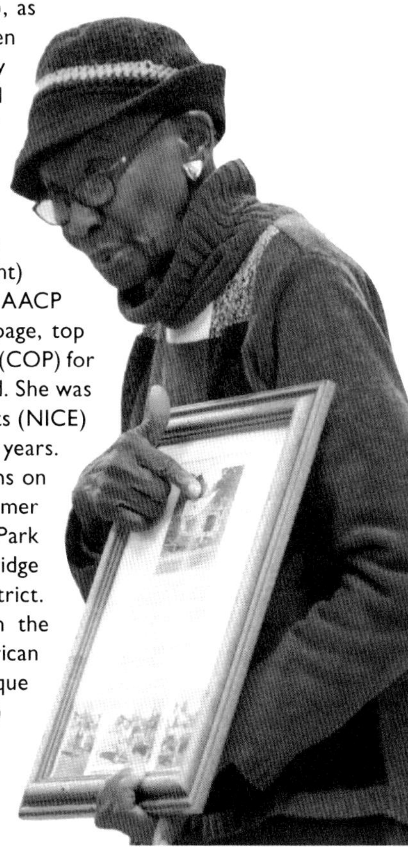

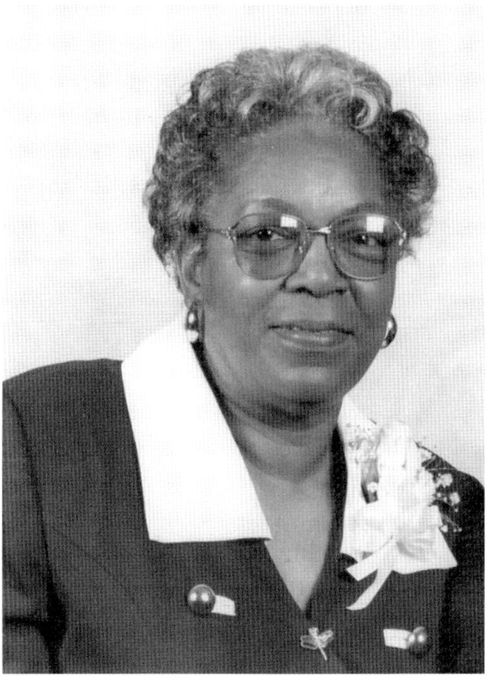

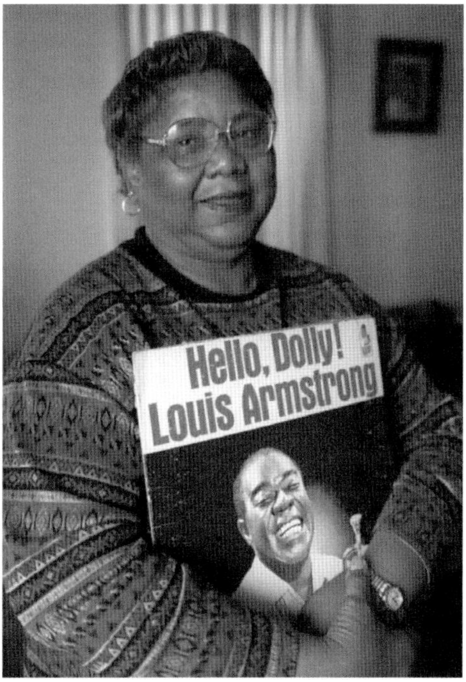
Hello, Dolly!
Louis Armstrong

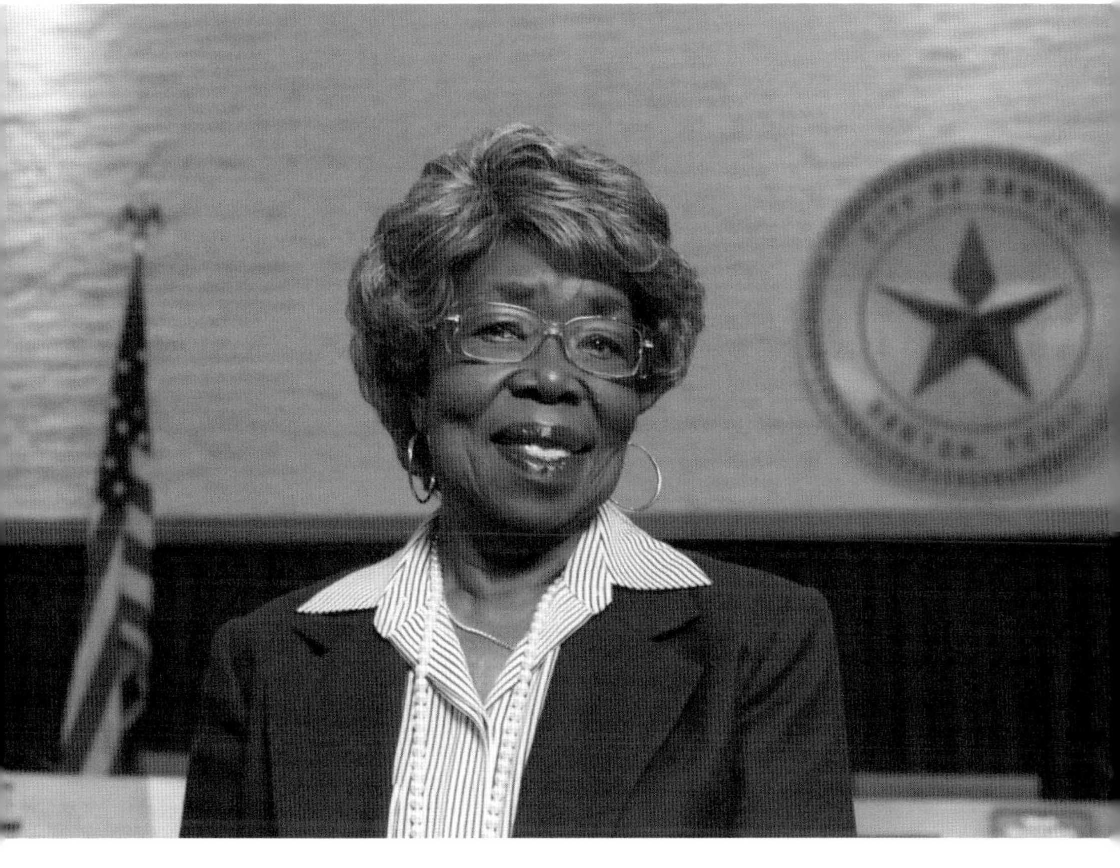

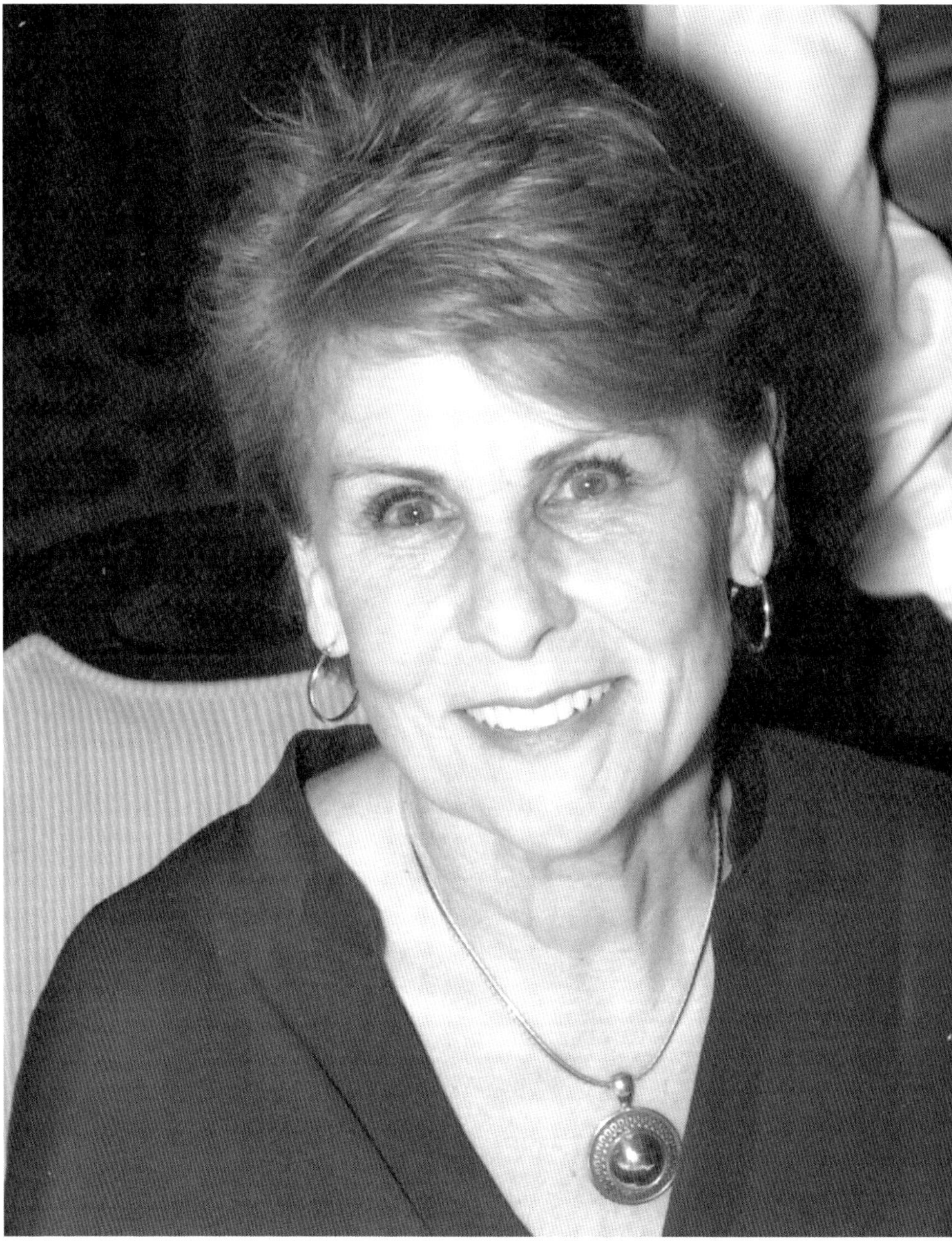

Guiding Light

Gayle Weber Strange's efforts span from civic leader, to philanthropist, to author. She has served as chairman of the UNT System Board of Regents and as a board member of countless community organizations, city commissions, and her church. Strange holds lifetime memberships in the UNT president's council and alumni association and is a major underwriter of numerous university and community projects, such as Cumberland Presbyterian Children's Home, the Denton Benefit League, Emerald Eagle scholarships, and the Denton Christian Preschool. One of the most admired businesswomen in the community, she still found time to write two books. The light from her tower of strength reflects her generosity of spirit. (Courtesy of Gayle Strange.)

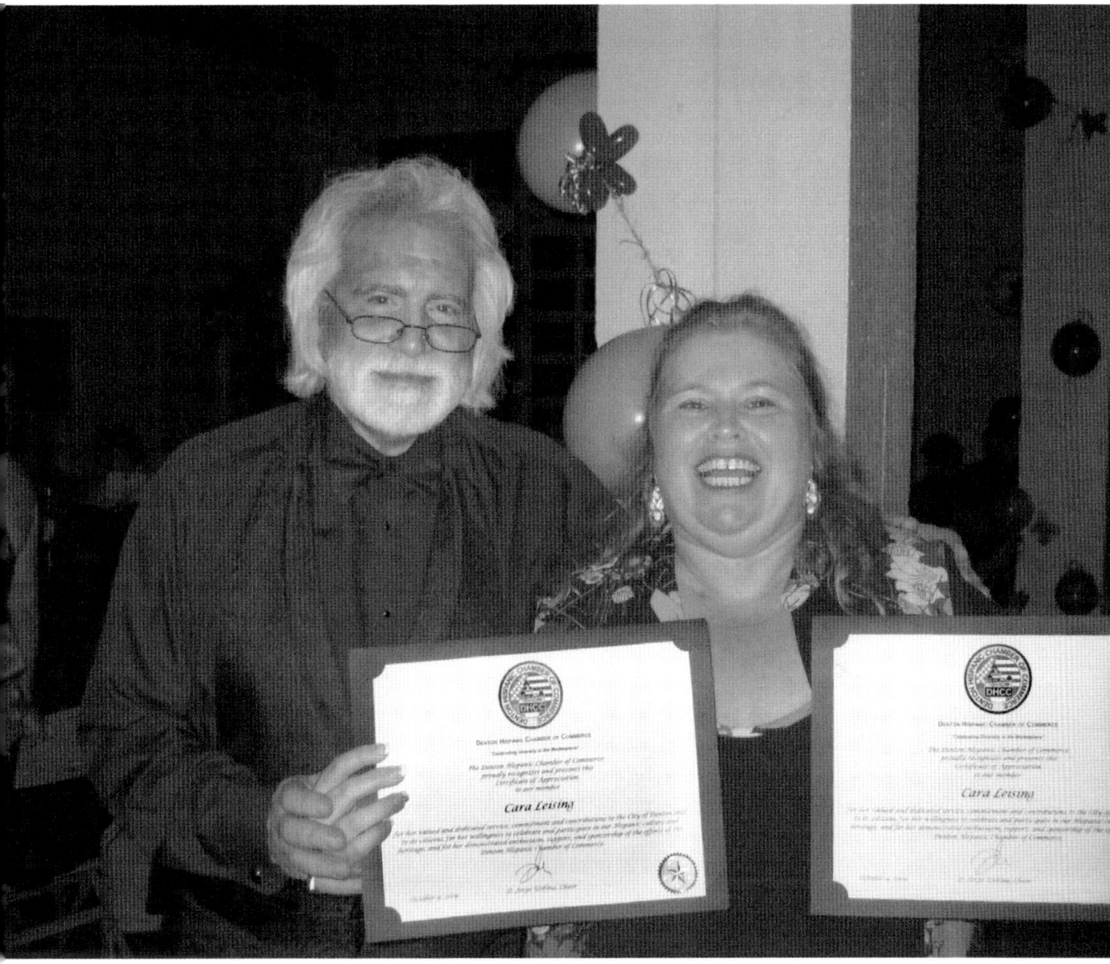

Lightning Leader of the Hispanic Community

David Jorge Urbina, lawyer and Hispanic community activist, served tirelessly as president of the Latino Urban League of American Citizens (LULAC) and the Denton Hispanic Chamber of Commerce to advance the economic condition, educational opportunities, political influence, health, and civil rights of the Hispanic population in Denton. During his leadership, dozens of scholarships were awarded each year to Latino high school students wishing to attend college. He has served on community boards and charitable committees too numerous to list. He was instrumental in founding the annual celebrations of Hispanic music, history, and dance, Fiesta on the Square and Cinco de Mayo. He leads by example in giving of the three "Ts"—time, talent, and treasure. He practices his mantra, "You must balance out giving and taking." However, most would agree that Urbina gives more than he takes from his adopted community. An enthusiastic Urbina can always be found in the middle of these activities, sparking ideas and energizing others to participate with him. Urbina is shown here presenting two awards to Cara Leising for her exemplary involvement with the Denton Hispanic Chamber of Commerce. (Courtesy of Jorge Urbina.)

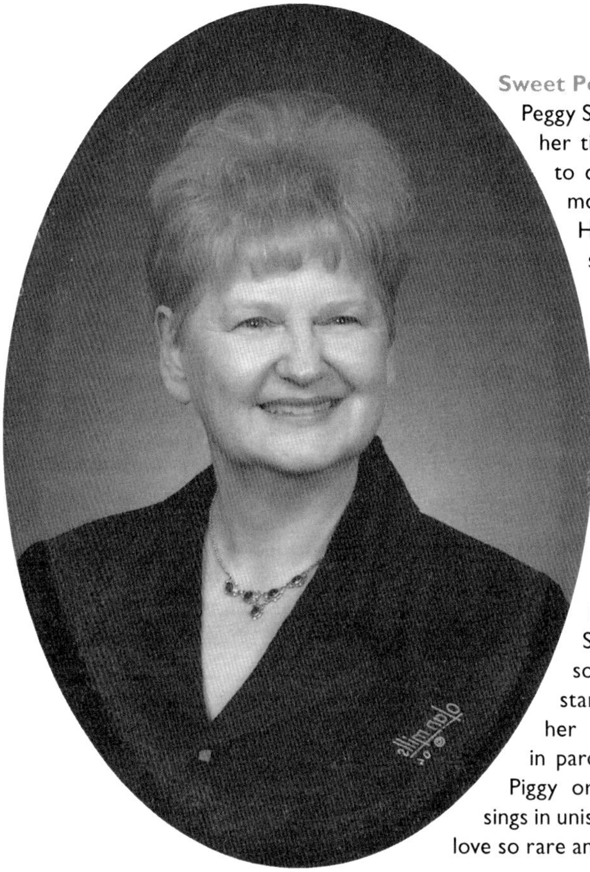

Sweet Peggy Sue

Peggy Sue Capps has boundless energy and gives her time, singing talent, and financial support to countless community events. She served more than 18 years on the Denton County Historical Commission, sharing her skills not only in preservation projects, historical events, and fundraisers, but also as chairman of the commission and chairman of the museum committee. As a member of the Denton Historic Landmark Commission, Capps was a historic house specialist, applying her knowledge of local history. She has been recognized with many honors, including the Community Arts Recognition Award, REALTOR of the Year, and the Leadership Denton Alumna of the Year. She enjoys singing with the Denton Bach Society and her church choir, where her soaring voice reaches to the stars. Her star power also sparkles when revealing her charming, mischievous interpretations in parodies and programs, performing as Miss Piggy or Richard Wagner's Brunhilde. Denton sings in unison, "We love our sweet Peggy Sue with a love so rare and true." (Courtesy of Peggy Capps.)

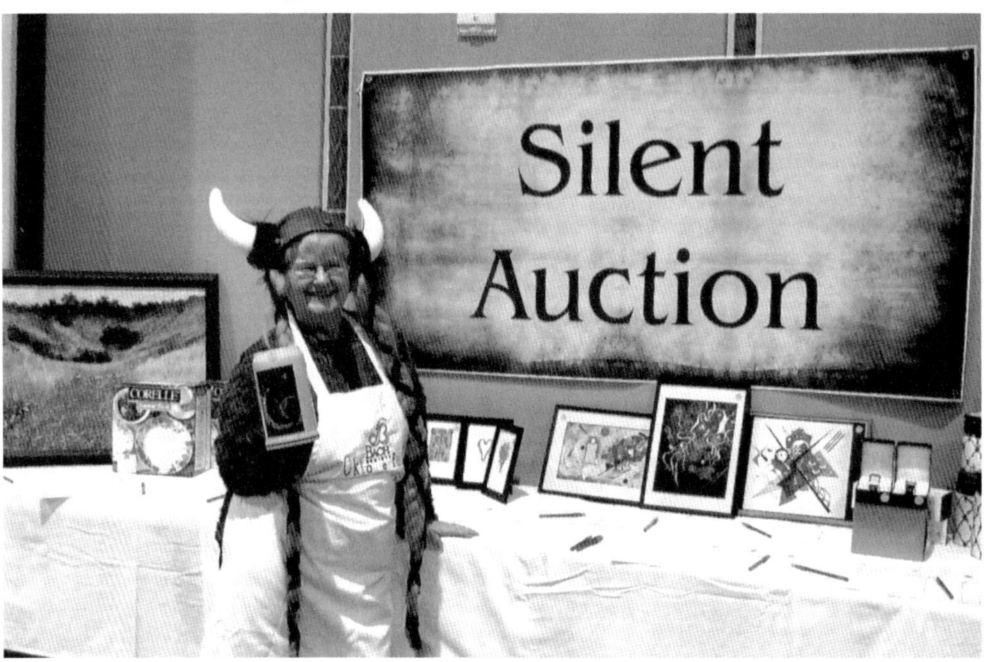

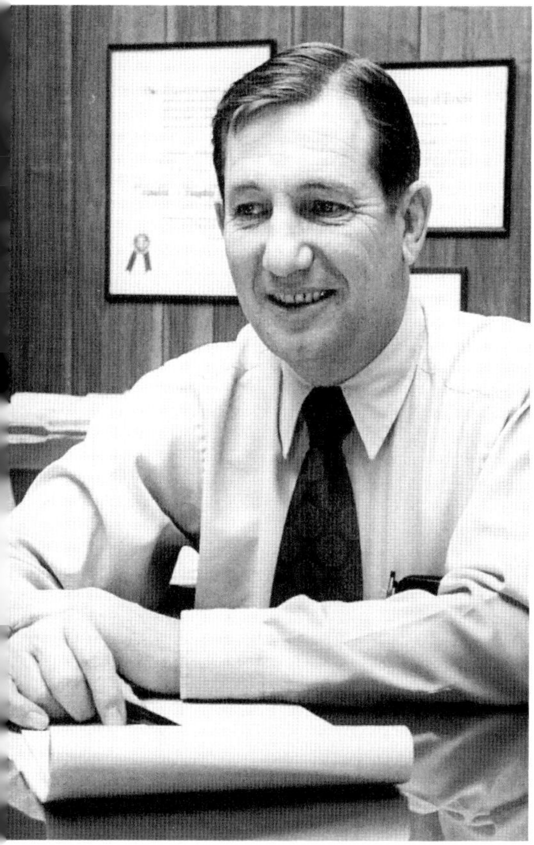

Devoted to Family, Friends, and Community

Luther Aldrich "L.A." Nelson (1926–2006) was a lawyer's lawyer, approached by inexperienced and experienced attorneys alike for his wise counsel. After serving in the Navy during World War II, he returned to Denton and Austin to attend college. He then came back to Denton to practice law for more than 50 years. He was acknowledged as one of the city's leading attorneys. As a civic leader, he served on the city council and as mayor. He was instrumental in the construction of a new city hall and the creation of Ray Roberts Lake. No less devoted to her community, Martha Len Nelson is a tireless volunteer who operated a successful catering business for many years while raising their family. There is little, if anything, that goes on in Denton that does not bear Martha Len's educated and nurturing touch. For her efforts, she was presented with the Community Arts Recognition Award. If there were such a title as "modern-day mother of Denton," it would go to Martha Len. This couple was awarded the UNT Ulys Knight Spirit Award in 1986 for their commitment to the university. For 60 years, L.A. and Martha Len Nelson were an integral part of the fabric that makes this city the special place it is. (Courtesy of DRC.)

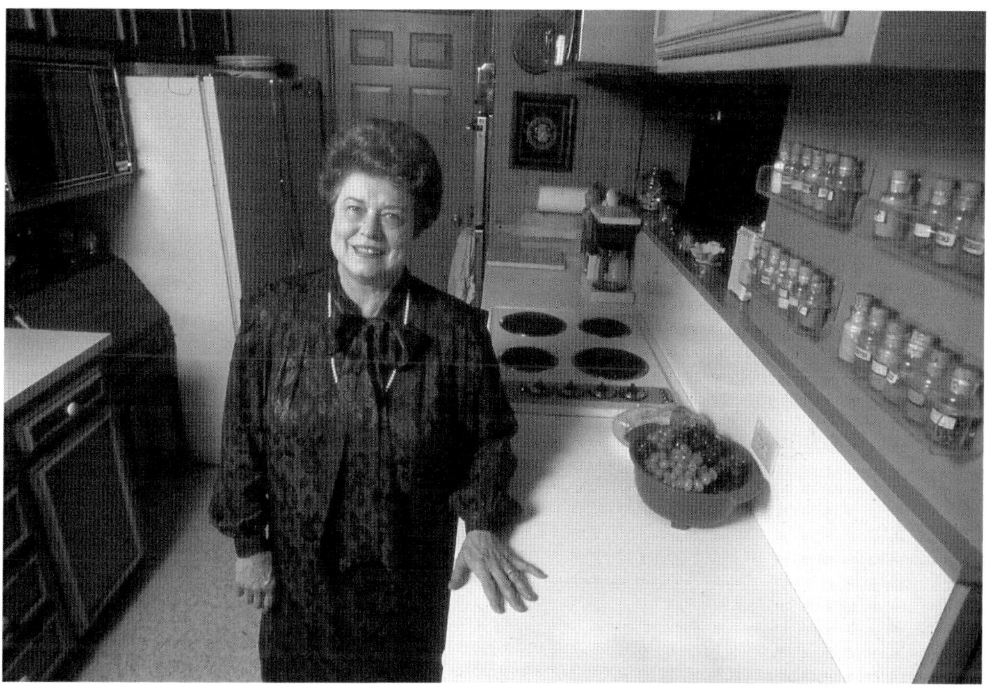

INDEX

INDEX